80 EXPERTS ON THE [S...] OF TURNING [80]

THINGS TO DO
WHEN YOU TURN 80

Edited by Mark Evan Chimsky

Associate Project Editor Laurie Moore Skillings

SELLERS
PUBLISHING

To Peter Oresick,
poet, teacher, artist, friend

Published by Sellers Publishing, Inc.

Copyright © 2017 Sellers Publishing, Inc.
All rights reserved.

Sellers Publishing, Inc.
161 John Roberts Road, South Portland, Maine 04106
Visit our Web site: www.sellerspublishing.com • E-mail: rsp@rsvp.com

Design by Faceout Studio
Production: Charlotte Cromwell
Managing Editor: Mary L. Baldwin

ISBN 13: 978-1-4162-4610-7
Library of Congress Control Number: 2016946054

The ideas and suggestions expressed in this book are based
solely on the personal experiences of the contributors and are
not intended as a substitute for the financial, legal, or medical
advice of a trained financial, legal, or health-care professional. All
matters regarding your health require medical supervision. Where
appropriate, consult your financial adviser, lawyer, physician, or
health-care team before adopting any of the suggestions in this
book. The publisher disclaims any liability arising directly or
indirectly from the use of this book.

10 9 8 7 6 5 4 3 2 1
Printed in the United States of America.

Credits: page 478

CONTENTS

INTRODUCTION 7

Making Each Day Count

PAT BOONE • *Turning Eighty* 13

TAB HUNTER • *It's All About Our Journey* 19

SALLY A. BREEN • *Pay It Forward* 25

THE AMAZING KRESKIN • *My Life Continues to Be an Adventure* 31

ELAINE L. NEWMAN as told to KATHY STOKES • *Keep On Keepin' On* 37

GORDON J. BAILEY, JR. • *Cultivating a Happy Life* 41

FRED WEINBERG • *My Life: An Audacious Adventure* 45

ELISABETH GRACE • *On Turning Eighty* 49

OLIVER SACKS, MD • *The Joy of Old Age. (No Kidding.)* 57

Being Resilient in the Face of Change

ROBERT ELLIS SMITH • *Eighty* 65

DORIAN MINTZER, MSW, PhD, BCC • *Changing Your Dreams:*
Talking About Life and Death 71

MORTON H. SHAEVITZ, PhD, ABPP • *Recovering from Injury and Illness:*
It's Up to Me, It's Up to You 77

KATHERINE GRIESZ • *How It Feels to Be Eighty* 83

DAVID BLACK • *The Stingray* 87

PJ COWAN • *Revisit the Dream, and Begin Again* 91

JERRY WITKOVSKY, MSW • *Life Is an Adventure* 97

ROGER LANDRY, MD, MPH • *Be All You Can Be* 103

GEORGE WOLF • *The Gift of Wisdom* 109

WALTER M. BORTZ II, MD • *Eighty Is Old* 115

DONALD HALL • *Losing My Teeth* 119

GEORGE LOIS • *How Your Work — and You — Can Live Forever* 123

Rules of Engagement

RUTA LEE • *Ruta's Rules* 131

WILLIAM A. SADLER, PhD • *Retuning Your Life Portfolio* 133

JOHN O'NEIL • *A Learning Life.* 141

BETTY ZIMMER • *Life Lessons for Your Eighties and Beyond* 149

THOMAS Y. CANBY • *"Rules for Old People"* 153

Challenge Yourself to Grow

FLORENCE LADD • *A Letter to My Younger Self.* 161

BETTY FINNEY • *Growing Young: The Formula* 167

GINNIE SIENA BIVONA • *The Heat Is Off.* 173

REV. MARGARET STORTZ • *A Work in Progress.* 177

FRAN MORRIS • *Seeking Wisdom* 181

BETTY MacDONALD • *All My Monsters Are Dead.* 187

NANCY K. SCHLOSSBERG, EdD • *It Can Happen to You:*
   My Online Dating Experiences 193

Doing Meaningful Work

ALICE CARTER • *Volunteering for the Peace Corps at Eighty-Six.* 203

JAN HIVELY, PhD • *Meaningful Work.* 211

ART KOFF • *Ways to Earn a Little Extra Money and Avoid Boredom.* 217

ROBERT MATULONIS • *My World at Eighty* 223

RICHARD ANDERSON BAMFORTH • *Aging into Selfhood* 229

Keeping the Creative Juices Flowing

CAROLL SPINNEY • *Looking Forward* 235

ELAINE M. DECKER • *Strike Up the Band* 239

DESIREE HOLT • *There Is Still Sex and Romance at Eighty!* 245

ANN STOKES NEFF • *Anyone for Their Own Toy Theatre?* 249

BARBARA BOLDT • *The Cycle of Nature* 255

WILLIS "WIZ" ARNDT • *Writing for Your Family* 259

JULIE KERTESZ, PhD • *Looking at Life with a Comedian's Eyes* 265

CAROL HEBALD • *The Joys of Solitude* 271

J. A. POLLARD • *Retirement? Nuts!*.................................277

KARL SINGER, MD • *Do Music!*.....................................283

ROBERT URBAN • *Free to Have Fun*.................................287

ROGER PEPPER, PhD • *A Second Life*.................................291

JENNIFER BIRCKMAYER • *Pleasures*................................. 297

JOAN PECK ARNOLD • *Writing Poetry in Our Eighties and Beyond* 303

PATRICE DOTSON • *Last Acts*..................................... 309

Staying Active

RICHARD ("Mr. Debonair") DWYER • *Axels at Eighty* 317

DR. RUTH HEIDRICH • *Making the Most of Your Eighties: Be a Triathlete!* 323

JAMESON SKILLINGS • *Stay in Shape: Eighty and Up* 329

NAOMI GOLDBERG HAAS • *Dance*.................................335

A. DAVID BARNES, MD • *Surprising Myself*...........................339

NANCY KING, PhD • *Wings, Not Weights*.............................343

Travel: What's on Your Bucket List?

WARREN STORTROEN • *On Earthwatch Adventures* 351

ED PERKINS • *Retire at Eighty? Fuhgeddaboudit — I'm Too Old to Retire* 357

CAROL SCOTT • *How Was the Food?* 363

DON SCOTT • *Cuba Is for the Birds* 369

JUDY MAGE • *An Eightieth Birthday Gift I Gave Myself.* 375

New Directions: Planning for Now and the Future

SALLY ABRAHMS • *Making the Most of Technology in Your Later Years* 383

ANDREW CARLE • *Planning to Be Eighty* 391

JOANNE TURNBULL, PhD, MSW • *Harvesting Our Wisdom* 397

TIMOTHY M. VOGEL, Esq. • *Look in the Mirror.* 403

STEPHEN JOHNSTON • *Aging2.0 – New Technologies Are Changing Aging
for the Better* 407

AUDREY S. WEINER, DSW, MPH • *How to Age Like a New Yorker* 415

RICK KIMBALL • *Eighty! OMG!* 421

BOB LOWRY • *A Fulfilling Life Is About Attitude, Not Age.* 427

Spiritual Lessons

REV. PATRICIA HOERTDOERFER • *My Turning Eighty "Day Walk in Nature"* 433

LaTRON S. BROWN • *Find Your "One Thing"* 439

GILBERT LECLERC, PhD • *Successful Aging Needs Spiritual Meaning.* 445

LANETTE H. THURMAN, PhD • *Life in the Eighties: Mourn or Celebrate* 451

LOIS C. ERNST, MSW • *"This Is Now"* 457

VIMLA KAUL • *Accept and Let Go* 461

REV. MARGARET L. CLARK • *Life Is a Gift — Live It Fully.* 465

DONALD F. MURRAY, MDiv, MTh • *On Joining the Over-Eighty Club* 471

ABOUT THE EDITORS 476
ACKNOWLEDGMENTS 477
CREDITS 478

INTRODUCTION

Welcome to this celebration of turning eighty. As the editor of *80 Things to Do When You Turn 80*, it is my intent to honor the inspiring voices and stories that are not often heard these days: of people in their eighties and older who are living dynamic and meaningful lives.

For more than a year my assistant Laurie Moore Skillings and I reached out to a diverse range of octogenarians and experts on aging to gather the eighty essays that follow. As I edited these thoughtful, moving, and sometimes humorous essays, I found a common thread emerge: most of the eighty-plus-year-old contributors saw the act of writing about their lives as a chance to explore the essence of who they are. They look at the challenges and achievements that have shaped them, and they address what makes their lives worthwhile now. Their stories form a wonderfully diverse mosaic of the vibrancy and wisdom of elders who have something important to teach all of us about making the most of our later years.

According to a 2015 UN report, *World Population Ageing*, "The global population aged eighty years or over is projected to grow from 125 million in 2015 to 202 million in 2030 and to 434 million in 2050." And yet even as America's older population grows exponentially, it still remains somewhat "invisible," marginalized both literally and figuratively in our culture. This is not the case in other countries, which make a point of venerating their elders.

In countries from China to Japan to India, as well as the Native American nations and in African American communities in the United States, families honor their oldest members, recognizing that they possess a wealth of experience that is often the best teacher. In her book, *On Becoming Fearless*, Arianna Huffington describes the way the elderly are esteemed in Greece and then adds, "The idea of honoring old age, indeed identifying it with wisdom and closeness to God, is in startling contrast to the way we treat aging in America."

Now more than ever there is a need for this book, which gives people in their eighties (and older) an opportunity to be heard. They defy all the stereotypes of how our youth-obsessed culture views aging, and reveal the ways, both large and small, that all of us can continue to make a difference as we enter our eighties and nineties. Some live each day to the fullest by engaging in passions that have defined them: Caroll Spinney still performs as Big Bird and Oscar the Grouch on *Sesame Street*, roles he has played since the show first aired in 1969; Richard Dwyer, the beloved "Ice Follies" star who is known to his fans worldwide as "Mr. Debonair," is still performing axels at eighty; Dr. Ruth Heidrich is an "Ironman triathlete" who is devoted to keeping active and still competing at eighty-one; writer Florence Ladd is working on new poems and other writing projects; and famous mentalist The Amazing Kreskin keeps up a personal and professional schedule that would tire out many who are half his age.

Others find their calling as they advance in years: Alice Carter started volunteering for the Peace Corps at age eighty-six; George Wolf does social work with The Blue Card, a nonprofit that assists destitute survivors of the Holocaust; and Jerry Witkovsky became a grandparenting activist, setting up Grandparents Connection programs in Chicago.

For some contributors, their essays provide an opportunity to express gratitude. Music legend Pat Boone urges us to thank God and to tell the people in our life that we love them; he even includes a special bonus in his essay: the lyrics to a song that sums up his philosophy of life. Movie icon Tab Hunter writes about finding joy in the simple things in life: walking his dogs with his life partner, watching PBS, and treating himself to a bowl of oatmeal with "cream all over it."

The essays in 80 *Things to Do When You Turn* 80 cover all aspects of life. A number of the most moving essays are by contributors who write about dealing with loss — and finding the resilience to forge ahead. Robert Ellis Smith describes the heartbreak of losing his twenty-one-year-old son Gregor, and how he rebuilt his life and found renewed focus and community by pursuing his interest in acting at seventy-three. Legendary art director George Lois reflects on losing his twenty–year–old son Harry, "the joy of our life," and how that led him to devote his life to fighting "racial injustice . . . and anyone or anything corrupted by money and power."

An author who looks at personal loss through the lens of humor is the great American Poet Laureate Donald Hall, who gives a hilarious account of how he soldiers on, even when his dentures go missing in action.

I felt it was also important to include advice from experts on aging in this book, and I am delighted that we have contributors like Sally Abrahms, Stephen Johnston, Andrew Carle, Dorian Mintzer, and Tim Vogel, among others, who offer practical suggestions on how to improve the quality of life in one's later years. Sally Abrahms's essay is chock-full of Web sites and useful tools that can provide support to all of us as we grow older, helping to safeguard our well-being and giving peace of mind to families and caregivers. Stephen Johnston, co-founder of Aging2.0, details the creative innovations, startups, and cutting-edge advances in technology that are available now — and are on the horizon.

I am especially grateful that we received permission to reprint the late Dr. Oliver Sacks's wonderful essay "The Joy of Old Age. (No Kidding.)." He was a renowned neurologist and best-selling author of *The Man Who Mistook His Wife for a Hat* and *Awakenings*, and his passing at eighty-two left the world a diminished place. But he exemplified a boundless curiosity and a love of life that can be a role model for all of us.

My hope is that you will find essays in this book that will enlighten and inspire you, and that your next chapter will be as fulfilling as the ones you read about here!

Mark Evan Chimsky
October 2016

MAKING EACH
DAY COUNT

Turning Eighty

By Pat Boone

Pat Boone has become a legend in his own time. His titles of movie star, gold-recording artist, best-selling author, Broadway show headliner, and television star certainly qualify him. Charles Eugene "Pat" Boone (born June 1, 1934) has sold more than 45 million records, has thirteen gold discs, two gold albums and a platinum record. Fifteen of his songs have hit the top ten and his song "Love Letters in the Sand" was on the charts for thirty–four consecutive weeks. Pat has appeared in fifteen feature films including: *April Love*, *State Fair*, *Journey to the Center of the Earth*, and *Bernadine* and he played David Wilkerson in *The Cross and the Switchblade*. He has also written fifteen books including *Twixt Twelve and Twenty*, which sold more than one million copies. Pat and Shirley reared and guided their daughters, Cherry, Lindy, Debby, and Laury in the midst of Hollywood's spotlight. They have sixteen grandchildren and three great–grandchildren and celebrated sixty years of marriage in November 2016.

B een there, done that!

Now, to all the fortunate ones turning eighty, I recommend the following:

a. Drop to your knees, raise your hands high, and thank God that you're breathing!

b. Get up, if possible, and thank God that you're now vertical, and still breathing.

c. If you're not already, for God's sake (and yours), get on a conversational basis with your maker — you'll be seeing him face to face before long. I wrote this very thing to H.L. Hunt, Howard Hughes, and Ross Perot, all acquaintances who died soon thereafter. I hope they took my advice.

d. Tell everybody around you that matters to you, "I love you — I hope you know that." Especially your wife, if you're as fortunate as I am, and still have her with you.

I knew a man named Horace Lipscomb who read the Bible admonition, "Greet one another with a holy kiss." He took it seriously, and in his later years, after he was eighty, very unashamedly would kiss male and female friends on the cheek. He kept it holy, and it was truly an expression of honest devotion and appreciation. And it was appreciated and memorable.

e. Try to categorize and assign to others all your "junk."

Somerset Maugham, noted author, wrote, "The older a man gets, the fewer things he needs or wants." Don't force your loved ones into "garage sales" of all the stuff you've collected and couldn't decide what to do with. Decide now. So treasure things with other people who will treasure them.

f. Read the words for a song I wrote years ago, as I contemplated this coming time. I think they are profound, and should interest everybody who realizes that he or she is going to die. I call it, appropriately, "Everybody Dies."

Everybody Dies
by Pat Boone
Everybody dies, everybody dies.
It's a sad but true fact of life.
Everybody dies.
And everybody knows that everybody goes.
You just sing your song, then move along.
Everybody dies.
Wish I didn't have to think about it.
Wish it wasn't so.
But if Einstein couldn't get around it, I'm sure I'll have to go.
So will Mom and Dad and Uncle Harry — baby sister too.
And if death could take the Virgin Mary,

Ya know it won't miss you.

Cuz everybody dies, everybody dies.

It's a sad but true fact of life.

Everybody dies,

And everybody knows that everybody goes,

You just get in line until your time.

Everybody dies.

Read it on a bumper sticker,

Pondered it for months.

Born just once, and you'll die twice.

Born twice, you just die once.

Heard folks say they're born again

And they haven't even died.

Others laugh to hide the funerals goin' on inside.

Heard God saw that we're all dyin'

He sent His only Son.

He died, too — but lived again.

Said "I'll show you how it's done."

Think I'd better take the offer — best one that I've found.

Cause after all my slippin', slidin',

Feels like solid ground!

Cause everybody dies, everybody dies.

It's a sad but true fact of life — everybody dies.

And everybody knows that everybody goes.

So meet the Son. He's the One.
Cause everybody dies.

If I do say so, the song itself is quite moving. I'd like you to look for it on iTunes. It's extremely good advice set to music — and I'll feel better knowing others are hearing it.

See you in heaven, hopefully!

Pat

2

It's All About Our Journey

By Tab Hunter

A product of Hollywood's golden age, Tab Hunter became Hollywood's golden boy. He starred in over forty major motion pictures, including *The Pleasure of His Company*, *Ride the Wild Surf*, *The Loved One*, *The Life and Times of Judge Roy Bean*, *Damn Yankees*, *Polyester*, *Grease 2*, and *Lust in the Dust*. He teamed up with Allan Glaser to produce *Lust in the Dust* and *Dark Horse*. Multitalented Tab also enjoyed a very successful recording career that culminated with one of the top records of the rock and roll era. His recording of *Young Love* zoomed to number one on the charts worldwide (knocking Elvis out of the top spot) where it remained for six weeks. He subsequently starred in his own television series for NBC, guest-starred in dozens of television shows, and was nominated for an Emmy. Tab's autobiography *Tab Hunter Confidential* was a national best seller, and an award-winning documentary based on the book was released in 2015.

Eighty things to do when you turn eighty? You've got to be joking. Perhaps if I strained the brain I could come up with some rather interesting things, but at this moment, my mind has drawn a blank. So many things to do, and so few hours left to do them in. Are you thinking, *I'd like to do this . . . or maybe that*? Perhaps you're wondering, *Haven't we done enough*? My answer is, no, not really. We only come down this road one time so let's relish the journey and make it a good one.

I'd probably start off with a martini on the rocks, then look up and give a heartfelt "Thank you." After that, I'd head out to the barn to be with my horses, and later that evening, my partner Allan and I would head out to dinner.

If we are fortunate enough to be alive and kicking at eighty, I'd say we definitely qualify to be put into the oldie but goodie category. Of course we need to keep our minds and bodies active. We can't overlook our aches and pains. That goes with the territory, so don't dwell on them. Just keep moving. Get out and take a walk and be aware of things around you. I'd say we are pretty darn lucky, right?

Five mornings a week I take my dogs, Olivia and Hattie, to the beach for a walk. I've slowed down a bit since I started doing this back in 1994. It's great seeing other four-legged friends and their owners. We make small talk. "Sure wish it would rain." "Did you see that pod of dolphins playing in the surf?" "Are we lucky living here, or what?" Interacting with others is so very important. Often, we are afraid to make eye contact with one another. We just drop our heads and keep on walking. Pick up your head. Give a smile and a nod. We all like that.

On Sunday after church, I can't wait to come home and fix breakfast. It's my favorite meal. I usually prepare multi-grain hot cakes and pour 100 percent maple syrup all over them. I keep telling myself that it's only once a week. A lot of older people don't feel like cooking for themselves. Don't get lazy. Get in the kitchen and fix yourself something. A bowl of oatmeal. No, not that instant stuff that tastes like wallpaper paste, but the unprocessed, real stuff. And if you want to splurge, pour cream all over it. I know it sounds decadent, but be good to yourself. You deserve it.

Do you like to read? I read three papers daily. It's sometimes tough digesting all the drivel that's out there, but we should keep up with what's happening in the world, and be able to discuss these events with others. We need to listen to what's being said. That doesn't always mean we have to agree. My hard-headed

German mother use to tell me, "If people don't like what you have to say, that's their problem, not yours."

What TV shows do you watch? I'm addicted to the morning and evening news, but I become inflamed with their spin on things. I switch channels a lot. But I stay tuned to PBS: *Masterpiece*, plus a good cooking show, and most certainly shows on travel.

How do you feel about music? I like just about everything except rap. Good music touches the soul and we all need our souls to be touched.

Let me throw out a dirty word. Procrastination. I hate the word. You have no idea how much I admire people who get things done. People who don't let grass grow under their feet. You need to call a family member or someone else? Don't just think about it. Pick up the phone, or maybe even write a note. A note? A handwritten note? Nobody writes notes anymore. It's all e-mail. Everyone does it. Everybody but my friend, Kate. She doesn't want to learn. She's lazy and that really bugs me. If she would just take the time to learn it, it would open up a whole new world for her. There is so much out there for us to absorb, to keep the mind active. Who was it who said, "Use it or you lose it"?

I've just taken a good look at my desk and it's filled with slips of paper. Lists of things to do. A pile of stuff that needs to be taken care of. Who am I to write about what we should and should not do? Excuse me, I'll be back shortly . . .

How do you feel about travel? When I was a young actor and the studio was paying for everything I just loved it. They sure knew how to impress an impressionable kid. Well, times have changed. Everything about travel today seems to be a problem. So what are we supposed to do? Elevate our thinking. Take the high road. No matter what street we take a stroll down or what gangplank we struggle to get up, headed for parts unknown, it's all onward and upward. Let's not cheat ourselves of that enlightening sense of discovery as we go along. It's all about our journey. Bon Voyage.

3

Pay It Forward

By Sally A. Breen

Sally A. Breen grew up in the gun-totin' culture of Texas. She married young and after her three children were grown, she began a ten-year odyssey to earn a bachelor's degree in English from Texas A&M. Her children well remember the time when their mother became an environmentalist, decided that nuclear weapons and nuclear power were immoral, and that war is not the answer. After moving to Maine, she worked as an office manager at a large hospital, and became a radical Unitarian Universalist who felt duty-bound to live the life of a committed activist. That included being arrested five times for civil disobedience. Sally and her husband, Dr. Keith Williams, travel to exotic places, such as the Amazon and the Inca Trail in Peru. For the past nine years, she has written a column, "Earth Speaks," for a local newspaper. In eighty years of living, she gets up every morning with the attitude, "Carpe Diem."

I t can't be helped. My Irish roots go back to the days of Cromwell's persecution of the Irish Catholics. The Breen coat of arms reads "Comrac an Ceart," meaning "Fight for Right." This motto has shaped me as I've lived my life from the United States border with Mexico to the border with Canada.

As I told the staff at MD Anderson in Houston while recovering from a lengthy surgery for an extremely rare and deadly form of cancer in 2012, "I'm not done yet. The world still has nuclear weapons."

So I'll live yet for a while longer, understanding that my goal of a nuclear-free and peaceful world will not be realized in my lifetime.

My remaining time will be as a cup full of opportunities. My cup is a world cup, overflowing with more than eighty options.

Perhaps I'll add to my list of five previous civil disobedience arrests in my continuing work with Peace Action Maine and Physicians for Social Responsibility. We seek a sane worldwide policy regarding the future of nuclear weapons.

Education is the key to many of the world's problems. Beginning on our home front, we must work together in supporting innovative policies to reduce high school drop-out rates, provide new-parent training, and Head Start for all children. Our prison population is full of grown "children" who have been left behind. Let's commit to providing them with meaningful education so they can rejoin the "free world" as productive members of society. We must welcome our influx of refugees and asylum seekers with job training, and, indeed, for all our own citizens who need updated job skills.

My Irish ancestry and education has gifted me with a love for writing. It gives me abounding joy. For the past nine years I've contributed columns for a local newspaper. The title of my articles is "Earth Speaks," and they focus on my concern for the future of our heavenly planet Earth as if it were the Greek living Gaia. Like my ancient Celtic forebears, I feel an abiding pull to honor and protect that which nourishes and gives us life. We have strayed afar. It is past time to creatively move forward in a communal way with the vision of the world as one.

More concretely, my greenhouse is a few steps from my kitchen door and provides my family with organically grown vegetables. We call our little cottage in the woods "Paradise Maine," where we protect the stream in our backyard and my husband is the scientist-protector of our nearby lake and other lakes in Maine. It is not unusual to find jars of algae in my refrigerator awaiting transport to the University of New Hampshire for assay. I've heard rumors that when visitors at our church, which is environmentally aware, ask why the congregation doesn't use paper products at its frequent potluck meals, the answer is, "Watch out for Sally Breen! She feels honor-bound to make sure our church lives its environmental values!"

"Paradise Maine" continues to be a healing haven for ex-prisoners, for many seeking solace from family tragedies, for fatherless grandchildren, for left-leaning United States presidential candidates, and even some simply wanting to live in this ever-entertaining household. When our small house is a full house, we have friends living in the camper (only in Maine's cool summers).

Once, after my husband and I hitchhiked in Honduras after the Contra Wars, my boss asked me "Why do you go to the war zones for your vacations?" In that vein, we thrill to the experiences of hiking the Inca Trail in Peru, boating and snorkeling down a stream in Brazil while the *jacare* (caiman) lurk on nearby river banks, joining scientific Amazon tours where we are warned to wear our hard hats to protect us from iguanas free-falling from the trees as our small boats pass below. The accounts I write of our adventures and the stories I've gathered through a half-century of family genealogy research will live on after me.

I'll continue to join my friends at the Jam Shack in my neighborhood and play my djembe drum. There, they speak their own foreign language about E-flats or C-sharps. Oh, and they smoke pot and drink liquor, and use the "F" word, too. It all just passes me by. But, damn, do I have fun!

The love of my family, friends, and communities enriches my life. It enables me to carry on into this new eighty-year-old phase. On my eightieth birthday, I earned the nickname of "Badass Sally" from my granddaughter. That story accompanied me to Ireland on my latest adventure.

After my last party, my cup will be empty. I've paid it forward.

4

My Life Continues to Be an Adventure

By The Amazing Kreskin

With a showman's flair, a comedian's wit, and the capacities of a bona fide mentalist or thought reader, The Amazing Kreskin has, for six decades, dramatized the unique facets of the human mind . . . his own. His very name has become an integral part of pop culture throughout the world. Through the past fifty years Kreskin has had a television series, his own board game by Milton Bradley, nineteen published books, and a major motion picture inspired by his work. In the 1970s Kreskin headlined his own television series for five seasons called *The Amazing World of Kreskin*, which can now be viewed on hulu.com. Since the series, Kreskin has traveled over three million miles, performing in front of millions his unique brand of mentalism. Kreskin has also been a recurring guest on shows hosted by Johnny Carson, Regis Philbin, David Letterman, and most recently, Jimmy Fallon and Howard Stern. In November 2015 Kreskin released his twentieth book, *In Real Time*, featuring his major predictions for the next several hundred years. He also has a radio show called *What's on My Mind*, currently airing on Satellite Radio.

At age eighty-one, I am not writing a suggestion of what I think an eighty year old should do, but instead I'd like to share with you what yours truly does on an average day. The sequence is pretty much exact, though not rigid, as there are other factors involved such as business visits and various appointment meetings. What I am not including is everything I do when I am on tour; that, of course, incorporates multiple other factors like traveling on a plane or in a car to the many different cities where I perform. What I am including are the kinds of activities that allow me to relax and replenish myself so that I'm able to keep up a busy schedule of writing and touring. So, then, let me share what an "average" day at home is like for me.

If it's a weekday, I rise at about 8:30 or 9:00 a.m., with the expectation that I will sit down with my secretary and other members of my staff after a light breakfast. We reflect upon the communications of the previous day, what's anticipated by me whether they be by phone, by e-mail, or written letters, etc.

Later, I make time to pore over four daily newspapers; however, that number can change if I've been away on a tour or trip for a sustained amount of time. The newspapers for each day pile up and when I return I try to go through all of them. Sometimes that means catching up on dozens of newspapers. Rather than rely on the Internet, I prefer to see the written word on paper as it tends to awaken new ideas, stories, and perspectives in me that I've never thought of before.

I've always enjoyed the company of animals and at the present time I have two kitty cats, and I see to it that I play with them — for about twenty minutes or so, twice a day. Certainly I will not miss seeing them in the evening, when I can pinpoint a dancing light on the floor and have them chase it.

Usually, the day is filled in part with interviews that yours truly does with newspapers, radio stations, and TV and online journalists. This can encompass as many as two or more hours for each interview. They are often scattered throughout the day, since some programming is done live and can take place in the morning, afternoon, or evening.

I usually have lunch between 11:00 a.m. and 2:00 p.m. and dinner sometime from 5:00 to 7:00 p.m. — that is, when I'm not traveling. I will often have a single glass of red wine after 8:00 or 9:00 p.m.

Now that my most recent book In *Real Time* is published, I am able to turn my attention to a variety of new writing projects, which I will dictate in the future. Part of this process involves analyzing stories, incidents, etc., from the headlines that I may wish to comment on. This hour is an important part of my daily activities.

I often spend forty-five minutes or so doing research in my library on various issues and topics. My personal library consists of over nine thousand books, covering many areas of interest. I take pleasure in reading two to four books a day.

Cat naps are a convenient tool for me and I will take one or two a day, lasting approximately ten minutes each.

At night, I relax by watching no more than an hour of television, especially news broadcasts. A favorite of mine is *The Bill O'Reilly Report* on Fox television.

Later in the evening, often around midnight, I will sit at the piano for one to two hours and play. One of my favorite composers is Chopin but I also have a love of popular songs. (I've written music as well, including my theme song called I *Can Read Your Mind*. I'll always remember hearing my song played by "Skitch" Henderson and his orchestra on NBC's

The Tonight Show as I walked on camera after Johnny Carson's introduction. I've even played the song with orchestras including the New London Philharmonic and the Carnegie Hall Pops!)

After finishing up at the piano, I will jog for thirty minutes each evening, usually at one or two in the morning. Then, finally, I go to bed, but rarely will it be before 2:00 a.m. and it could be as late as 4:00 a.m.

Yours truly is still excited about living a dream, the fulfillment of which has been against all odds, considering the challenge of my work, which is reading people's thoughts in audiences all over the world. It continues to be a learning experience because I'm listening to the thoughts of people that are part of my audiences. Today people are not taking advantage of the golden opportunity of "listening" to (and by that I mean "hearing") what others are saying; if they did, they would gain remarkable insight into people's inner feelings. When I reflect on the contents of what I perceive from others each day, I find it to be a learning experience. Furthermore, every day one can find a touch of humor in life, and that doesn't mean necessarily watching a comedian on television. There are incidents and remarks if one listens carefully that will have a touch of comedy or humor. If you don't find it in the people you're with that day, turn on the television or radio and listen to the remarks of a politician: the ludicrous expressions, the obvious, defensive remarks, and the false promises become a comedy of words, contradictions, and insults to our intelligence.

Yes, there will be times when you can have an internal smile, without revealing at that moment the comedy you perceive. You see that's the beauty of quiet humor, you don't have to be politically correct.

5

Keep On Keepin' On

By Elaine L. Newman as told to Kathy Stokes

Elaine L. Newman was the first executive director of the Maryland Commission for Women in the 1970s. Some of her accomplishments include getting credit for women in their own name at financial institutions and changing sex-segregated employment ads. She served as a policy analyst for the Office of Human Resources Management at the Environmental Protection Agency where she worked with the legal office to establish a nationwide Expert Witness Program. Elaine was also the assistant director of Equal Employment Opportunity at the National Labor Relations Board, and she has been the Federal Women's Program Manager for the Public Buildings Service at the General Services Administration. In addition, she was vice chair on the DC Advisory Committee on Consumer Protection, a member of the National Association of Commissions for Women, and a member of the Maryland Advisory Committee to the U.S. Commission on Civil Rights. For ten years she was vice president for programs at the Woman's National Democratic Club. She is currently the chair of their Nominating Committee.

I'm supposed to share ideas with you about things to do when you turn eighty. Well, I'm ninety-one years old, and I have so many things to do that it's hard to make time for everything! I feel very lucky to be living independently in a co-op in Washington, D.C. Our complex was once considered a "Naturally Aging Community" and they sponsor a lot of different activities that I try to fit in. We have a listserve, making it easy to keep informed about our neighbors and events, and a volunteer neighbor network of which I've been a floor coordinator for twenty years. I help people with things like getting rides to medical appointments. I'm trying to get more exercise, so I do water aerobics for seniors three times a week at a public pool. This is in addition to a regular aerobics class I take twice a week, where they are teaching us to use weights. I believe it's important to build strength. It helps me keep up with myself!

I'm happy to live on the subway line, because I use public transportation a lot, whether it's to go to a book reading at my local bookstore or to usher for a play or musical. (I usher for four different theaters, which is fun and allows me to see the plays free.) When I'm waiting on the metro platform, I almost always see someone I know. Over the years, I've been involved with so many groups and organizations that I now see familiar faces everywhere.

One of the highlights of this year was my trip to India. I went on a tour with a group of about forty people. And wouldn't you know I met up with someone on the tour that I knew! We visited the Taj Mahal, Gandhi's house, and the city of Hyderabad in southern India, which is a technology hub. It was exciting to take in all the sights and sounds. We saw people riding on cows and once I even saw five people riding on one motorcycle! I plan to do more traveling.

Living in a city like Washington, D.C. gives me the opportunity to pursue my interests, whether it's attending a lecture at the law center that's connected to the University of the District of Columbia, or going to meetings at the Alliance for Justice. And, of course, being here in D.C. makes it easier for me to stay involved in national politics.

As a lifelong Democrat, I still volunteer with the Woman's National Democratic Club. Until a few years ago I chaired the Program Committee, which meant I was responsible with committee members for deciding on which guest speakers to invite, and then lining them up for eight to ten luncheons a month. I still book speakers and help out when I can. I went to the Democratic National Convention in Charlotte, North Carolina, in

2012. This year, I stayed up late at the Woman's National Democratic Club to watch the historic 2016 convention. I wouldn't have missed it for the world, even if I wasn't there to see it in person! To my surprise, a reporter from the British Broadcasting Company took my picture and featured me in an article the next day. I continued to work hard for Hillary's campaign, including making phone calls to get out the vote.

I have a wonderful life, filled with the activities and people I love. I'm thankful to have so much to look forward to, including the Barbra Streisand concert I have tickets for! I hope you'll continue to live your life to the fullest, too.

6

Cultivating a Happy Life

By Gordon J. Bailey, Jr.

Gordon J. Bailey, Jr., Chairman of the Board of Bailey Nurseries, Inc., grew up in the horticultural industry. Bailey Nurseries — founded in 1905 by Gordon's grandfather, J.V. Bailey — remains family-owned. Today, the St. Paul-based company is an industry leader, serving more than 4,500 customers worldwide. Though "retired," Gordon, who turned eighty-one in 2016, continues to play an active role in the business, maintaining about a half-time work schedule. He also plays a pivotal role mentoring emerging leaders in the nursery industry, including fourth- and fifth-generation Baileys working at the family business. In addition, Gordon and the entire Bailey family continue to have close ties to their community, contributing their time and talents to a number of philanthropic and community organizations. His other favorite activities include spending time with his family, reading, traveling, and doing such outdoor pursuits as hiking, biking, cross-country skiing, hunting, fishing, as well as cutting brush and gardening at his rural Minnesota farm.

At eighty-one, I'm very grateful for the life I've had and I believe I owe it to the "three Fs": family, friends, and faith. I've been blessed to have a great wife (we've been together fifty-six years), seven wonderful kids, and seventeen terrific grandchildren. I try to see my friends often, as I believe it's important not to isolate ourselves from others as we get older. As for my faith, I say prayers of gratitude every day for the blessings I have.

Our nursery business in St. Paul, Minnesota, has been an important part of my life for fifty-nine years. I continue to chair the board and I still go to the nursery a couple of days a week to help out. We sell our branded products worldwide and they include our Endless Summer hydrangeas, our Easy Elegance roses, and our First Editions premium collection of shrubs, trees, evergreens, vines, and perennials.

Continuing to be part of the nursery business that bears my family name and that I helped to grow and nurture means a lot to me. I believe that each one of us needs something to get up for every morning. The best way to have a meaningful life is to do something meaningful for others: visit a friend (or even just call them up to tell them you love them), be productive in some way, or pursue some kind of volunteer work.

I volunteer at a number of organizations: I'm back on

the board of the University of Minnesota Landscape Arboretum, one of the best-known plant and garden attractions in the country. More than 450,000 people visit the arboretum every year.

I also believe in staying physically active. I'm restoring my farm in southern Minnesota and it's truly a labor of love, planting 110 acres of restored prairie and eliminating several invasive alien plants. I climbed Mt. Kilimanjaro in 2015 and I'm hoping to go on an eighty-one mile bike trip to celebrate my recent birthday.

I think everything starts in our mind. If we see ourselves doing something, we can make it a reality. So, I'm definitely seeing myself completing that upcoming bike ride! And living a long and happy life!

7

My Life: An Audacious Adventure

By Fred Weinberg

Fred Weinberg was born and raised in Paterson, New Jersey. After graduating from Eastside High School in 1950, he attended Tulane University. He subsequently was awarded a BSW from New York University's School of Education in 1957 after serving in the army for two years during the Korean War. His forty-five-year career in criminal justice was highlighted by thirty years as a parole officer in New Jersey and New York. He graduated from the FBI's National Academy in 1973. Following his retirement from the New York State Division of Parole, where he held the position of Chief of Special Services, he worked for the Vera Institute of Justice and as a Senior Detective Investigator for the Kings County District Attorney for twelve years in programs focused on alternatives to incarceration. For the past ten years Fred has been affiliated with a hospital social work program in New York as a patient advocate. In 2014 Fred self-published *Social Workers with Guns*, an account of his career as a parole officer.

N anci Hellmich got it right in her article "How to Find Your Passion After You Retire," featured in the October 15, 2014 issue of USA *Today*.

"Take Fred Weinberg of New York City," she wrote, "who retired at age fifty-five in 1988 after working almost three decades as a New York State parole officer. Since then, Weinberg now is eighty-one and has had half a dozen different careers. He volunteers one day a week in the pediatric social work department at a hospital in New York."

My dad died in his mid-fifties. I never expected I would make it much beyond, let alone into my ninth decade. I wasn't conscious of my compulsive need to make every day count until I heard myself telling Hellmich how important it was for me to stay active and be prepared for the physical adjustments and restructuring that define the aging process. So Instead of accepting the premise that eighty was old, I would flaunt it. Why not? How often was my ego assuaged hearing, "Gee, you don't look that old."

The idea of "retirement" was anathema to me and I came across as somewhat of a bore with my haughty attitude. On more than one occasion I was called to task by retired friends for bragging about my latest job. The insinuation was, of course, "look at me, I'm still capable of working." I needed to believe that I could still compete in the job market and it became a challenge. It was a game I was now playing. Could I still convince a prospective employer I would be a good fit for the job, my age notwithstanding?

Two years ago that plan backfired after I resigned from a very desirable part-time job in a hospital social work department to accept a job that turned out to be a bad match. I resigned at the end of the first day. Once I was able to step away from that situation I realized I faked my way through the pre-employment process. I obviously wasn't at peace with myself. What was it I was looking for?

Then, something happened when I turned eighty-three earlier this year. For the first time since my mid-twenties I found myself not working. Instead I'm volunteering at the hospital and taking classes in an adult education program three days a week. I recently self-published a memoir, *Social Workers with Guns*, an account of my thirty-year career with the New York State Division of Parole. I'm a part-time caregiver for Fran, my wife of thirty-two years, who is bravely dealing with Parkinson's Disease. Besides lots of reading, attending concerts and movies, and writing, I maintain close ties to my three daughters and two grandchildren and (hopefully) I'm finally breaking free of that uncanny and irrational, obsessional need to prove myself.

I believe that having reached my ninth decade is a blessing and as the days now seem to pass so swiftly, I'm aware how important it is to make every day count. I've set a goal for myself of accomplishing something positive each day, no matter how insignificant. Time is short. I'm now in Act 3 and this is not a dress rehearsal.

8

On Turning Eighty

By Elisabeth Grace

Elisabeth Grace is a retired clinical social worker, having continued to work one day a week in private practice until a few months after her eightieth birthday. She was born in the UK, but has lived in the United States since 1972. She has resided in rural upstate New York since 1975. Elisabeth's interests in retirement include reading, writing, politics, and animal welfare, and her activities include birding, gardening, hiking, and canoeing.

On a certain day in April 2014 I was still seventy-nine years old. A look at the calendar confirmed that the very next day, I would turn eighty. It seemed kind of exciting — a new decade, a nice round number divisible by four, a neat and tidy figure. Thinking about it even gave me a slight sense of achievement; not everyone is lucky enough to arrive safely at that destination, and I was active in many fields, healthy, and for the most part comfortable with my station in life. Of course, I had suffered my share of losses: my life partner, family members, and beloved friends; animal companions; several teeth, and most of my hearing. I had weathered the C's and M's of late middle age, the cataract surgeries and colonoscopies, the Medicare choices and memory lapses. I slept less and read more. Some of the A's of old age might lie in wait for me, arthritis and the grim prospect of Alzheimer's, but I nevertheless felt very fortunate. I remembered with a smug smile the gloomy remark of an acquaintance twenty years before: "It's all downhill after sixty." *Not so!* I'd thought then, and I said it to myself again on the 364th day of my eightieth year.

I had gone online a few weeks before, wondering who else might share my birth year, and made a list of the celebrities who had already turned, or were about to turn, eighty. I was pleased to share a 2014 anniversary with Judi Dench, Bill Moyers, Alan Bennett, Barry Humphries, Madhur Jaffrey, Marilyn Horne, Gloria Steinem, Shirley MacLaine, and others whose names were less familiar to me. I was particularly happy that my compatriot Jane Goodall would have her eightieth birthday a couple of weeks before mine, and I had even sent her online greetings like hundreds, perhaps thousands, of her other admirers. To join such an impressive list of active octogenarians made my imminent move into another decade seem challenging rather than troubling.

A few more hours passed on the day in question, and suddenly I was eighty. I was on vacation in New Mexico, which somehow added to the feeling of unreality I experienced. I awoke in my room in the Santa Fe Inn, dressed and went down to breakfast, to be serenaded with a round of "Happy Birthdays!" spoken and sung, a greeting that would be repeated throughout the day. Never comfortable with being the center of attention, I filled my plate, poured myself some coffee, and slunk into my seat, glad when conversation turned to the group's plans for the day.

Since that day at the end of April, I have had time to reflect on what it feels like to be eighty, and have observed that I now view that milestone a little differently. How could the passage of twenty-four hours have changed my perception, and will I recover my seventy-nine-year-old's optimism? I remember how often in the past, while canceling a plan or ruling out a possibility, I have thought or said, "There's always next year." Now I feel inclined to add, "I hope!" when I postpone something. How many more "next years" will I have?

A few weeks into my eighty-year-old life, I sat on the porch steps at dusk as I have done many times each spring, watching for the bats, which arrive almost without fail as the sky pales. They crisscross the space high above my head, hawking for insects. I was reassured when two appeared, the onslaught of the fatal white-nose syndrome having decimated bat colonies across much of the United States. I count on the constancy of certain things like the nightly arrival of the bats, while noting that many things in my environment have changed. There is a spruce tree close to the house that must be cut down soon, having grown from twelve feet tall to a threatening thirty-five feet over the past forty years. The house itself now stands centered in an amphitheater of tall trees; even twenty years ago we could look westward over their crowns and across the valley to fields full of grazing cows. Now the view, the cows, and the farm itself are gone. Of course, the changes did not occur all at once, but at a rate so reassuringly slow that I only gradually became aware of them. A year or two ago, considering a move, I caught myself thinking, *How could I leave this house and give up my view*? I had to laugh at myself as I acknowledged that my view no longer exists, stolen by those ever-growing trees.

Around the same time that I sat watching for the bats' return, I came across an article about a British study. Two thousand residents of the United Kingdom over the age of forty were asked what they considered "old." The average answer was eighty, an advance on the age of sixty-eight suggested by previous generations. The respondents were influenced by the active lifestyle of older people, the fact that many delay retirement, and even by familiarity with happily working and playing octogenarians. Just as I did, many people noted names of celebrities who had celebrated their eightieth birthdays and saw that for them, as for the population in general, it no longer made sense to link "old age" to retirement. Ninety-three percent of the people surveyed said that "you're only as old as you feel," and 82 percent said that they themselves felt, on average, eleven years younger than their chronological age. I've taken questionnaires that distinguish between chronological age and "real" age, measured in terms of both physical and psychological health; I imagine that the 82 percent in the survey — a whopping 1,640 respondents! — reflected that distinction.

So I must, and will, come to terms with being eighty. I will relish the things I enjoy doing just as much as I did at sixty-nine or seventy-nine, but accept that there are some things I will decide not to do. I will accept that my physical strength has decreased, but take comfort from the fact that my trust in my own judgment is enhanced by years of experience. I will not beat myself up when I notice that I have become less confident in tackling new things, driving unfamiliar routes. I will allow myself to take time in making major decisions, and to claim the right to change my mind, and to say, "No!" I will try to cultivate, in the words of the Serenity Prayer, the "wisdom to know the difference" between the things I can change and the things I can't. Some of the things I can change are adaptations that have made my home safer and more convenient; a handrail alongside some steep stone steps, a new garage door with an automatic opener, another handrail, this one in the shower stall.

The biggest practical concession to my increasing years was the one I had the most difficulty making. A friend, still partnered but aware of my single status, had long urged me to buy some kind of device to wear in case of an accident, one that might necessitate my calling out, in those well-worn words, "I've fallen and I can't get up." I argued with my friend, I argued with myself, but eventually I saw the wisdom of that piece of advice and, after reading an advertisement in the *AARP Bulletin*, made the necessary telephone call. The product I selected was one called Splash, marketed by GreatCall. Not only does it operate when wet — hence the catchy name — but it will work in any part of the United States and has a built-in GPS system. If I get stuck in the bathtub at home as a friend of mine once did, or trip and break a bone while hiking somewhere, I can, with the push of a button, notify the company of both my plight and my location. Only days after I placed my order, UPS deposited a small package beside the handsome, new, lightweight, automatic-opener-equipped door to my basement garage. Now I just have to keep it charged and remember to wear it.

I did not like the fact that the average answer given by those two thousand Brits was that eighty equals "old"; I preferred the opinion of the one in five who said that you might be considered "old" when you reached ninety. I'll drink to that — and at least for now, it won't be from a can of Ensure.

9

The Joy of Old Age. (No Kidding.)

By Oliver Sacks, MD

Oliver Sacks, M.D., was born in London and educated in London, Oxford, and California. He practiced neurology in New York City, where he was a professor of neurology at NYU. The feature film *Awakenings* and Harold Pinter's *A Kind of Alaska* were both based on Dr. Sacks's work, and he was a regular contributor to *The New Yorker* and *The New York Review of Books*, as well as to many medical journals. He held honorary doctorates from numerous universities, including Queen's College, Oxford, the Karolinksa Institute, the Universidad Catolica del Peru, Gallaudet University, and Georgetown University. His work has been translated into more than two dozen languages worldwide. He died in August 2015.

L ast night I dreamed about mercury — huge, shining globules of quicksilver rising and falling. Mercury is element number 80, and my dream is a reminder that on Tuesday, I will be eighty myself.

Elements and birthdays have been intertwined for me since boyhood, when I learned about atomic numbers. At eleven, I could say "I am sodium" (Element 11), and now at seventy-nine, I am gold. A few years ago, when I gave a friend a bottle of mercury for his eightieth birthday — a special bottle that could neither leak nor break — he gave me a peculiar look, but later sent me a charming letter in which he joked, "I take a little every morning for my health."

Eighty! I can hardly believe it. I often feel that life is about to begin, only to realize it is almost over. My mother was the sixteenth of eighteen children; I was the youngest of her four sons, and almost the youngest of the vast cousinhood on her side of the family. I was always the youngest boy in my class at high school. I have retained this feeling of being the youngest, even though now I am almost the oldest person I know.

I thought I would die at forty-one, when I had a bad fall and broke a leg while mountaineering alone. I splinted the leg as best I could and started to lever myself down the mountain, clumsily, with my arms. In the long hours that followed, I was assailed by memories, both good and bad. Most were in a mode of gratitude — gratitude for what I had been given by others, gratitude, too, that I had been able to give something back. *Awakenings* had been published the previous year.

At nearly eighty, with a scattering of medical and surgical problems, none disabling, I feel glad to be alive — "I'm glad I'm not dead!" sometimes bursts out of me when the weather is perfect. (This is in contrast to a story I heard from a friend who, walking with Samuel Beckett in Paris on a perfect spring morning, said to him, "Doesn't a day like this make you glad to be alive?" to which Beckett answered, "I wouldn't go as far as that.") I am grateful that I have experienced many things — some wonderful, some horrible — and that I have been able to write a dozen books, to receive innumerable letters from friends, colleagues and readers, and to enjoy what Nathaniel Hawthorne called "an intercourse with the world."

I am sorry I have wasted (and still waste) so much time; I am sorry to be as agonizingly shy at eighty as I was at twenty; I am sorry that I speak no languages but my mother tongue and that I have not traveled or experienced other cultures as widely as I should have done.

I feel I should be trying to complete my life, whatever "completing a life" means. Some of my patients in their nineties or one hundreds say *nunc dimittis* — "I have had a full life, and now I am ready to go." For some of them, this means going to heaven — it is always heaven rather than hell, though Samuel Johnson and James Boswell both quaked at the thought of going to hell and got furious with David Hume, who entertained no such beliefs. I have no belief in (or desire for) any post-mortem existence, other than in the memories of friends and the hope that some of my books may still "speak" to people after my death.

W. H. Auden often told me he thought he would live to eighty and then "bugger off" (he lived only to sixty-seven). Though it is forty years since his death, I often dream of him, and of my parents and of former patients — all long gone but loved and important in my life.

At eighty, the specter of dementia or stroke looms. A third of one's contemporaries are dead, and many more, with profound mental or physical damage, are trapped in a tragic and minimal existence. At eighty the marks of decay are all too visible. One's reactions are a little slower, names more frequently elude one, and one's energies must be husbanded, but even so, one may often feel full of energy and life and not at all "old." Perhaps, with luck, I will make it, more or less intact, for another few years and be granted the liberty to continue to love and work, the two most important things, Freud insisted, in life.

When my time comes, I hope I can die in harness, as Francis Crick did. When he was told that his colon cancer had returned, at first he said nothing; he simply looked into the distance for a minute and then resumed his previous train of thought. When pressed about his diagnosis a few weeks later, he said, "Whatever has a beginning must have an ending." When he died, at eighty-eight, he was still fully engaged in his most creative work.

My father, who lived to ninety-four, often said that the eighties had been one of the most enjoyable decades of his life. He felt, as I begin to feel, not a shrinking but an enlargement of mental life and perspective. One has had a long experience of life, not only one's own life, but others', too. One has seen triumphs and tragedies, booms and busts, revolutions and wars, great achievements and deep ambiguities, too. One has seen grand theories rise, only to be toppled by stubborn facts. One is more conscious of transience and, perhaps, of beauty. At eighty, one can take a long view and have a vivid, lived sense of history not possible at an earlier age. I can imagine, feel in my bones, what a century is like, which I could not do when I was forty or sixty. I do not think of old age as an ever grimmer time that one must somehow endure and make the best of, but as a time of leisure and freedom, freed from the factitious urgencies of earlier days, free to explore whatever I wish, and to bind the thoughts and feelings of a lifetime together.

I am looking forward to being eighty.

2

BEING RESILIENT IN THE FACE OF CHANGE

10

Eighty

By Robert Ellis Smith

Robert Ellis Smith is a journalist who uses his legal training to report on the right to privacy, including electronic surveillance, credit, and medical records. Since 1974 he has published *Privacy Journal*, a monthly newsletter, and has been a frequent speaker and Congressional witness. He began the newsletter in Washington, D.C., but since 1986 he has lived in Providence, Rhode Island.

When my twenty-one-year-old son died, I knew that I needed a new focus. Otherwise, the grief and my longing for him would overwhelm me. I decided to become an actor. I was age seventy-three at the time, in 2013.

What we call grief is an organic force that comes and goes in our lives. It may disappear as quickly and as irrationally as it comes. I had to accept its presence, almost detach myself from it, and turn it into positive memory. Acting allows me to do that.

Eight weeks after Gregor died, I signed up for a once-a-week acting class for beginners and found myself in a roomful of young people, from fourteen to thirty years of age, and a lone man in his forties. There was nothing to lose. I had signed up for a class out of town and had told no one of my plans. After the horror of losing a loved one, a little stage fright or embarrassment wasn't going to faze me.

Death in a family, ironically, means losing a lot of friendships. People think you are toxic *and* contagious. Yes, many of them avoid you. Acting is the opposite. It is a bonding experience, regardless of age or gender or prior experience. Each of us comes together with varying life experiences to unite in a common enterprise, to make our friends and neighbors laugh or cry or simply enjoy a night out.

So here was an activity bringing me friendships — of all ages — and letting me exploit my creative interests. Hanging around young actors made me forget my age. After six weeks, the instructor looked at me and said, "Bob, you and Nancy there should be auditioning." Even though I realized that I had an inclination for acting (I had always envied actors and wanted to be bold enough to act), I had no idea what I was doing right.

I discovered that acting can enhance physical fitness; perhaps it maintains memory.

I had found an intense new focus in my life: absorbing all that I was learning about the theater, reading books about it, chattering about it with my (still remaining) friends, and becoming eager to get into a play and give it a try. The instructor recommended a fine book, *Audition* by Michael Shurtleff, which has tips for coping with life's challenges as well as those on the stage.

For instance, Shurtleff writes, "It is possible for an actor to get himself into such a healthy frame of mind that he enjoys auditioning. It gives him a chance to try on the role, to show his stuff, to practice his craft, to give himself a high, to experiment and take a risk, to meet a challenge."

I scoured the Internet for audition opportunities. I discovered that the area within a seventy-five-mile radius was teeming with community and regional theaters that were endlessly looking for talent. And there were plenty of short roles for newcomers. I enjoyed preparing the mini-scripts that are often required in auditions for theater roles. I incorporated my life experiences into the character that I was to play.

After two unsuccessful tries, I was cast as the elderly Juror Number Nine in *Twelve Angry Men*. The director was a retired police detective who prided himself on coaching newcomers; of the cast of thirteen men, he had selected six applicants with no prior experience. At the first rehearsal, I whispered into the ear of the man next to me, "I'm worried about memorizing the lines. I'm not sure I can do it."

"Aw. It comes to you," he said. "Once we walk around the stage (called "blocking," he told me), it comes to you. And your fellow actors are a great help."

"You been doing this long?" I asked.

"My second play," he replied. "The first one was great; so I came back."

In rehearsal, I felt really comfortable doing what I was doing. I kept calling it a "new focus." Indeed, I was focused. There was no opportunity during rehearsals to dwell on my loss negatively. On the other hand, I regularly invoked the loss of Gregor, in private moments, to direct my performance, to inspire it, to use it to bring emotion to the role.

Each night, before going onstage, I focused on a red

light somewhere backstage and said to myself, *Get me through this, Gregor.* I still do it. I have had nothing but success, in nine roles in two years, including singing in a couple of musicals. I even took two film roles, one of them about a father whose thirty-year-old son dies at sea. "I have experienced the real thing," I told the director. "How bad can make-believe be?"

Changing Your Dreams: Talking About Life and Death

By Dorian Mintzer, MSW, PhD, BCC

Dr. Dorian Mintzer is an experienced therapist; retirement transition, relationship, and executive coach; consultant; writer;
teacher; and speaker. Her expertise in adult development, life
planning, and positive psychology combined with her life experiences have led to her passion for helping individuals and
couples navigate the "second half of life." She is founder of
two virtual communities, one of which is the Fourth Tuesday
"Revolutionize Your Retirement" Interview Series for professionals and the public. She is coauthor of *The Couples Retirement
Puzzle: The 10 Must-Have Conversations for Creating an Amazing New
Life Together*, has contributed to a number of other books, and
has been featured in a variety of media such as the *New York
Times*, *Wall Street Journal*, CNN *Money*, ABC *Evening News*, and the
Today Show. Her Web site is revolutionizeretirement.com. She
lives in Brookline, Massachusetts with her husband and son.

I'm a "do it today" person and always have been.
Many of my friends are *mañana* people — there is
always tomorrow. By the time one reaches his or

her eighties, there are less *mañanas* ahead to defer to, even with the greater longevity that's occurring and the fact that middle age has recently been expanded to be age fifty to seventy-five. Among my husband, friends, clients, and colleagues in their eighties, I note a sobering sense of time passing. Their realization that they are eighty often elicits some profound changes. Even with retained vitality and resilience, priorities as well as expectations of self and others often begin to shift. Eighty years old reflects many years lived, many experiences, many hills and valleys, curveballs, disappointments, challenges, wisdom, and joys. It's a bit mind-boggling to think of how the world was in the 1930s, when many people age eighty-plus were born, and all of the changes that have occurred since then.

First disclosure — I am not eighty. I'm a decade younger. I write from the perspective of a therapist, coach, teacher (of geriatrics) and spouse of an eighty-plus year old. Until the past few decades there hasn't been much interest in adult development or people in their eighties and older. Now this is the fastest growing segment of our population. Aging isn't always easy. As young as we can feel inside, there are changes that happen in our bodies; and with it comes an awareness of slowing down and of the finite number of years ahead. It's easy to say be present, be positive, savor each day; but sometimes it's hard to do that. It can be frightening to think about *not* being part of the world and missing important milestones of those we love.

On a personal note, this is the second marriage for both my husband and me. Neither of us had children before and we became parents later in life. This has been part of keeping us young. As a family we traveled extensively; primarily hiking, skiing, biking, and sailing. Over the years we began to change some of our dreams. When my husband had trouble with high altitudes we gave up skiing on high mountains and much of our hiking. We both liked boating and always had our own sail boat until we sold it a few years ago when my husband's balance issues made sailing our own boat feel too stressful. We never imagined that taking cruises would work for us, but it does. We're able to see parts of the world we want to see, but with the comfort of only having to unpack once. We can have time together or apart. I may want to go on a shore excursion and he may want to stay on board and exercise or whatever.

As an observer, it seems to me that turning eighty

is challenging. It's a big number. My husband, for example, has many things he wants to experience. One was the high school graduation of our son from his own alma mater, which happened last summer. This "rite of passage" helped my husband decide it was time to have the heart surgery he was putting off. We had known for many years he would eventually need the surgery. He had the luxury of waiting to find the "right time," when symptoms were developing and quality of life was being compromised. Some milestones had been achieved, and my husband was deemed "strong enough" to withstand very invasive surgery. I know this can happen at any age. It just so happened that my husband was in his early eighties, still working part time in the field he loves, and still engaged fully in life with me, our son, family, and friends. It was a challenging time. We had to more fully confront life and death issues and take time to reflect on our lives. My husband, not a religious person, sought some guidance from our rabbi. He wrote an ethical will; a letter to our son. It felt comforting to me that we planned our summer so we could be together as a family to support each other.

Given my background and field, we've talked about life

and death issues over the years, but it was different this time given the immediacy. It wasn't just a hypothetical exercise. It was time to do all of the things I support my clients doing; to have the difficult conversations, and be sure that legal and financial issues are in order, while at the same time putting as much closure on relationships as possible. It was difficult to say good-bye and leave each other when my husband was wheeled to the operating room, not knowing if he would survive, and if he did, what quality of life he would have.

Some friends questioned the timing of the surgery since they felt he was "doing pretty well for a guy his age," but he was aware that he was developing more symptoms that compromised his life. I fully supported his decision in the hopes that his remaining years would be vital and full for him and us. We were lucky. He came through the eight-hour surgery with a new aortic arch, repaired aneurism, and new aortic valve. He didn't lose cognitive function (this had scared him even more than the idea of dying). The healing was slow, but three months later he returned to his part-time work and feels better and stronger than he has in the last twenty years. We're ready for another cruise and we're talking about a bicycle trip (although, being honest, we've discovered electric-assist bikes which are a boon for people who need a little extra push to be able to keep bicycle riding).

So, it's been an eye-opening experience for me to see the resilience that's still possible. My husband has taught me that the key is to stay alert, vigilant, and open to being realistic and also optimistic. None of us will live forever, and the older we get the clearer it is that there are fewer years ahead. Perhaps one has to confront death in order to fully live! This doesn't mean having a life or death experience, but it does mean recognizing our mortality so that we don't take a moment for granted. We need to cherish every day we are given and most of all, spend time with people we love.

12

Recovering from Injury and Illness: It's Up to Me, It's Up to You

By Morton H. Shaevitz, PhD, ABPP

Morton Shaevitz, PhD, ABPP, is a psychologist, author, and consultant. For more than three decades, he has been inspiring individuals and organizations to grow and change through his clinical practice, organizational consulting, training programs, and presentations. His current interests are assisting individuals to explore new models of productive aging and helping organizations develop transition programs for their valued older employees. His latest book, *Refire! Don't Retire: Make the Rest of Your Life the Best of Your Life*, coauthored with Ken Blanchard, was published in February 2015. He serves as an Associate Clinical Professor of Psychiatry (V) at the University of California San Diego (UCSD) and chairs the Geriatric Section of the California Psychological Association. Morton's other publications include four books, a number of audiotape series, and numerous journal articles.

After a month of denial and uncertainty, I agreed to have a surgery to address my severe back pain and decreasing ability to walk. My surgeon did a really good job, managing to remove the herniated disk with limited invasion and no fusion of vertebrae. However, while the surgery was successful, I was woefully disabled. Getting in and out of bed without further injury to my back involved a complex series of maneuvers: rolling onto my side, pushing up with my arms, and onto a walker. I needed help dressing, bathing, and going to the toilet. Everything was a challenge, everything was new, and everything was hard.

With no appetite, I lost more than twenty pounds, and sadly all of it muscle mass. I had difficulty sleeping, cycles of mild to moderate pain, and felt totally helpless for the first few weeks. Thanks to careful planning and Medicare, a physical therapist came to the house and slowly got me upright and moving. (By the way, physical therapy is covered by Medicare, but your physician must order it.) After a few weeks, it became clear the skills of my physician and team were responsible for a successful surgical outcome.

My surgeon was enthusiastically optimistic.

"You'll be up and about in a couple of weeks, walking in a month, driving again in two months, and back to yourself in three."

HA!

No way did that happen. It became abundantly clear that I needed to be the responsible party and not assume that things would get better on their own.

Partially mobile, still on a walker, but able to get around, I began searching for a physical therapist and visiting different settings.

I found the right person in the acting Associate Director of the UCSD Outpatient Physical Therapy Program. After an assessment, a program consisting of twice a week supervised physical therapy in the outpatient clinic, five days of at-home exercises, and daily walking (first with a walker, then with a cane, and then on my own) was prescribed. (Important: any physical therapist that starts out working with you before they've done a thorough assessment should be avoided.)

For decades, I had been focused on helping medical patients address their long-term chronic health problems such as diabetes, cardiovascular disease, and yes, post-trauma disabilities via behavior change. The research on patient follow-through is actually quite dismal — one in three patients does not get their prescriptions filled, and of those who do, only around half take their medications as prescribed. And this is easy — just take your medicine.

When we look at the more difficult behaviors like regular exercise, sleep, hygiene, food volume and type, weight-loss, and stress reduction, follow-through is even worse. Part of this, I believe, is due to the current paradigm, which talks about "patient compliance" and "patient adherence." Frankly, I don't think these are useful concepts. No one that I know wants to adhere or comply. Most people don't like to be told what to do. A more compelling concept is "patient empowerment," which the World Health Organization defines as:

> a process in which patients understand their role, are given the knowledge and skills by their health-care provider to perform a task in an environment that recognizes community and cultural differences and encourages patient participation.

So, it was up to me! I want to say that I'm not a jock and I've never been one. As a matter of fact, I was significantly overweight as a child and adolescent. Aside from being a physically large presence on the line of an intramural football team, I did not play team sports in high school or college. Even as an adult, I didn't begin exercising until I was in my late thirties and that was to accompany my newly pregnant wife on her daily walks so she could have a healthy pregnancy — and it worked for her.

But what I was doing then was relatively easy and totally pain-free. After my back surgery, what was asked of me was very, very, very difficult and, at times, quite painful. I was having difficulty standing, sitting, walking, and balancing. But I found that after I started doing what I was asked to do I began to feel better, stronger, and more in control of my life. So, I had a choice. Do nothing and hope for the best, or begin taking slow steps forward.

So, what happened?

Eventually, I was able to throw away my cane.

Eventually, I was able to dress myself.

Eventually, I was able to step into a shower, stand on my own, and step out to dry myself.

Eventually, I was able to get back to a number of projects that I was working on and complete a book on aging with Ken Blanchard (refirebook.com).

Eventually, I began to rebuild my clinical and consulting practice.

Eventually, I was able to fly to New York and to Eugene, Oregon, to visit my other two adult children.

Understand this was not a superhuman feat. I was simply fortunate enough to have a good outcome from the surgeries, make a commitment to recovery, and was (and still am) living a happy life filled with friends, family, and meaningful things to do.

So I say again, it's up to me, it's up to you, and it's up to each of us to do whatever we can to make a difference. Learn what you need to do to get better and do it. Take charge of your recovery. By taking action, you get to determine, in part, what that future will look like.

13

How It Feels to Be Eighty

By Katherine Griesz

Katherine Griesz was born and grew up in Budapest, Hungary, and is a Holocaust survivor. After the war, she left the country of her birth, attended school in Switzerland, and subsequently settled in Sydney, Australia. After many years, she felt a strong desire to return to Europe and she chose London as her new home. Eventually, Katherine came to the United States via marriage, having met her husband in Vienna. He was also a native of Budapest, but had moved to New York. After working in a number of interesting jobs, Katherine retired and decided to turn her hand to producing a memoir. Having been recently widowed, she is now surrounded by many friends and leads a quiet life, reading, writing, and lecturing.

We all know that old age is not easy to bear, but like everything else in life, how we handle growing older is a very individual thing. Some people do it well, others less so. How often do we hear the malcontents complain about aches and pains, and the other negative sides of being elderly? They look back and compare their present age with the times when they were young, but fail to put youth in its proper context. They forget all the problems they once experienced, which fortunately do not exist in old age.

For example, we no longer have bosses to give us orders, and we no longer have to adhere to strict timetables, or have difficult coworkers to contend with. In addition, we no longer have to look for a partner to share our life.

The other day, a sentence I read on the Internet caught my attention. It said: "Do not regret growing older, it is a privilege denied to many." How true! So many people die young, without ever having tasted the joys of life. Love, parenthood, middle age, and full maturity were not granted to them.

I am no stranger to life's dark sides. I was born in Budapest, Hungary, and survived the Holocaust and other political upheavals. Emigration and living in different countries followed, and I had to learn how to fight for myself. I have spent the last five decades here in America and at age sixty-five "officially" became elderly, that is a "senior citizen."

I kept on working as a multilingual tour leader, showing foreign visitors New York City. I was so proud of "my" city. It was a glamour job that I loved very much. Then, I reached the age of seventy and retired from work, but I knew that I could not be idle. I had to do *something* with my life, so I started to look around for a new project.

But what? And then it hit me! I started to look back over the years and realized that by no means had I lived an "average life." I realized I needed to put my story down on paper and so I focused on writing my memoir. This project took well over ten years, because a tremendous amount of historical research needed to be done in order to fill in all the background details of my life story. In my book, I describe what it was like to endure the horrors of the Holocaust in Budapest, followed by several years of Communist dictatorship.

I self-published my book, *From the Danube to the Hudson*, about three years ago and I was deeply gratified with its success. A strenuous effort at publicity followed and it included a good number of lectures. By that time I was eighty-two years old.

The clock, thankfully, did not stop at that age. Even

with the loss of the only person I had in my life — my husband — who passed away very recently, I know that I have to go on. But, hey, at eighty-five years old, I am still only a kid.

Reaching one's eighties can be wonderful, provided you are physically and mentally well, have many interests, love people, and recognize that being old is not a punishment. On the contrary, it is the greatest privilege the good Lord can bestow on us.

14

The Stingray

By David Black

David Black has been a violinist, opera singer, award-winning salesman, CIA covert intelligence officer, actor, Tony Award-winning producer of eighteen Broadway shows, director, playwright, and author of *The Actor's Audition*, *The Magic of Theater*, and *Falling off Broadway*. He is also an artist and his paintings hang in the residences of American ambassadors. Hillary Rodham Clinton called David Black "an honorary diplomat" for introducing Tunisian Collaborative Painting to the United States.

When my good friend and favorite editor Mark Chimsky invited me to contribute to his book, 80 *Things to Do When You Turn 80*, I was already eighty-four years old and I had done quite a lot in the preceding years, including producing and directing, painting, and writing three books. I wanted to do something new to write about for this essay so I asked my wife if she could think of something. She told me she had heard of a place in the Cayman Islands where you could wrestle a stingray. That sounded like an adventure!

We went to The Cayman Islands and stayed in a lovely house on a beach. The next morning we got on the boat that took us out to where the stingrays were swimming. When I saw my first stingray I decided to find something else to do for this book. The stingray looked like a giant kite with a long electrified tail. The rest of him resembled a military airplane in the shape of a triangle capable of supersonic speed. He also had two enormous red eyes embedded in what appeared to be a wet, expensive fur coat.

While I was trying to think of something else to write about for this book, my wife jumped in the water and got in line to wrestle the stingray. She has always been more adventurous than my city-boy cowardly self. Then I realized if I didn't do it I would have to live the rest of my life listening to her telling our friends how she wrestled the stingray.

When it was my turn the stingray looked me over carefully with his revolving red eyes. For one brief moment I thought of the affection I never received from my mother. Then I was suddenly surrounded by the gigantic wings of the stingray squeezing my head and chest. I began finding it hard to breathe. But just as I thought I was about to experience my last gasp forever, he let me go.

The morning after we got home I had a stomach ache that would not go away. I was rushed to a hospital where the doctor asked me if I had done anything unusual lately. I was afraid to tell him the truth so he began investigations on his own. After checking me out he told me I had gallstones, which would have to be removed. He also told me they would have to remove my gallbladder, but he said they were having trouble locating it. I realized the stingray might have pushed my gallbladder to a new location when he hugged me.

While I was in the emergency room being prepared for my surgical procedures, a nurse told me that a reporter from the New York Times was on the telephone and wanted to speak with me. I imagined he had heard about the stingray and was contacting its victims. When I picked up the phone the reporter told me he had discovered an interesting story about one of the shows I had produced on Broadway and he wanted to talk to me about it. (One of the eighty things I did *before*

I turned eighty was to produce eighteen Broadway shows).

The reporter had discovered that the Broadway play I produced in early 1970, *Paris Is Out*, listed a well-known person as my co-producer. I told him the story of the twenty-three year old who appeared in my office and invited me to lunch. During the meal he offered to invest $70,000 in my show, if I would put his name next to mine as the co-producer. When the show was a flop he asked me, "David, what should I do now?" "Why don't you try real estate?" I suggested. The young man's name was Donald Trump.

The story appeared with photographs in the *New York Times* the day after my surgery. I was not only minus my gallbladder but I was minus most of my friends. Since then I have decided that the next time Mark asks me to write something, it will be about one of the things I did *before* I turned eighty!

15

Revisit The Dream, and Begin Again

By PJ Cowan

PJ Cowan is a self-published author of forty children's books who, using a forty-two-inch monitor and magnifier, battled her way through dyslexia and macular degeneration to get her stories written. She didn't let her handicap stop her from reaching her goal of writing stories for her great-grandchildren. She also gives her books to children in hospitals, shelters, and free libraries all over the United States.

From the very beginning, our lives are filled with struggle. First, we struggle to be born. As toddlers we struggle to learn to walk, talk, and deal with our surroundings. We endure the onset of puberty, and the bullying that is part of the life experience. As teens we hone our social and academic skills, and learn to deal with the handicaps that come with the package that is us.

By the time we are at the threshold of midlife, we should have set, worked for, and hopefully met our goals. But, sadly, if we aren't rich and/or famous by eighty, chances are we never will be.

I was blessed with a singing voice, but, try as I may, I was not able to learn to read music. This, I was told, was because I had dyslexia, a condition diagnosed by my third grade teacher after she discovered I was able to memorize the stories she read to us, but could not read them myself.

In time I discovered the little tricks that help one overcome that particular handicap. I learned which numbers and letters turned themselves upside down and switched places relentlessly. It worked for me in school and on the job. I got away with it for sixty-some years. In my late sixties I developed macular degeneration. So much for the tricks; they don't work when your middle vision is absent.

I love to write and always wanted to create the "great American novel," but sadly, my brain only produces short stories that tell themselves, starting and ending whenever they please. I decided to go with that, and by the time I was writing in earnest, the great-grandchildren were beginning to arrive so I wrote for them.

By this time however, my two handicaps had united as one and were fighting my efforts. I could no longer see the text on the small screen, and what I could see fought for a place in my vision. Not wanting to give up, I called upon an expert, who directed me to buy a forty-two-inch monitor that he programmed with very large icons. I was able to set the font as large as I needed it to be. In addition, I began to use another tool, the magnifier, so I could write once again.

Funny thing, the more I wrote, the more I found that little stories began presenting themselves to me. Before I knew it, there were ten short books waiting to be illustrated. So I went on a search. It took me awhile but I found a site that employed illustrators at expensive, but not exorbitant prices, and sent off my first book.

If you write, you know that it's not easy to get published. After struggling to find a publisher and getting only a series of rejections, I decided that I didn't have time for this game and would take a chance on self-publishing. I had some savings, so my adventure began.

Way back in the twentieth century, self-publishing was one of the dirtiest terms in the publishing industry. If your story wasn't accepted and published by a well-known publisher, you were not a true author, just a "wannabe." One had to go to a "vanity" press to publish, and they took full advantage of the author by charging outrageous prices.

I could not afford the print prices offered by local printers. I was about to give up my search when I received a colorful postcard in the mail advertising a small print shop in St. Louis, Missouri. I liked their prices and sent them a book to print.

I list my books on my printer's Web site, but I give them away in order to get them into the hands of as many children as I can. In 2009 I got in touch with a fellow author who advised me to look at giving them to shelters. I obtained a list of local shelters from my church and was off and running. The list of places to which I donate my books has grown to thirty-four shelters, children's hospitals, and free libraries all across the United States.

As I turned eighty, I found a graphic designer who was willing to take on the burden of designing my books for a small salary. His wife has already translated seven of them into Spanish for me.

If, at eighty, you want to write, but have not done so, this can be a new beginning for you. Nowadays self-publishing is as easy as writing your story or your book, and uploading the electronic file to an online self-publishing company for the world to see. Do it! You will have a great time creating it, and you won't be sorry.

16

Life Is an Adventure

By Jerry Witkovsky, MSW

A social worker by training, Jerry Witkovsky has been a beloved mentor to thousands of individuals and generations of families, thanks to forty-seven years of professional leadership, including eighteen of them as General Director of Chicago's Jewish Community Centers. In 1995, Jerry was named one of the city's "Most Effective Nonprofit CEOs" by *Crain's Chicago Business* magazine. Since retiring in 1997, Jerry has focused his considerable energies on being a grandparenting "activist," setting up programs at area schools and being featured on radio, TV, and in the news. His joyful commitment to his six grandchildren (ages thirteen to thirty-one) and to their parents, and his passionate belief in the transformative power of becoming a "Teaching-and-Learning" family, is at the heart of his book *The Grandest Love: Inspiring the Grandparent-Grandchild Connection*.

I met my wife Margaret when I was a senior at George Williams College in Chicago. She was a freshman. Her parents would not fund her college education unless she wanted to be a nurse or a teacher, and she didn't want to be either one of those. Maybe it was fate, or maybe it was her strength, confidence, and creativity, but she worked in an office for three years, saved her money, and came to George Williams, setting the perfect timing for our paths to cross.

I had to take a dance class for my degree. And, there she was. Beautiful, charming, good moves. The full package. After the dance class I asked her out. In Chicago's Hyde Park neighborhood there were a lot of different places where college kids could go to get a drink or hang out. As we sat down at the table she said proudly, "I can drink you under the table, Jerry." And I said, "I only drink root beer."

Six months later we were married.

After our daughter graduated from the University of Illinois and our son was still a sophomore at Carlton College in Minnesota, my wife declared she was going to do a double major in Psychology and Art History at Roosevelt University. At Margaret's behest, the university worked out a program with the Art Institute of Chicago, which was just down the street. She arranged to take classes at both schools, and she earned her BA.

In 1997 Margaret was diagnosed with breast cancer,

and in 2003 she passed away. I wallowed in loneliness for a long time after Margaret's death.

I knew that Margaret and I had shared a beautiful life together. But, repeating a phrase that I often use with other grandparents at speaking events, I reminded myself, "Don't die until you are dead." Despite my sadness, I wanted to move on.

I figured I could just wallow or I could do something about this. I decided to join a support group for those who had lost their spouses to cancer. We met for fourteen months, one night a week.

I met a woman there. Her name is Felice. We started dating, and we're still dating. We travel, we go to concerts, and we go out with friends. We hold hands watching television.

It was through this time that I wrote and published a book, *The Grandest Love: Inspiring the Grandparent-Grandchild Connection*. Now well into my eighties, I've been traveling across the U.S. speaking to grandparents about how to enter their grandchildren's world. I've been to Rochester, New York to speak, Manhattan, Phoenix, and Los Angeles. I even have a Web site, over 1,200 followers on Facebook and Twitter each, and my own YouTube Channel, all connected to *The Grandest Love.*

I have always advocated for a culture of Teaching-and-Learning, one in which knowledge and experience are shared in all directions, from young to old or old to young; where individuals take their passions and teach those around them. All involved not only learn new skills or gain new knowledge, but get insights and more closely connect with loved ones, at any age. I had promoted a culture of Teaching-and-Learning as a business leader, as head of the Jewish Community Centers of Chicago, and had both preached and practiced this at home.

I am passionate about the power of grandparents to unleash their creativity and transform their families. I have successfully set up Grandparents Connection programs in the schools in my hometown of Deerfield, as well as at other schools and synagogues across the Chicagoland area.

What's next? I want to see armies of grandparents actively volunteering and supporting their grandkids in school. How? I've written a step-by-step "how-to" kit to help grandparents mobilize and connect to their own local schools. The kit would show grandparents how to ask their grandchildren's teachers about the classes and subjects being taught. For example, the head of our local high school's English department gave the grandparents of freshmen in the school a list of all the books they'll be reading over the next four years. I turned eighty-eight in March of 2016, and my goal is to find sponsors and partners to have the kit published and distributed across the U.S. before I'm ninety.

Some look at life as an arc, where you are young and learning in the beginning, achieving and producing in the middle, and winding down or even diminishing toward the end. But I say, life is an adventure, from start to finish. You can wallow or you can move on and do things.

You are never too old to stop and smell the roses. I do that almost daily, literally, with walks year-round in our nearby botanic garden. I find peace and joy in nature. It replenishes my spirit and brings me tranquility and time to think about what's next.

At eighty-eight, I'm still going — and I'm going to keep going!

17

Be All You Can Be

By Roger Landry, MD, MPH

Dr. Roger Landry is a preventive medicine physician, author of the award-winning *Live Long, Die Short: A Guide to Authentic Health and Successful Aging* and president of Masterpiece Living, a group of multi-discipline specialists in aging who partner with communities to assist them in becoming destinations for continued growth. Trained at Tufts University School of Medicine and Harvard University School of Public Health, Dr. Landry specializes in building environments that empower older adults to maximize their unique potential.

There's no sugarcoating it. Aging is about loss. We lose friends to geography, to sickness, or to different life pathways. We lose abilities — both physical and intellectual. It's as if we are no longer really being seen and heard. We become invisible.

Okay. Before you slit your wrists, PLEASE NOTE, *loss doesn't have to be the whole story.* As long as we have a pulse, we can grow. We can grow physically, actually building vitality and resilience. We can improve our memory and reduce the likelihood of ever having the symptoms of dementia. We can, in fact, significantly alter the trajectory of our aging experience so that we live our lives at the highest level of functioning possible until our time is up.

Me? I want to age like a leaf. I want to get more colorful as I age. I want to blend with others to make more beauty than I can alone. And when my time comes, hopefully, I'll just fall off the tree. No long chronic loss, no expensive long decline, and no loss of independence and dignity. So, how do I do this?

The Research Is Clear

It's been more than twenty years now since the seminal work that smashed the stereotype of aging first came to light. The MacArthur Foundation's ten-year-long Study on Aging clearly showed us that it is not genes, or fate, or serendipity that mostly determines how we age. It is *lifestyle* — the choices we make every day — that plays the major role, up to 70 percent, in what our aging journey looks like. All subsequent research has validated the finding that how we age is mostly up to us.

At this point, you're assuming I'm going to launch into

a sermon about exercising more, losing weight, and eating better . . . not exactly. I'm first going to talk about our distant ancestors.

Since humans have walked the earth — in fact, about 99 percent of the time we've been around — we lived a radically different lifestyle; one that, despite marked advancement in our societies, is what we still require to be healthy and age well. Nothing exotic, nothing difficult, nothing expensive. This lifestyle of our hunter-gatherer ancestors that has been bequeathed to us is in our very DNA, but we're getting further and further from living it, and so we're suffering the consequences.

Squeezing the Most Out of Our Lives

Being all that we can be for as long as possible, like my leaf wish, is called in public health terms, the *compression of morbidity*. Morbidity is when we're sick and impaired. We want to compress that time. Another growing concern for many is learning how to be vital until our time is up. It doesn't happen because we're lucky. Life has curveballs waiting for all of us. It's about how *resilient* we are to take life's hits and keep on truckin'. Resilience comes from that simple lifestyle we all have written in our DNA. We don't have to become hunter-gathers; we just have to make sure the key components are there.

The Path to Your Best

Any changes you plan to make have to be in small steps or they will end up in the same bin with your New Year's resolutions of the past. What do you want to change? What's the *smallest* thing you can do to start moving toward that goal? THAT small thing is your goal. Achieve that, and then take the next smallest step. Didn't make it? Set the goal back a bit. You cannot fail. By taking small, realistic bites, you can indeed eat the elephant.

Now, the first thing you must do to be all you can be is to *MOVE*. Notice I didn't say exercise. You can do that, but to begin a lifestyle that is based on movement, like our ancestors, you must begin to move naturally — walking, climbing, bending, stretching — throughout the day. Think 10,000 steps a day.

Next, *be with people*. Friends, family, new friends, friends of friends. Eat with them. Walk with them. Converse with them. Forgive them. Care for them. Alone time is good, but isolation is deadly.

Learn new things. Yes, forget fear of failure. Who cares? Be a beginner every day. Scare yourself by getting out of your comfort zone.

You must *find your purpose*. You must have a reason to pop out of bed in the morning. Usually that involves other living things: people, animals, the environment. No purpose, no *joie de vivre*.

And yes, *eat a little less overall and eat more plants*. Our bodies jump for joy on our ancestors' diet.

Not Rocket Science

Come on now, that's doesn't sound difficult, does it? You can do it. Then, you'll be more likely to be able to do the other seventy-nine things in this book! Live long. Live well.

18

The Gift of Wisdom

By George Wolf

George Wolf was born in Brno, Czechoslovakia (now the Czech Republic), into a large, well-off family. When Germany occupied the rest of Czechoslovakia in March 1939, George and his mother and father drove to Prague, and obtained one of the very few exit visas the Gestapo allowed. Overnight, he and his parents became homeless, stateless refugees. By sheer luck, they found refuge in Switzerland. Later, they received word that most of their family had been herded first into the Theresienstadt concentration camp and eventually murdered in Auschwitz. Near the end of the war, George worked for the American Consulate in Zurich. In the summer of 1946, as an interpreter and translator, he attended the Nuremberg War Crimes Trials, and decided not to go back to Czechoslovakia. In 1950-52, George was part of a Cold War intelligence project of the U.S. Army. Back in civilian life, he became a fashion industry designer, consultant, and eventually manufacturer. At age eighty, he found a new career and a much more fulfilling life of social work with The Blue Card, aiding destitute Holocaust survivors.

The most surprising thing about turning eighty is how quickly it has come about. Of course it does not require much — just hanging around, avoiding trouble and illness, and not doing anything stupid.

I never considered "retiring," that is, not continuing to being active and creative. I had seen neighbors, retired from meaningful work and positions, become depressed from doing nothing constructive, and die off soon after from a variety of illnesses, vascular accidents, and car accidents. Consequently, I started a new business at age sixty-seven, domestic manufacturing of upscale fashion knitwear in the economically impacted area of the Bronx, New York, after a career of consulting and creating new businesses in the field of fashion. By 2005, after thirteen years, that business, like so many others, went to China.

At age seventy-nine, despite vast experience and ability, I found myself unemployable. My impressive resume elicited rapid invitations to interviews, only to have my gray-haired appearance lead to sudden embarrassed excuses, the fastest interview lasting only two minutes. A fortunate consulting gig ended when that business also went to China. I needed a new direction, and became involved with Encore.org and their Purpose Prizes for older people creating socially productive new ventures. Through Encore, I came across a New York City nonprofit called ReServe, now also active in other cities. ReServe provides the many nonprofits that need otherwise unaffordable help with retired professionals, looking to remain meaningfully busy in part-time work at nominal stipends.

I had some fascinating interviews, some leading to several weeks or months of work with a wide variety of nonprofits that specialized in such areas as prelitigation arbitration; child-care; the promotion of small businesses to recent immigrants; and, most important of all, domestic abuse prevention. Another job involved working with a small ballet troupe, responsible for revitalizing an economically depressed upstate community. One interview led to a lasting relationship with The Blue Card, a charity that aids destitute Holocaust survivors. I am now eighty-eight, and I've been with them for seven years; I fully expect to remain there until the end. The one constant in all of these endeavors has been the element of helping those who need it the most.

Originally from what is now the Czech Republic, I was lucky to have escaped Hitler, whom I saw in person in Prague, and avoided the camps as a refugee in neutral Switzerland. I worked for the U.S. State Department, at the American Consulate General in Zurich at the end of the war. I spent time at the Nuremberg War Crimes Trials as an interpreter in 1946, and then at the end of that year, at age nineteen, I came to America without any family. After a stint in a Cold War intelligence project with the U.S. Army, I went on to have a varied career in fashion design and production.

Eventually I met and married a brilliant young pianist, and through her I became involved in classical music, making friends with performers, teachers, and composers. The leadership and organizational aspects I learned in the business world come in handy at The Blue Card, where I now do indirect fundraising, organizing their charity marathon teams at the New York City Marathon, and in other cities like Miami and Jerusalem. I do extensive outreach and lecturing, sometimes making two presentations in one day. My other responsibilities include writing, representing the organization at events and conferences, and advising on policy and programs, especially as it concerns geriatric problems with which I have direct experience. I'm also a member of a committee adjudging applications for financial assistance. This gets me involved in aspects of social work, bereavement counseling, and more, and provides me with a large circle of new friends and collaborators outside of New York, from Prague and Vienna to Boston and Jerusalem, and including journalists, professors, writers, composers, diplomats, and government representatives, all of whom help me sustain my cultural interests.

My never-less-than interesting and exciting marriage of fifty-seven years came to a sad end with the death of my spouse after a long illness and caregiving, which largely consumed the last three years. It now requires reimagining life without her. Besides my work, I am attending and organizing concerts and poetry readings, supporting a major music school, maintaining a busy social schedule, and even enjoying a new romance. In sum, my life has changed full circle, and I can confidently say that despite my recent grief, I am now more productive, respected, and appreciated than ever. At age eighty-eight, I am happier in some ways than I was in many of my younger years.

19

Eighty Is Old

By Walter M. Bortz II, MD

Walter M. Bortz II, MD, is a Clinical Associate Professor of Medicine at Stanford University School of Medicine and a graduate of Williams College and the University of Pennsylvania School of Medicine. Recognized as one of America's most distinguished scientific experts on aging and longevity, Dr. Walter Bortz's research has focused on the importance of physical exercise in the promotion of robust aging. He has published over 130 medical articles and authored numerous books, including *We Live Too Short and Die Too Long*, *Dare to Be 100*, *Living Longer for Dummies*, and *Diabetes Danger*. Dr. Bortz is past co-chairman of the American Medical Association's Task Force on Aging, former President of The American Geriatric Society and is currently Chairman of the Medical Advisory Board for the Diabetes Research and Wellness Foundation, as well as a Senior Advisor to Healthy Silicon Valley, a community collaborative effort, which addresses the soaring incidence of obesity and diabetes.

Knowing that the maximum human lifespan is 120 years lends itself conveniently to subdivisions. Zero to forty is young, forty to eighty is middle, and eighty-plus is old. So I am now almost six years into my "old" era. There is more time to look back upon than ahead.

By any standard, looking back yields treasure chests full of special shining memories. Most of them have to do with family, some with work, many with friends. Unfortunately, most of these positive memories are smirched by the death of my wife last July. We were together sixty-two years, a big chunk of my life, so it's inevitable that I would feel lonely now. But Father taught me what Robert Browning wrote:

then welcome each rebuff
that turns earth's smoothness rough
that bids each man not sit nor stand
but go.

As I reflect back on the years I spent married and fathering and grandfathering I see too that there is a future. I am determined that this is where the binoculars must focus.

As a geriatrician I am firm in my projection of one hundred healthy years as our birthright. Millions of years of evolutionary shaping have given this as the human potential. So if one hundred is out there as my destination, and I'm only eighty-five now, that gives me fifteen years of opportunity to be pursued.

When I showed this projection to my Stanford colleague Albert Bandura and asked him when I could stop working on my "self-efficacy," he answered, "Never."

All of this helps me to confirm Bortz's Law: "It is never too late to start, but it is always too soon to stop." I resonate with this exhortation. The world needs my fifteen future years.

I have been given eighty-five glorious years. I owe much, but much remains to live and to do.

20

Losing My Teeth

By Donald Hall

Donald Hall, eighty-seven, is the author of Essays After Eighty and The Selected Poems of Donald Hall. He was Poet Laureate of the United States in 2006-2007. In 2011, President Obama gave him the National Medal of Arts.

When I was eighty-five my last teeth wiggled loose in my bottom jaw and I was toothless. For decades an upper plate had sufficed but now I needed a lower if I were to gnaw meatballs into my gullet. Dental machinery is difficult for me because my jawbones and gums are so thin that the hardware can't find a purchase. My uppers stay stuck with a touch of glue but not the lower plate. My tongue flails up through the dental horseshoe and the plastic teeth fly out even though I have applied a pound of adhesive. Sometimes they slip loose while I'm chewing in a restaurant. I hold a napkin to my face and tuck a loathsome slimy pink object into a jacket pocket.

Other diners at Piero's or the Millstone gag as they avert their eyes.

Between meals at home, I kept my lowers on a shelf beside my blue chair and every day I lost them. I lost them because I couldn't stand them. Since I don't go outdoors, they had to be nearby. I don't have a dog that eats dentures. If I walked a dog, every day I would break two hips. My cat's mouth is too small. Each time I lost my teeth, I stared at every tabletop and shelftop. I looked at places where they couldn't possibly be, and once or twice that's where they were. My trainer Pam comes Tuesday and Thursday to stride me on a treadmill and punish me with weights. Once as I was pacing through cardio my teeth shot out. I tucked them into a small tray beside the treadmill's panel of knobs and buttons. Did I hide them on purpose? I gummed my food for two days until Pam came back. Only a woman can find what I lose. A few years ago I spent three months in New York. I had my own teeth then, and never misplaced them, but I wore bifocals and when I couldn't find them I telephoned my assistant Kendel in New Hampshire and she told me where they were. (I don't lose my bifocals now because I no longer wear them. I won't tell you why.) Once I was in my bedroom when the telephone rang on the far side of my bed. I was talking to my investment guy Jeff when my teeth flew out. Talking often flies them out. Linda sleeps on that side of the bed and found them.

Another time I couldn't find them anywhere and Linda was soon to arrive. My fecklessness shamed me. I remembered putting them on top of my rollator under a throwaway piece of cardboard next to a mug of cold coffee. I tossed the cardboard, set the mug beside the coffee maker, and when I got back to my blue chair my teeth were missing. I checked out the wastebasket where I threw the cardboard. I checked out the coffee maker. When Linda walked in I told her I had lost my teeth and she reached behind her chair and picked them up.

It was a week before I lost them again. I heated up supper one night, take-home flatbread with shaved steak and stewed tomatoes and hot peppers. I warmed it in the toaster and brought it into the parlor where every night I watch the Red Sox. Often I eat supper in my mechanical chair, so I keep a tube of glue beside it. This time I found the glue but not the teeth. They weren't among the strategic piles of papers, tucked away so that I would never forget them, where I forget them. The flatbread went cold and I stuffed it into the take-home box and back into the refrigerator. I gummed a banana, not difficult, and tried gumming cheddar, not easy. When Kendel brought me my breakfast sandwich I wrapped myself in a bath towel and chomped my oozy meal, slithering sausage and fried egg and English muffin into my mouth and my beard and my lap. When Linda dropped by at noon she picked my teeth out of the wastebasket.

She also had a great idea. Since my teeth flopped out after every meal, she said that I should lift up my rollator seat — my rollator confronts me at all times — and plop my pink horseshoe (horseshoe crab, crabby horseshoe) into the bin under the rollator's seat. Her great idea is virtually foolproof but some fools can outdo any proof. Since Linda made her suggestion, I have lost my teeth twice. Staring at the empty bin of the rollator I wail out loud, "Where are my teeth?" The wailing does it. My teeth are in my mouth.

21

How Your Work — and You — Can Live Forever

by George Lois

The legendary George Lois is the most creative, prolific advertising communicator of our time. Running his own ad agencies, he is renowned for dozens of marketing miracles that triggered innovative and populist changes in American (and world) culture. In his twenties he was a pioneer of the landmark Creative Revolution in American Advertising. Additionally, thirty-eight of his iconic Esquire covers from the 1960s have been installed in the permanent collections of the Museum of Modern Art in New York.

Growing up in a loving, Greek immigrant family in the Bronx, it was understood that the only son of Haralambos and Vasilike Lois would finish high school and take over his father's flower shop. But my drawings at P.S. 7 caught the eye of my eighth grade art teacher, Mrs. Engle, who handed me a black, string portfolio filled with my drawings, which she had saved, and sent me to the High School of Music & Art (a brilliant, specialized school in Manhattan founded in 1936 by Mayor Fiorello LaGuardia). After my first day at Music & Art, I knew that I would never be a florist.

In my first term at Music & Art, Mr. Patterson taught a basic design class where he asked us to create abstract design compositions each day. The more we ripped off a Malevich (or Klee, Bayer, Albers, or Mondrian), the better Mr. Patterson liked it. Bo-r-r-ring!

In the last class of the term, when Mr. Patterson sternly asked us to create a design on 18" x 24" illustration board using only rectangles and called it a final exam, I made my move. As my twenty-six classmates worked furiously, cutting and pasting, I sat motionless. Mr. Patterson, eyeballing me, was doing a slow burn as he walked up and down the classroom, peering over the shoulder of each student. Time was up. Growing apoplectic as he stacked the final designs, he went to grab my completely empty board, when I thrust my arm forwards and interrupted him by casually signing "G. Lois" in the bottom left-hand corner. He was thunderstruck. I had "created" the ultimate 18" x 24" rectangle design! I had taught myself that my work had to be fresh, different, seemingly outrageous. From then on, I understood that nothing is as exciting as an idea.

Four years later, with savings of thousands of ten-cent tips delivering flowers in the lace-curtain Irish, Kingsbridge section of the Bronx, I paid for my first term at Pratt Institute to further my designing ability, shocking my father, who had expected me to work full-time to prepare for the inheritance of his beloved flower shop that had sustained my family throughout the days of the Great Depression.

In 1949, on my first day at Pratt, I spotted Rosemary Lewandowski, a second-generation, Polish-American who had come to New York City from a working-class family from Syracuse, New York, to build an artistic career and meet cultured people. Instead she met me. I saw her face, and after a lo-o-ong check of her legs, I knew she would be at my side the rest of my life.

For sixty-five years, she has loved me, fed me, raised our two sons, nurtured our two grandsons, was one of the few female art directors of her time, has a career as a dynamic easel painter, and sees, and okays, everything I produce, and then some — working with me as a thinker and copywriter on ads, TV spots, slogans, and brand names I usually take credit for. What a dame!

In 1978, sixteen days after my son Harry's twentieth birthday, he was struck down by an undetected heart disorder, Long Q-T Syndrome. Harry, whose name means "joy" in Greek, was a powerfully strong young man, a living incarnation of the great Herakles, a warrior on the athletic field with a love for living, a probing mind, and already a talented film producer.

Since losing the joy of our life, the grief stricken Rosemary, Harry's younger brother Luke, and I have gone on, living, working, remembering, and constantly smiling at the images of him in every room of our home. As Abraham Lincoln said after the death of his son Willie: "If I did not engage in levity, my heart would break."

Having a mate who understands and contributes mightily to your ethos of life and work is a blessing beyond measure. Now in our eighties, our love for each other remains absolute. And I continue to diligently, and passionately, work a full-time schedule, side-by-side with my talented son, Luke, as we continue to fight racial injustice, Wall Street greed, political demagogues, government that benefits the wealthy at the expense of the poor and powerless, and anyone or anything corrupted by money and power.

At the age of eighty-five, I have finally decided to give my archives to a hometown university. The City College of New York (CCNY) has always been a melting pot of Big Idea thinking in all intellectual and creative-driven professions, graduating many of the most distinguished people in the world, including ten Nobel Laureates, derived from one of the most democratic student bodies in America.

My beloved Music & Art was located on the very edge of the CCNY campus, so my archives, headed for CCNY, makes me feel like I've truly come home.

CCNY most reflects my belief that as a graphic communicator, imbued with the melting-pot ethics of my city, my mission in life is not to sedate, but to awaken, to disturb, to communicate, to command, and even to provoke.

My archives will be open to the public and available for educational and research purposes, but most importantly, they will ensure that my life's work will continue to inspire a heroic ethos in the souls of thousands of students throughout the world.

RULES OF
ENGAGEMENT

22

Ruta's Rules

By Ruta Lee

Ruta Lee is one of Hollywood's most glamorous ladies, and also one of its most multifaceted and top-notch civic contributors. She has appeared in such illustrious films as *Seven Brides for Seven Brothers*, *Funny Face*, *Witness for the Prosecution*, and as Frank Sinatra's leading lady in *Sergeant's Three*, to name but a few. Her extensive television credits include *Murder She Wrote*, *Love Boat*, *Roseanne*, *High Rollers*, *Hollywood Squares*, and the *Bonnie Hunt Show*. In addition, she has headlined around the country in many musicals, and lists her starring roles in *The Unsinkable Molly Brown* and *Goodbye Charlie* among her favorites. Ruta is highly acclaimed for her leadership role in The Thalians, a charitable organization that is committed to good mental health. She is also the proud recipient of a star on the Hollywood Walk of Fame, and was honored as a "Woman of Achievement" by Northwood University, joining a roster of some of the most prestigious women in America.

I don't do long essays! I figure when you reach eighty and are of sound mind . . . prove it!!! SPEND IT ALL!!

My words of advice . . .

Don't wait for the mortician to give you that facelift you've been wanting.

Spend your heirs' inheritance . . . it avoids arguments!

Be generous to your favorite charities.

Above all, be generous to yourself . . . you deserve it!

23

Retuning Your Life Portfolio

by William A. Sadler, PhD

William A. Sadler, PhD, is a leader, teacher, author, consultant, and elder. Since receiving his doctorate from Harvard University, Bill has been teaching sociology, business, and interdisciplinary courses for over fifty years in the United States and Canada. Widely recognized for excellence in teaching, he continues to teach leadership courses at Holy Names University (Oakland, California) and a fall course in the OLLI Program of the University of Southern Maine about redesigning life after fifty. He has also held several senior administrative posts and served as consultant for leadership and organizational development. He was a founding member of The Center of Third Age Leadership and is currently on the Board of North Oakland Village. Bill is the author of dozens of articles and six books. He and his wife, Sallie, have raised five children, have six grandchildren, and share many professional, cultural, and outdoor interests. His Web site is: changingcoursebook.com and he can be reached by email at: sadler22@pacbell.net

"Do not regret growing older.
It is a privilege denied to many."

— Author unknown

During twenty-five years leading up to my turning eighty I engaged in research, focusing on longitudinal studies of individuals who were creatively redesigning their lives after fifty. From this research I learned Six Principles of Growth and Renewal that lead to vibrant, purposeful living and personal fulfillment in the Third Age. I described these principles in three books and many articles; and I have tried to follow them in my Third Age. Aging has not been a vivid concept in my life-planning until I passed eighty. At that point I felt that I had been dropped into a different country without a map or a trustworthy guide. It has taken me half of this ninth decade to figure out what I need to do in my Fourth Age.

Reflecting on my research, I began to see that a central issue after fifty is to shape a new identity. The major question is not "What should I do?" but "Who do I want to become?" I saw that in others; and it has also become a central question for me. To develop a new, mature identity leads into a creative process of designing a complex life. I have called this process *shaping a life portfolio*, similar to the creative process of artists who assemble their most important, different art forms. In shaping our life portfolio, we ask ourselves: What do we want in our future? What is most important? How can we best express our core values in making a life that matters? And as we add new elements, we have to ask: What should we drop or cut back on doing? I've been learning that I have had to revisit and retune my Third Age life portfolio to better apply it to the challenges and changes I experience aging in my ninth decade. The first step has been to develop a positive, searching mindfulness that promotes being wide open to life *now*. A second step is to identify core values, crucial endeavors, and cherished relationships. This will guide me as I try to answer the question: "What should I put in my future that will make it more meaningful?"

Research and experience show us that people age in different ways and at their own tempo. Every person's life is different. But looking at the lives of others, we can often learn something that helps us sculpt our own. I'm hoping that what I share in this brief essay can help you design a full life. Without suggesting a formula, I'm learning that much of what I want to put in my future, in my retuned portfolio, can be categorized by "L" words. Here are seven of them.

Live consciously in the present. Be here now! Reflections

from the past and anticipation of the future can be wrapped into now; but it's most important to pay attention to the day. I often ask myself after arising: what can I do today to have a good day — or even a great one?

Longevity is adding a new dimension to our lives. Our upbringing has not really prepared us to live so long. Even in our eighties many of us may have a long, bright future ahead of us. We should ask: "What is the purpose of this longevity?" For many of us, it offers us a chance to keep developing our full potential, giving us time to fashion a better version of ourselves. This venture also calls for sustained self-care, to keep as healthy as possible so that we can continue growing and contributing to the world.

Legacy is a term that shapes a sense of purpose and meaning. With longevity, we've been given new opportunities to enrich the lives of others by how we touch their lives and by how we model value-based aging. A challenge is to commit ourselves to what my friend, Meg Newhouse, calls *legacies of the heart* in the title of her inspiring book. To start this process, it helps to reflect on the positive legacies we have received from others. I'm finding this prompts gratitude that opens my heart to do to others what so many people have done for me. As we live our legacy we build a way to age that is the opposite of the disengagement that a previous theory of aging declared was natural and inevitable. The way forward to positive aging is through engagement, involvement, and generous investment in individuals, communities, events, families, and a future enriched by our contributions.

Leadership can still be an important part of our portfolio, as we recover the ancient tradition of elders who set examples of right living towards a good end. Our society needs role models of people who are still reaching towards a fulfilling, purposeful life. I believe elder leadership is more about leading by example than by control. It can be especially powerful as we show young people a way forward that benefits others instead of exploiting them.

Laughter is a distinguishing expression of happiness in humans, especially in children. In aging it often seems to be fading away. We need to bring it back into our present. Healthy aging calls for reduction of stress, where the level of cortisol is reduced by laughing. A friend who now practices making serious statements with humor put his changed outlook this way: "When I was younger I wanted more sex; now I want more laughter." Well, it doesn't have to be either/or, does it?

Learning continues to be vitally important to me. It should have a large part in a senior life portfolio. It's essential for us to keep our minds healthy and alert — to combine brain training along with physical exercise. Gaining knowledge is a deeply important part of being human. Of all creatures on our planet, we are the most expert at it. This process keeps us engaged in the world and directed towards future well-being. It also informs and sustains our friendships, work, and leadership. As an academic whose life has been shaped by disciplined learning, I know that its most important forms occur outside the class room. Lifelong learning feeds our understanding and imagination, nourishes novelty and our creative productivity, develops our curiosity and sense of wonder. If we give up on learning, we really give up on life.

Love is the heart of a good life, and my retuned portfolio needs to have more of it pulsing through every aspect. It points me outwards to people who mean the most — wife and family, friends both old and new, communities, and the world. Love also directs me towards life in varied forms, to beauty in nature and art, to activities of *flow* where I experience wonder, fun, and exhilaration. And increasingly love leads me on an inward, spiritual journey to revere the mystery and connections with everything.

In my eighties I'm retuning my life portfolio as a response to the challenges of aging. I sense I'll have to do this all over again in the next decade; and I look forward to the opportunity.

24

A Learning Life

By John O'Neil

John O'Neil is currently the President of the Center for Leadership Renewal. He serves on several boards and is an author, speaker, and adviser on leadership issues, providing leadership advisement and development services to senior leaders serving across a wide range of organizations from start-ups to mature enterprises. John's book *The Paradox of Success* (G.P. Putnam's Sons, 1993) has been a best seller in the U.S., Europe, Asia, and Australia and was reissued by the publisher in 2004 as one of the best business books of the decade. His book *Leadership Aikido* (Crown/Harmony, 1997) focuses on the practices of enduring and creative leaders. *Seasons of Grace* (John Wiley & Sons, Inc., 2003) coauthored with Alan Jones, Dean of San Francisco's Grace Cathedral, won the Nautilus Prize for Best in Spirituality category in 2004. John is at work on a new book on learning and renewal for organizations and individuals.

Beware of adding interesting and innocent-looking projects to your life. For example: last summer I began to write poems as a diversion from a badly stuck seven-year writing project. My topic,

The Future of Learning, was too big and dynamic. E-learning was changing the rules and players weekly. I was flummoxed by the sheer scale of it. So, I thought, I'll *write a few poems — what's the harm*? I didn't even bother to add it to my to-do list or tell my editor. No big deal, right? Now at forty poems and counting, the exercise has morphed into a book on changing life stages (with a smile).

At eighty-four, healthy, with a brilliant wife and delightful children and grandchildren, I still hadn't learned how to stay on task. My entire life was comprised of "mini-careers." Each one had seduced me with shining learning challenges. I was like poor Odysseus heading home from Troy with the sirens beckoning him off course.

Here were my mini-careers in a nutshell:

- Serving as an Air Force Training instructor teaching pilots to survive in Korea;
- Going to U.C. Berkeley and rushing to finish in record time;
- Working as an AT&T team member on large, switched networks, like the airline reservation system SABER;
- Doing early-stage investing in Silicon Valley with two partners;

- Attending graduate school while going through psychoanalysis and serving as Vice President of Mills College;

- Leading a four-campus graduate school of psychology with 2,500 graduate students;

- Writing and hustling three books on leadership and gratitude;

- Developing "Good Life Seminars" with associates;

- Advising leaders engaged in dynamic changes in their lives and careers;

- Working on a slippery nonfiction project and writing poems.

In the middle, muddle of my life, Merlin appeared in the form of John Gardner, a leadership maven who taught me how to respect my learning compulsions. Joe Henderson, Jungian analyst, who had actually studied under Jung, taught me how to make creative learning healing. My wife Pat showed up to guide and support me, and many dear friends and children taught me and rescued me.

Winston Churchill, a learning hero, wrote about how creativity changed his own second-half of life. Jung had said, "The first half of life is getting ready for the second half." Churchill, tossed out of government and power, retreated to his country estate, Chartwell.

In a lovely, small book, *On Painting*, he describes the transition: "Like a sea beast hoisted from the depths — my veins threatening to burst from the lack of pressure — it was then the muse of painting came to my rescue."

Writing became my muse. But in order to balance competing, glittering prospects, I established some rules of engagement, to wit:

Make lists!

When you turn eighty it is important to have lots of lists: to-do's, should-haves, apologies, and big ideas. Any damned fool can make a to-do list, but at eighty it can become an art. For example, in earlier years you could write down "gym" on your calendar. Now you should put down all of the stuff you will need, such as the book to read on the stationery bike, and the ear buds to listen to music or an inspirational topic as you walk or run the treadmill. And, don't forget Ace bandages!

Hang with young people!

The beauties of the art of mentoring are spelled out in Ricardo Levy's book *Letters to a Young Entrepreneur.* Find younger people who will become learning partners, including your children and grandchildren. Be sure and include new and diverse people on your list (yet another list!). It is amazing how many young people will find your experience and life lessons of value. But this is true only if your stories are carefully curated to be of value to them. Reminiscences, homilies, and moral tales can be heavy, boring, and devoid of learning values for your partners. Also, don't try out your new rap music on them, as good as it might be.

Create a learning plan!

If you want to fashion a bucket list, that's okay, but only if it's about learning voyages. Learning should be exciting, adventurous, deeply satisfying, not just another trip. Remember what Carl Jung said about the second half being the creative half.

There are several new learning curves to consider. What dreams and ambitions have you set aside that might be revisited? Who do you admire and want to learn with? (They can be present or dead.) Dig deep inside. You may want to learn to meditate so you can reclaim those outrageous aspirations you put aside as not realistic.

Perhaps your next learning challenge can be an interior one. Helen Luke, in her powerful book, *Old*

Age, tells of Odysseus finally returning home from his dramatic adventures only to start a new journey. Luke, a Jungian, insists that the weary warrior must now go inside and discover who he really is. So must we all.

Do a Workout!
The evidence mounts up that good workouts are needed for mental health. A well-functioning cortex needs oxygen. Too simple? Try it. It just may make you feel good. There are several things in favor of workouts besides feeling righteous. Your abs may look better, at least when you hold your breath.

Another advantage: put on a headset and escape from all life's noise and demands. Some might say that workout clothes are stylish so you can wear them all day, sweaty or not. Finally, you can make new friends who are buff — or not.

Practice Gratitude!
It was Cicero who said, "Gratitude is the highest human virtue and the mother of all virtues." If you are still motoring, be grateful. Be grateful for friends and family, freedom, opportunities, beauty, sunshine, small flowers, animals, poems, mighty trees. Create

rituals of gratitude. My favorite one is Thich Nhat Hanh's gratitude walks. Try them today.

My friends, and over-eighty wunderkind learning partners Pete Thigpen, Chuck Frankel, Dick Gunther, Burt Marks, Bill Sadler, and of course my brilliant wife, Pat, are always grateful for every learning occasion. When Pete and I teach the Good Life seminar we start with a gratitude walk. It clears the mind and readies the soul for learning. As I fashion two new books, I crave and receive ideas, research, critiques, from all of my trusted learning partners of all ages. I am so grateful.

25

Life Lessons for Your Eighties and Beyond

By Betty Zimmer

In 1950, Betty Zimmer was living in Hollywood and working at a local TV station, when friends invited her to visit a little Hindu temple (Vedanta Society) there. It quickly became her spiritual home and still is to this day. Determined to reach a level of consciousness unknown to most people, Betty read ancient scriptures translated by the Swami. Soon after, she met her second husband, an announcer for ABC network. He didn't want her to work as his hours were at night. So she attended UCLA, receiving a BS degree in Fashion Design. After working for designers in Hollywood, Betty moved with her husband to New York City, where opportunities for him were greater. Betty put her design skills to work by making costumes for the Village Light Opera Group. Near their house in the Catskills was the Zen Mountain Monastery, which she joined. Later, she attended The New Seminary and became an Interfaith Minister. She became a Group Leader and taught Science of Mind. Betty believes we are responsible for making ourselves happy, and that no one can do that for us.

After eighty, many have retired from a regular career. Mothers may feel no longer needed. There's time on one's hands. Often a professional man or woman has so identified with a role, they no longer know who they are or what their purpose is. We are not our roles; we are much more than that. Here are eleven important things to do to make your later years meaningful.

l) **Work out.** I realized I could not meditate unless I had a strong body. My husband and I both worked out daily. I still do: I lift heavy weights at a gym, have a personal trainer, and work out daily in a class at my senior residence, sitting in a chair. Do what you can, but do your best. We need to keep the joints moving.

2) **Meditate or take a class in Mindfulness.** It's not a religion — it can be done in any tradition. It helps give peace of mind and relieves stress. A simple meditation is to count the breath. On the count of one, inhale; on the count of two, exhale; and so forth until you reach ten. If a single thought or distraction comes into your mind, start over. Don't get discouraged: it can take years to get to ten! What is important is the effort to stay focused. Try it for

ten or fifteen minutes — don't make a big deal out of it.

3) **Read something every day, a paragraph or two of something that inspires you and lifts you beyond everyday concerns.**

4) **Forgive yourself for any insensitivity; we are all guilty of unknowingly hurting others.** Forgive everyone who ever hurt you. Free yourself of old resentments that keep you from being happy. Don't weigh yourself down with old stuff from the past.

5) **Cultivate younger friends.** They often have interests that you can participate in. Even though my poor eyesight prevents me from doing creative things I used to do, I volunteer to "stuff dolls." It's a project started by a young woman who sends them all over the world to poor children.

6) **Give young people encouragement; don't try to impress them.** Someone once said to me, "If you want to be interesting, you must be interested."

7) **If you can't do the hobbies or creative things you once did, do what you can.** I try to crochet every day. It does keep my hands supple, and it's creative: I make baby blankets.

8) **Play games.** My favorite game is Rummikub. It's the card game of Rummy but with plastic cubes. In concentrating on moves, one has to be present. There's no time to drift off into thoughts of the past or worry about the future.

9) **No matter how you feel, be cheerful and show a smiling face.** It's better to say, "It's nice to see you," rather than, "How are you?" After my mother had a stroke, she said, "I feel so bad that Father has to wait on me. I can't do anything — but I can be cheerful!"

10) **Do puzzles or quizzes to sharpen the mind and improve memory.**

11) **Do something new!** Half of my life was spent in warm climates. The second half has been in New York City. All these years, with a house in the Catskills, I never made a snowman! This winter, at ninety-two years of age, I have promised myself to make a snowman!

26

"Rules for Old People"

By Thomas Y. Canby

Thomas Y. Canby was born in 1930 in Sandy Spring, Maryland. He attended the University of Virginia on a Naval ROTC scholarship and served as a Navy communications officer. After working for and editing a Maryland weekly newspaper, he joined *National Geographic* as a writer, then became Science Editor, writing twenty-two articles and editing many more. He resigned in 1991. Since then, he has written extensively about Quaker-founded Sandy Spring, including two plays. His hobby is gardening-landscaping. He is married to Susan Fifer Canby, and he has two sons by an earlier marriage and three grandsons.

W hen my sister Vertrees and I were little, we had an ancient great aunt — Aunt Millie. She lived her final years with our family in our modest Maryland farmhouse. Aunt Millie was then in her late eighties, was wobbly physically and financially, and — to our young eyes — was pretty far over the hill. Her disturbing behaviors would inspire impressionable Vertrees to compile a list of thirty

"Rules for Old People" — a child's take on things *not* "to do upon turning eighty."

In her heyday a youthful Millie had cut quite a figure. Entering society as a Baltimore belle, at eighteen she married a rich and dashing gentleman who ran Baltimore's German-language newspaper. A liveried coach bore them to racetracks and evening balls; they mingled with Baltimore's celebrated Duchess of Windsor. Millie shampooed her hair in champagne.

Then the Depression wiped them out, and the dashing husband died of tuberculosis. In time, Aunt Millie took in sewing, and married a nice enough man who sold neckties door-to-door. Now she washed her hair in beer.

By the time venerable Aunt Millie arrived on our farm, she endured mounting infirmities. These manifested themselves unpleasantly at our table and in other unwelcome environments. To sister Vertrees and me, these lamentable manifestations were avoidable — if only Aunt Millie made the effort. That others might benefit from her observations, Vertrees, sensitive and precocious, put pencil to paper and codified her "Rules."

Now, finding myself deeply ensconced in my eighties, I occasionally reread those rules, just to be sure I'm not straying. Here they are, in all their transcendent wisdom:

1. Do not suck in soup or other liquids. You may not be able to hear yourself doing it so just keep it in mind.

2. Do not chew with your mouth open, particularly when eating mayonnaise.

3. Don't talk when you are chewing.

4. Try to avoid sleeping with any relatives (outside of your husband, of course).

5. If you do sleep with them, never suggest sleeping in the same bed, etc.

6. Try to arrange things so you don't have to get up in the night to use a potty or go to the bathroom.

7. Try to put your belongings where you can find them. Other people hate to hunt for them for you.

8. Keep up with the times. Don't refer to things in the terms used many years ago.

9. Develop interests such as Solitaire to entertain yourself.

10. Change your clothes often. Do not get slovenly. Wash your hair often. (Every two weeks.)

11. Do not speak in a trembly voice.

12. Do not act cute. Pattering around, imitating drunkards, etc., may have been funny when you were young, but now people only laugh at you.

13. Do not go off into long harangues when talking to people. Try to be witty, not cute.

14. Try to avoid telling the same stories over and over.

15. Don't talk about your health, etc.

16. Don't talk about your hobbies continually.

17. Don't talk about your anatomy.

18. Look for any aversions the people around you may have.

19. Do not be self-pitying.

20. Don't be a stick-in-the-mud. Don't hold your relatives back.

21. Try to be helpful without forcing yourself on people.

22. Don't talk about the past or your dear deceased.

23. Carry a handkerchief with you at all times and never use your finger.

24. Don't get right up in people's faces when you talk.

25. When you make your will, don't continually change it. Don't promise things away too soon.

26. Keep clean.

27. Don't haunt parties.

28. If you live with another family, don't butt in on family arguments.

29. Remember — you have had your life.

30. Stop short of murder to get attention.

(This excerpt is adapted from the author's recent memoir *Crooked Furrow*, available via Amazon.com, with proceeds benefitting Maryland's Sandy Spring Museum.)

4

CHALLENGE
YOURSELF
TO GROW

27

A Letter to My Younger Self

By Florence Ladd

Florence Ladd's novel, *Sarah's Psalm* (Scribner), received the 1997 best fiction award from the American Library Association's Black Caucus. Her novel, *The Spirit of Josephine*, was published in 2014; another novel, *Jason Henderson's Senior Year* (Atria), appeared in 2016. Finishing Line Press published *Reclaiming Rose: A Suite of Poems* in 2015. Other poems have been published in *The Women's Review of Books*, *The Progressive*, *The Rockhurst Review*, *Sweet Auburn*, *Beyond Slavery*, *Transition*, and *River Stories*. With Marion Kilson, she is the coauthor of *Is That Your Child? Mothers Talk About Rearing Biracial Children*. She lives in Cambridge, Massachusetts and Flavigny-sur-Ozerain, France.

Dear Florence,
I wish you had known then what I know now — about aging. Much of the sand in the hourglass of our life has trickled into the lower bulb, as I advance in the eighth decade. Alas.

If I had a bucket list, the first item on it would be my unfinished business: finishing incomplete writing projects. Among them are two novels and a bushel of poems. As you may recall, I'm an undisciplined writer. Correspondence (letters like this) is my warm-up practice for a writing session. Only after writing notes and letters to relatives and friends do I turn to a writing project. Well, it's time that I review abandoned projects with the intention of completing them or declaring them unworthy of more time. I hope you would agree.

What, you may well ask, is worthy of my time at this age and stage? I find I'm increasingly concerned about my (our) health and well-being — a concern that should have been more central decades ago. Maintaining sound physical health requires more hours each week than in previous years. Physical therapy, water aerobics, medical and dental appointments are on my agenda frequently. I had a knee replacement operation recently. While a new knee may increase my mobility, I don't expect to ice skate or cross-country ski again.

Other activities and opportunities now invigorate my life. Again, yes again, I'm studying French. Upon turning eighty, I began meeting with a French coach every Friday morning at a chocolate boutique in Harvard Square. There are pragmatic reasons for this practice. As you know, during the college years, travel abroad became a meaningful part of my life. Since 1984, Bill Harris, my third and last husband, and I have vacationed in a village in Burgundy where we have a house. Our son, Michael, lives in Paris with our Parisian daughter-in-law and our two young grandchildren whose first language is French. So I continue to try to improve my French. Studying a foreign language late in life is a frustrating process. Failure to recall a regular verb in the present subjunctive can bring on chagrin. The effort, however, continues to sharpen my mind. An occasional chess game with Bill also quickens my wits and revives my competitive spirit.

It should not surprise you to learn my trips abroad now are limited to France and England. No more adventure travel to exotic destinations you visited in your thirties and forties, and that I now only vaguely recall.

Reading and writing are still essential to my mental and intellectual well-being. Although I usually prefer to read fiction and poetry, works selected by the other eight women in my book group expand the range of my reading, as they sometimes propose biographies and historical works. I am challenged by women in my writing group who suggest reading books that influence and perhaps improve my prose. Members of the poetry workshop I attend enlist my interest in making language dance. Yes, I've returned, with some satisfaction, to writing poems. A decade ago, I joined The Saturday Morning Club, a Boston women's club that requires a scholarly essay annually of members. I have presented essays on such topics as forgery, trust, textiles, and masterpieces. As a social psychologist, I recognize my need for belonging in groups that offer a variety of face-to-face relationships. I suppose I have grown more gregarious lately. Participation in these groups has expanded and enriched my social contacts and friendships, important in the post-retirement years. The day-to-day association with office colleagues formerly provided sufficient interpersonal stimulation.

Concerts, films, public radio, and a few television programs are my primary means of entertainment. Occasionally, Bill and I visit art galleries and museums, where I find I need my glasses to take in details of exhibitions. In the first balcony at Symphony Hall, I miss the nuances of the string section's performances.

A front seat at lectures and in theaters makes for better hearing. I worry about my sensory decline.

Less taxing are televised games of the Red Sox, Patriots, Bruins, and Revolution. I generally view sports in the closing innings or last half of events, if Boston is winning. Bill and I attend Harvard football games. He insists there is more drama on the field than onstage at our local theater.

I could bore you with my quotidian routines that provide the foundation of life, like the harpsichord's *basso continuo* that supports the flow of a composition. There are countless, essential errands and chores, too banal to mention. And there are days punctuated by serendipity when an encounter with a new work of art or a conversation with a stranger takes me outside my zone of the ordinary. I treasure unplanned moments of novelty and surprise. But that's not new for me or us, is it?

Well, enough about life in my eighties. As ever, it is always useful to connect with you as I glance back and gaze ahead.

Yours truly,

Florence

28

Growing Young: The Formula

By Betty Finney

Betty Finney has spent her life going "against the grain," and delights when friends and family refer to her as a "rare bird." Don't tell her she can't do something, because "she knows she can, and she will." Born in Jeffersonville, Indiana, the daughter of florists, she married Charlie in 1957, and together they raised seven children, who have since given them sixteen grandchildren. Betty was promotion director for Kathrine Switzer's Avon Running events in Cincinnati. She also was one of the women who broke the "men's only" restrictions at Cincinnati area restaurants. Betty operated her own advertising and public relations firm for years, well into her sixties, with such clients as Avon, AT&T, Panasonic, and Time Warner Cable. She received several outstanding sales awards at sixty-four, sixty-five, and sixty-six from the *Cincinnati Enquirer.* Betty launched her "Growing Young" campaign online in the summer of 2016.

I n the past, men and women searched futilely for the Fountain of Youth. But they looked in all the wrong places. And the wrong kind of fountain. The fountain that restores youth is all around us. And it's inside us.

Today more people are drinking deeply from the water of that fountain, enjoying youthful vigor and an outlook that eluded those in previous generations. For the first time, Americans sixty-five-plus represent one-eighth of the nation's population. Not too many years ago anyone sixty-five or older was considered "old" — ready for the rocking chair, retired from working, retired from life itself.

Because of the "The Growing Young Formula" that Third Age group (sixty-five-plus) are making history. They are transforming the mindset of aging to the mindset of agelessness. In the ranks of on-the-go citizens today are people in their seventies, eighties, nineties, and beyond, and they are showing youngsters in their fifties and sixties how to stay active. The Growing Young Formula shows that the real fountain of youth is one we create, proving that age is really "just a number." The secrets to long-lasting health and agelessness lie in these eight steps:

1. Leave Your Comfort Zone and Be Willing to Try a New Way

Check in with yourself on a regular basis. A lot of

us greet our retirement years with "aha at last!" It's what we assumed because it's been handed down to us as a hardened concept. Stop living this automatic perception of retirement. Paint a new picture for your life. It's a challenge, but oh so exciting.

In my own life, I've gone outside my comfort zone many times:

At seventy-one, I performed in a tap dance show;

At seventy-seven, I went zip-lining and "Tarzan swinging" with my husband Charlie in Costa Rica;

At seventy-eight, I wrote my book *Growing Young*;

Throughout my sixties, seventies, and eighties, Charlie and I have set off on our own for self-guided adventures in countries throughout Europe, the Caribbean, South America, and Iceland.

2. Be the Architect of Your Life

Live the life you want. Think outside the box. Bring your experience and wisdom to the forefront. Overcome the myth that you are physically and mentally unprepared for life's Third Age. Reviewing all your life experiences to date will give you a new perspective of your skills. It's like letting the genie out of the bottle. If you surprise yourself, then you'll likely surprise others. Now, with your refreshed frame of mind, you'll be ready to create your own vision of the future.

3. Shape Up!

Oh yes, exercise. Get off the couch and awaken your body to this new challenge. Live instead of existing. Put together a realistic plan that will fit your vision for your future activities. You may need a professional trainer or assistance from a local gym.

4. Become a Nutrition Warrior

To have high performance every day, you need to fuel your body so it lasts those extra years you have projected. Take some appreciation time daily for this great machine. Your body is a miracle. It works 24/7 and we forget that. Think about it. It never stops. To fuel this machine we need to develop a defense fortress. To do this we must put the right amount of real foods (you know what they look like — an apple, a carrot) into our fortress. Forego the philosophy that there are only four food groups — fast, frozen, junk, and processed. Go for healthy foods and give this miraculous body a boost.

5. Get Over Terminal Seriousness

Laughter is a must, for your biological health. Not only does laughter make you feel good, but you get a free massage for every organ in your body. The big bad monster that has consumed our world is stress. It has become an epidemic. Stress can compel us to action, but it can also be brutal to our physical and emotional well-being. As they say, "Laughter is the best medicine." It can provide a way to get over the speed bumps of stress. Anyone can join the laughter movement. All it takes is a willingness to let go and have some fun.

6. Check Out Your Future Assets

No matter what your age, yearly tuning into your finances is necessary. The Third Age brings new activities and an ever-changing lifestyle. "Be prepared" is the motto.

7. Put Together a Reinforcement Team

Involve those that support your new mission. Include some young blood in order to keep your ideas fresh and current. Get crystal clear in your own mind about what you want to achieve. That will help you get your message across to others. Update your challenges regularly. Be willing to adapt to new insights that are suggested.

8. Hang in There

Small changes are extremely valuable. Often we give up because we cannot accomplish the task we set for ourselves. Even incremental steps can trigger progress. They will eventually lead you to your desired goals. Change will bring choices for happiness, fulfillment, and new beginnings.

Seek Your Dream

As you reach eighty and beyond, make sure that hardened old concepts don't derail your plan. Tell your family and friends that you are Growing Young. Keep this idea in the forefront of your mind. And here's one final secret to the Fountain of Youth: Become a master of exploration. You'll discover exhilarating adventures!

29

The Heat Is Off

By Ginnie Siena Bivona

Ginnie Siena Bivona has created *Ageless Authors*, a series of anthologies by writers and artists over the age of sixty-five (agelessauthors.com). Ginnie also helps other authors by editing and producing their books for self-publication. As a published author, Ginnie's first novel, *Ida Mae Tutweiler and the Traveling Tea Party* was the inspiration for a Hallmark TV movie, *Bound by a Secret*, starring Meredith Baxter, Lesley Ann Warren, and Timothy Bottoms. In addition, she has written a humorous cookbook, *The Seductive Chef: A Cookbook and More for Lovers*, and her other recent releases include *The Secret Lives of Ordinary Women* and *Reality Check: The Work of a Part-Time Poet*. Her book, *Notes from a Chameleon: Sort of a Memoir*, is a finally finished project that she has been living, writing, and illustrating for the past forty years. It was a finalist in the 2008 Eric Hoffer Awards.

Like everyone else, when I was a whole lot younger, I always looked at aging as The End. No more fun, no more adventures, I'd go dobby in the head, wobbly in the knees, and other body parts would sink to new lows. Turns out, like on several other occasions in my life, I was wrong. Now that I'm in my eighties, I find that it's actually almost like being six again, only this time there's nobody bossing me around. And the even better news is that I'm finally free to be the creative person I have always been. In the past I was just too busy to find the time for all of the fun, artistic, and rewarding ideas that were bubbling around in my head. Sadly, I pushed them aside for what I thought were the more pressing duties of the day. But what a difference it makes to follow our bliss!

I'm absolutely convinced that we can learn new skills at any age, and I have some powerful evidence to back me up on that. Her name is Barbara Mott, and she is a shining example of the loving wife and mother. Her life and goals were all about her family. She did do an occasional bit of china painting, and even a little oil painting or two for the walls of her home. But it was just a form of entertainment for those rare un-busy hours now and then in her busy life.

Then, about nine years ago, when Barbara was eighty-two, her beloved husband decided to write his memoir. He asked Barbara to take dictation for the book (since she used to be a secretary in the days before they were married). Well, how antiquated can you get? Everybody knows that nowadays you have to write a book on computer. So she went to the local junior college and learned how to use one. Yep. Just like that. She didn't say I'm too old, she didn't say I can't; she just did it. And she wasn't the only student in the computer class. I met her when the book was finished. She brought the manuscript to me to help get it self-published. Because that's what I do.

After we proudly held the printed memoir in our hands I began my new campaign. I encouraged Barbara to do her memoir. (She says, I "harassed, hounded, and begged" her!) After refusing more than several times, insisting that she had no story to tell, she finally caved in and began to write. And write and write. Her book is about 106 pages longer than her husband Bill's book. That was about six years ago. Recently, we published *Petals and Thorns*, a collection of her essays, poetry, and fifty-word *really short* stories that are funny as all get-out! Barbara will celebrate her ninety-second birthday this year. Don't tell *me* you are too old to learn something new!

Recent research has shown that the human brain never stops adding new synapses, the tiny little connecting bits of brain where we store what we learn. And the biggest reason we seem to be slow in remembering is because the file boxes of a long life are so full, it takes a bit of time to go through everything, to dig out the exact file you are looking for . . . and I can see you smiling and nodding at that!!

So, remember these three points — one: you are never done till you decide you are done; two: you never stop learning; and three: the heat is off, now it's time to have fun!

30

A Work in Progress

By Rev. Margaret Stortz

Rev. Margaret Stortz is a minister and practitioner of Religious Science. She has been both chair of the International Board of Trustees and president of the United Church of Religious Science. She has two popular books, both available from Amazon.com, entitled *Essays on Everything* and *More Essays on Everything*. Margaret lives in El Cerrito, California, and may be reached at margaretstortz.com. Read her blog at margaretstortz.blogspot.com.

While working on this article, I find that I've been thinking of my life in terms of decades rather than just years. A scattering of years seems indeterminate, but counting decades sucks me right into seriously accounting for my time. Equally daunting is the awareness that I now have much more of a past than a future to consider. Time has seemed to speed up as the years begin to clump together more. Do I fear what eventually lies ahead? I may have once, but not now. I don't spend a lot of time figuring out who I am; I've done enough of that already. What I do notice is that I have many days when I look into the mirror and ask, "How in the hell did this happen?" I haven't decided whether turning eighty is an accomplishment . . . or a shock!

The essays in this book involve doing things after you turn eighty, but that assumes we're approaching (or have approached) this milestone age with a full head of steam, and are *already* moving vigorously into advancing years. Must we delineate certain things to do now that the magic number has arrived? Maybe, and perhaps there are some glimmers of "newness" to be explored, perhaps picking up a few new dance steps, or maybe more pointedly, learning to bring more love into a caregiving circumstance. Hang gliding? Definitely not!

I am not sure that marking a special birthday is so much about what we *do* as much as what we have *learned*. If we continue to make the same, uninformed mistakes we made when we were younger, what is the advantage in just packing on years? Is being old and dumb more of an accomplishment than being young and dumb? Perhaps an honored birthday should be more about how to move into a boundary-blasting mind-set rather than just continuing to schlepp along by default. Actually turning eighty is different than it used to be. I am not my mother's eighty, and I am quite sure that my daughter's eighty will not be mine.

I have lived long enough now to have created a history of my own, and from it I have gained a thing called *perspective*. I discovered that I would not die of disappointment, although as a younger person I often felt that death on such occasions was imminent. It wasn't. I know this much: if the people who come into our lives do not get to be themselves, we will eventually be very lonely. Others cannot possibly be who we want them to be, and they cannot possibly fill the empty holes in us. They were never meant to. They walk with us, and we walk with them, along the multiple paths our lives will take.

We are, of course, making an assumption that we shall live to be in our eighties. A reasonable assumption, to be sure, given the many ways that are now available to us to maintain a healthy and longer life — if we choose to employ them. Nevertheless it is wise to take some sidelong looks at what and how we are creating expectations that do alter the flow of our lives. Then, of course, we keep dreaming and steaming . . .

When I look in the mirror at the face I did not plan on, I ask myself: A*m* I *growing old*? Then I remember a TV ad that asked: Doesn't growing old mean living longer? This is a really, really good question with multiple, sometimes complex answers. On the other hand, growing old is an established condition. Not much we can do about that . . . but growing old-*er* is a work in progress. It is open-ended, not fully established, still malleable. Given my choices, I think I'll opt for this because I certainly wouldn't want to miss something.

So, turning eighty? Nailed it. Now, on to ninety.

31

Seeking Wisdom

By Fran Morris

Fran Morris is a retired Clinical Professor of Psychiatry and Behavioral Sciences, Oklahoma University Health Sciences Center, and a children's mental health consultant/trainer. She is the past state president of Oklahoma Association on Children Under Six and Oklahoma Committee to Prevent Child Abuse, a founding member of Oklahomans Opposed to Corporal Punishment and the Oklahoma Association for Infant Mental Health. Fran wrote a column in the *Oklahoma Gazette* called "Speaking for Children" for eighteen years. She directed the Diagnostic-Therapeutic Nursery at OUHSC for ten years, was "Miss Fran" on local TV for twenty-six years, and has received numerous awards for her child advocacy contributions.

I n basic psychology, we learned that every stage of life has a goal. Erik Erikson gave us a chart that has helped many parents and teachers. The first year of life is to develop trust. Purpose, competence, and love follow. Then, finally in old age, our goal is to gain wisdom.

When I was asked to contribute an essay to 80 *Things to Do When You Turn 80*, I did some reading, some thinking, and then settled on three things that I believe are helping me toward wisdom.

1. *Take another look at all those things you've been told about old age.*

"It's all about reconciling with loss." No, it's not. With every goodbye, you can learn something positive and helpful.

"You have to either resist or surrender to change." No, you don't. You can accept and move along. Look at the Serenity Prayer again.

"You must be very careful." Why? If you can't be an active risk-taker in your eighties, when CAN you?

Well, you see where I'm going with this. We have plenty of time to read now. I have an amazing number of peers who read and reread old favorites because that's what we're supposed to do "at our age." Why?

I subscribe to a variety of magazines because I have learned that it is fun to discover new things and ideas on diverse topics. I enjoy it and it may be depositing something into my wisdom bank.

2. Relist memories that make you happy.

Once on a plane going through a stormy sky, I tried to find a way to distract myself (because I was absolutely sure that I was about to die). I started making a list of all the most spectacular loves of my life. I was single in my thirties and forties during the '60s and '70s, which was a fabulous time to be on my own, healthy, and moderately attractive.

The list I started writing has been modified a few times, but I still have it and several others as I have learned what joy one can derive from remembering highlights of your life. I have lists of some of the most spectacular plants that I have grown in my many years of gardening. I have lists of the dozens of birds I saw when I lived in a tree-filled neighborhood. And I have lists of children I knew when I worked in a nursery.

Have I listed every man I've ever loved? Every seed I ever planted? Every child I ever met? No. That's the best part of making lists when you're older. You can weed out your failures and focus on the most positive and successful endeavors of your life.

3. Recommit your time, effort, and resources to something you think is important.

Your choice: Religion? Education? Climate change? International relationships? Health? Mental health? Hunger? There are many ways that older citizens can get involved in these and other important issues.

For me, it's politics. In this country, that has come to include all of the above. I was fortunate to have been reared by parents who taught us that patriotism is not a spectator sport. We learned that the honor of being "born in the U.S.A." included responsibilities as well as rights. My father was a Baptist preacher who walked the walk. My mother was an intellectual pragmatist who taught school, planted a garden, milked the cow, tended the chickens, and made sure that her family of seven survived the Depression with an optimistic view of the future.

My heroes were Eleanor Roosevelt ("You must do the things you think you cannot do"), Will Rogers ("I belong to no organized party. I'm a Democrat"), and Adlai Stevenson ("My definition of a free society is a society where it is safe to be unpopular").

Later, I much admired the writings of Molly Ivins. I felt a kinship with this spirited author who wrote, "So keep fightin' for freedom and justice, beloveds, but don't you forget to have fun doin' it. Lord, let your laughter ring forth. And when you get through kickin' ass and celebratin' the sheer joy of a good fight, be sure to tell those who come after how much fun it was."

In midlife I was able to return to the university and via evening and Saturday classes, earn a master's degree in Human Relations. New doors opened and I discovered a lot of new thinkers, teachers, and heroes. Among them, the wonderful Rabbi Daniel Hillel who wrote, "I get up. I walk. I fall down. Meanwhile I keep dancing."

Let's remember to laugh and dance while we continue to seek wisdom.

32

All My Monsters Are Dead

By Betty MacDonald

Writer, actor, sculptor Betty MacDonald contributed to the writing of and performed in TMI Project's *What to Expect, When You're Not Expecting*. Her essay, "Before Roe v. Wade," appears in the anthology *Get Out of My Crotch*! published by Cherry Bomb Press. Betty frequently reads her work at gatherings of writers and readers in upstate New York. In July 2015 she presented her essay "First Love" at a Writers Read event in New York City's Cell Theatre. She has participated in story slams for Woodstock Writers Festival, StorySlams.com, and for TMI Project. Following her early career as a continuity writer and radio personality, she freelanced as a travel writer, unfortunately, she doesn't like to leave home and finds travel exhausting. For twenty-six years she has performed with Community Playback Theatre, an improvisational acting company in New York's Hudson Valley. Her memoir *Basking in the Glow of Her Golden Years* is almost completed.

I'm twenty-three years old. I've arrived in New York City on the night train from Richmond, Virginia. My dream to live in "The City" has begun. As I step to the curb a taxi stops right in front of me ignoring the line of waiting would-be-fares ahead of me.

"Me?" I gesture incredulously.

The driver yells, "Get in!"

I obey. Once I'm ensconced in the backseat he lectures me. The theme: "Use what you got!"

What I *got* or rather what I *had* are youthful good looks. Now, at eighty-two, it's what I no longer have. My subscription to youthful good looks has expired! I no longer deal in the currency of youth, the exchange that could stop a taxi without flagging it down.

What I've acquired is Age. Unlike my peers and a lot of people younger than I, I love being old. For one thing, no one expects me to do anything. I get a free pass. For another, whenever I do *anything* at all, I get extra credit.

No one expects me to carry my own groceries or packages.

"Shall I put this in your car?" says the young woman at the hardware store hefting a couple gallons of paint I could easily lift.

"Sure," I say, leading the way.

Later, in the parking lot of the feed store I'm transferring a twenty-pound bag of birdseed from the shopping cart to my car when a young man rushes over to help. Although I could've done it myself, I'm grateful for his assistance. I like having help.

After years of homemaking, earning a living, child raising, and frantically keeping it together with never enough time to do it all, now I have a lot of time. I do whatever I want. Ignoring the "to do" list, I go online. I read all the columnists I agree with, I disregard all the ones I don't.

I check out Facebook to see what my kids and their partners are doing, and what their ex-partners are doing.

I appropriate photos of my grandkids at the pool, at the beach, in a hat. I install them in the continuing slide show I spend hours watching on my computer, whenever I'm not reading or writing. I love gazing at their adorable faces.

While my kids were small, I longed for long, uninterrupted time to descend unfettered into the rabbit hole of creativity and lose myself in my work. During those years I kept the creative fires burning by producing small sculptures to sell at craft shows. I supplemented my income with freelance assignments for industry magazines, waiting tables, and house cleaning. Now with my children grown I have all the time I need to do whatever I want.

Back when I was sixty-five I discovered a photo in a magazine of a woman ten years my senior performing an exercise in a Pilates class. Jealousy overwhelmed me. *I could do that,* I thought. My envy opened a door, alerting me to what I wanted. Now seventeen years later, and a veteran Pilates student, I am stronger at eighty-two than I've ever been in my life.

I started writing my story a few years ago. Reading my essays aloud in a memoir-writing group empowered me. Soon I enrolled in a challenging workshop in which writers are encouraged to perform our essays on the stage of a local theater. Since then I've had many opportunities to read my work in local venues and in New York City. I love performing. For twenty-six years I've honed my acting skills as a member of Community Playback Theatre, a unique improvisational acting group.

Among the blessings of aging: I now have excellent medical insurance thanks to Medicare and I'm delighted with the senior discount at the movies, in the health food store, and on Tuesdays at ShopRite.

But the best thing about having lived this long: ALL MY MONSTERS ARE DEAD!

My parents, whom I could never please, no matter how I tried, are long gone.

My adoptive parents, although extremely generous to me, didn't approve of me from the get-go! They're gone too.

My brother, whom I adored, is dead from the trinity of Alzheimer's, Parkinson's, and a broken hip. My brother, my only sibling, tormented me when we were children and never stopped denigrating me after we were grown. I loved him deeply in spite of his attitude toward me. I weep over his loss.

On my last visit with him a few months before he died I sat beside him, pressing myself into him as close as I could.

Holding his hand firmly I willed my voice to direct my words to what shreds of memory he had left.

"I forgive you." I told him. "Do you understand?"

"Yes," he paused and nodded, "I think I do!"

He's dead these last five years.

All my monsters are dead.

I outlived them!

I love being old!

33

It Can Happen to You: My Online Dating Experiences

By Nancy K. Schlossberg, EdD

Nancy K. Schlossberg, EdD, spent most of her career as a professor of counseling psychology. She taught at Howard University and Wayne State University, and for twenty-six years at the University of Maryland, College Park. Nancy was the first woman executive at the American Council on Education, where she started the Office of Women in Higher Education. She is now a Professor Emerita from the University of Maryland. One of her books, *Retire Smart, Retire Happy*, was featured on a PBS Pledge Special. Her new book, *Too Young to Be Old*, will be published by the American Psychological Association. Her mission is to translate her work on transitions for the general public in order to help people negotiate the inevitable changes that occur in life. Her husband of fifty years died in 2011 and she now lives with a man whom she met on the Internet. As Nancy says, "There are always new adventures."

Sitting at a beautiful bar in a hotel in Prague, overlooking the city, yearning for someone to love — that was me three years ago. A very attractive couple came in and sat in my line of vision. They started kissing passionately. It was inappropriate for a public place but it was painful to watch. I wondered, *Will I ever be kissed like that again?*

Recently widowed, I went on a Viking trip down the Danube by myself. Wherever I looked I saw happy couples. The trip highlighted what I didn't have — a relationship with someone who cared for me and for whom I cared. I was a new widow, coming from a very long, loving relationship. I wanted more of the love and affection that had been such a constant part of my life.

As I look back on the last five years, I have experienced many transitions: retirement, years as a widow-in-waiting, loss of my spouse, grief, recovery from grief, returning to dating in my eighties, finding a new love, moving into a retirement community, and dealing with the failure of a nonprofit I was part of building. For most of these life passages, there are guidelines and roadmaps, except for one — dating in one's eighties. For that adventure, I was "flying by the seat of my pants."

During this period, I had a number of dates. One lived in another city, one's wife had Alzheimer's, another was boring, and the two most promising found me resistible. Everyone said how lucky I was to have dates but I felt sad and lonely that I did not have a relationship. I was getting dates; it was romance that was elusive. Despite the demographics — women age eighty-five and over outnumber men five to two — I had assumed that I wouldn't have any trouble. I had always been popular, in high school, college, between marriages, so why not now? However, my phone did not ring. I started telling everyone I would love to meet someone but most of my friends didn't know of anyone who was available. How did the men get grabbed up so quickly and what were other women doing that I didn't know about? I knew I couldn't join the casserole brigade because I didn't cook!

One night in bed I thought there must be something I can do. My son and daughter-in-law met online. Would that work for me? I was afraid of going to a dating Web site but I did need a "connector." Malcolm Gladwell wrote in his book *The Tipping Point* about the importance of connectors who are *not* part of your immediate circle. Obviously my immediate circle was no help.

My first step: I Googled matchmaking services and impulsively invested too much money in what appeared to be a first-class service. I had many conversations with the owner and their psychologist but after a year I had not had a single contact. I later discovered that the organization had been sued and had declared bankruptcy. Unfortunately, I had not checked out the service before using them.

I then proceeded with Plan B. I conquered my fear and joined five online dating services — The Right Stuff, eHarmony, Our Time, Match.com, and JDate. I wrote my profile to reflect the real me — I was eighty-three years old, politically liberal, and did not cook, clean, or sew. Rather, I was a writer and active in my community.

My online dating began to take on a life of its own. I spent time every night checking the sites. I enjoyed the process. Then I met Ron online and we started e-mailing. Eventually, I gave him my phone number. He went out of town to visit a daughter and e-mailed me daily. We made plans for lunch the weekend he returned. He suggested that he pick me up for the date. Now everyone knows not to let a stranger pick you up. But I said, "You can pick me up if you assure me that you are not a murderer or a rapist." He assured me he was not a murderer. I gave a friend all of the information I had about Ron, suggesting that if she did not hear from me by four p.m. to call out the troops.

We started seeing each other — slowly at first. We got along well. Ron made me laugh, and we discovered we had the same taste in music and loved dancing and the theater. When my internist found out I was dating an eighty-six-year-old man she said, "You must promise me that you will not go to bed with him until he has a test for HIV/AIDS." And furthermore, she insisted, "I will give you a blood test so you can show him you do not have AIDS." I explained there was no way I could have AIDS, having been in a monogamous, committed marriage for forty-eight years. Her point: you show your stamp of approval and he will have to get cleared.

Can you picture my discussions with my new friend? First of all, we had not begun a sexual relationship. So how was I supposed to suggest he have HIV testing? I began very theoretically. "Have you heard of the AIDS epidemic among the elderly?" I asked. No, he had not. I continued to try and alarm him about this. And then I added, "Well I would never have sex unless someone had been tested." He e-mailed me the next day saying he couldn't wait to see his doctor. However, when I casually asked later if he had seen his doctor, he said no but he would if I insisted.

My doctor had also told me I could have sex if my partner used a condom. Can you picture an eighty-six-year-old man being able to maintain an erection long enough to get a condom on? Well, I was not sure about his abilities in this area so I decided not to mention this possibility.

Ron invited me to his home in the Adirondacks. My daughter-in-law secretly gave me a birthday present before I went — a book written by Judith Sills, PhD, called *Getting Naked Again*. The title says it all. When I told a woman friend about the book she said, "I don't think I could do it. No one — not any of my friends or family — have ever been allowed to see my upper arms, which are profoundly jiggly." Based on advice from the book, my answer to her was simple — "Only undress in absolute darkness."

I met and visited Ron's children and he spent time with mine. We agreed that we would never marry (if we did our children would kill us), and that we would not live together. We traveled together. Eventually we changed our minds and we moved into a retirement community.

When I suggested it to him, he agreed but said, "We're not ready yet." I replied, "If we are not ready at eighty-six and eighty-nine years old, then when?"

When we meet people, how do I introduce him? He is more than a friend and more than a boyfriend. But what is he? He is the person with whom I hold hands when at a piano bar, a movie, or walking down the street. The other night when we were at the Fairmont in Washington, D.C., listening to light jazz and romantic music, I thought back to the bar in Prague when I wondered if I would ever again have a romantic connection. I smiled, knowing that some wishes do come true. But only if we take the first step, and put ourselves in the dating pool!

5

DOING
MEANINGFUL WORK

34

Volunteering for the Peace Corps at Eighty-Six

By Alice Carter

Alice Carter spent the first twenty years of adulthood raising six children and writing poetry. Her introduction to Christianity altered the direction of her life. Discovering that the Gospel explicitly demands renunciation of violence took her from a path of safety and comfort to resisting and protesting every war America fought, as well as protesting above-ground nuclear weapons — for which she was arrested. She opened her home to the homeless. While working with addicts and alcoholics she learned the skills of medical and dental assisting — skills she used for nearly thirty years. Alice helped begin a house for homeless mothers, a job both exhausting and rewarding. She coordinated the local food pantry for ten years while finishing college and later received her master's. In 2013, Alice attended a party in Vermont given by Peace Corps volunteers from the '60s and thus began her journey with the Peace Corps.

The huge dirt square in the center of town is filled with pick-up trucks, large vans all containing watermelons. Summer has begun in the "Dellah" capital of Morocco. This is the town in which I live and serve in the Peace Corps. As I weave my way through the traffic, several cows on one side, a donkey on the other, and everywhere people selling watermelons, I see small kiosks set up serving mint tea and *milwe*, a kind of pancake but not really. Impossible to translate, but delicious to eat. It is sprinkling, the rain comes and goes as I walk to the gas station to meet my friend and fellow volunteer Adelia, who has come to take our students on their Sunday hike, an activity my arthritic knees object to anytime it rains.

We meet the students at the Dar Chebab, the youth center, which is where I have been working for the past year. "Teacher, teacher" is the usual greeting, happier sounding as I begin to hand out snacks for their hike in the hills. They have been hiking for several months now in preparation for climbing Toubcal, the highest mountains in Morocco. This is one of the programs the Peace Corps offers to the youth. Our primary mission is to empower, train, and educate the youth here in every way possible. We use the acronym CLIMB: Creating Leadership in the Mountains and Beyond.

As I return home to my third-floor apartment, thinking about writing the story of how I got here at the beginning of my eighty-sixth year, it seems almost quixotic. Improbable. Unlikely. On the other hand — inevitable. In the fall of 2013 I went to New Hampshire to visit my friend Heidi, a once or twice-a-year event in our sixty-year friendship. Heidi teaches in an Ashram in South India every winter, something she began while teaching at Antioch and continued on retirement. As usual her schedule was packed with parties, meetings, and lots of talking together. We went to Brattleboro for a gathering, which included returned Peace Corps Volunteers from the 1960s. I remembered how much I wanted to join in that era, especially after hearing President Kennedy describe it.

I had been searching for work in Boston without much success. So, even though I doubted that the Peace Corps was an option at my age, I decided to ask the young recruiter who was there what the age limit was. "None" came the reply. That was the magic word. It stayed with me on my return to Boston. Googling Peace Corps, I found the online application and began the first step of the journey that brought me to this amazing country.

The application process was immensely challenging, including many forms needing MD signatures, especially since I had survived colon cancer five years before. Then came the French test, a daunting online test featuring the latest improvements in agricultural fertilizers. I had studied up on history and literature but not this. I just made the minimum score. Seven months later, after almost daily conversations with the wonderful Peace Corps nurse, Carol, I received the letter inviting me to serve in the Youth Development program in Morocco. "Click 'Accept' if you want to go." I clicked "Accept" in a New York minute. The improbable, impossible adventure began.

I have rather a large family and they were happily assuming that the Peace Corps would let me apply, but they also assumed that common sense would rule out an actual invitation to serve. Now we had a new reality to deal with. Of my six children and one stepdaughter, and fifteen grandchildren, just one granddaughter was adamantly opposed. One daughter was worried about what might happen to me in a Muslim Arab country. The others came out of their initial shock and began to support me. I am happy that my daughter and two of my sons' families have come to visit me here. Even the granddaughter who voted no to my joining the Peace Corps has made peace with me being here. As for the concern about safety in Morocco, it is the safest region in all of Africa and most of Europe. No terrorist attacks here. Also no armed civilians, guns are outlawed.

After "staging" in Philadelphia, a small Peace Corps exercise to prepare us, our service began with a great training at a beach hotel near Rabat. We were all so jet-lagged that we slept through the first morning session, but gradually came to life and began to meet the others, over one hundred of us. Three days later we were on our way to our "culture-based training" (CBT) site. Five of us were sent to M'Haya for six days a week of language classes, visits to the local youth center, learning the culture in the café over *kawa nus nus* (coffee with milk) or *lavoca* (avocado smoothies). That was the routine.

We were housed with host families; mine had three of the best cooks in the world and provided me four meals a day. However, after three months of training, it was clear I had acquired very little language and that I was a big disappointment socially. It is hard to learn a new language at my age, or maybe it's just me. The five of us trainees, now really close friends because we shared the same miseries and small successes, were on our way to Rabat to be sworn in by Ambassador

Bush. We had a very good teacher, a Moroccan, Badr, and we hated to say goodbye to him. I am happy he is still my tutor.

The Peace Corps trainings are amazing, as is the staff, both the Moroccans and Americans. The medical staff, in particular, has been a blessing beyond expectation. I never had three doctors take me to an appointment in the U.S.A. They have kept me well. The Moroccan diet is extremely healthy, which helps.

We were all sent to our permanent sites to begin our work after being sworn in. After a good amount of partying, for the young anyway, we dragged our roller bags, backpacks, impedimenta to our new homes. Here we had to register with the gendarmes, apply for our *cartes de sejours* (work permits, aka IDs), find homes, meet the people, and begin teaching. I found out I hate to teach English grammar but I did it for the first semester. In the fall I decided to teach human origins and migration (my Moroccan students were happy to find out that everything began in Africa), Native American history from the Native American perspective, and Amazigh history, comparing two experiences of colonizing. We studied conflict resolution, and the genocide in Rwanda, which none of the students knew about.

They were so forgiving of my language handicap. The French and English and Deriga (Moroccan Arabic) got mixed together in my effort to teach. I have a Moroccan counterpart who speaks English and without whom nothing could happen.

In the new year, we had a camp for the girls in the winter break, and a writing contest with three winners from our group.

Now the CLIMB program is getting closer to Toubcal all the time. In June, Ramadan begins, which means we won't be hiking. Instead, we will present science films, which gives them the chance to sleep if they wish (they eat and drink nothing from sunrise to sunset). Life is segmented by the calls to prayer on a daily basis but Ramadan is the big month-long call to practice Islam.

Owing to my family visits I have seen much of the country, including the ancient city of Fez, and the other Imperial cities of Meknes, Rabat, Casablanca, and Marrakech. Last August we went to the mountains in Azrou and Irfran. It is beautiful and peaceful here. The Moroccan people are hospitable, generous, and unpredictable. I am thankful that the Peace Corps took a chance on this eighty-six year old!

35

Meaningful Work

By Jan Hively, PhD

Jan Hively, PhD, describes herself as an "encore entrepreneur." In Minnesota, after a career in city planning and administration, Jan Hively earned her PhD in 2001 at age sixty-nine with a dissertation on "Productive Aging in Rural Communities." Since then, she has focused on raising awareness about new opportunities and challenges for older adults, based on twenty-first century trends and research. Jan has cofounded several thriving networks that support positive aging, including the Vital Aging Network (vital-aging-network.org), the SHIFT Network (shiftonline.org), and a global-program exchange, the Pass It On Network, (passitonnetwork.org). As a Purpose Prize Fellow, she is an internationally known presenter and consultant for programs that engage older adult leadership and support "meaningful work, paid or unpaid, through the last breath." Jan's academic degrees were earned at Harvard University and the University of Minnesota.

What would *you* do if you were asked to describe "one thing to do when you turn 80"? I did what I most often do when faced with a challenge. I asked for help from a friend! In this case, I wrote to my friend Mary and said, "You know me well. Does anything come to mind?"

Mary responded with something better than I could have come up with, as usual. She wrote: "Speak your truth. It's never too late to do that. When you hit eighty it's time to look at what's important to you at your core and use your time to make your passions known in the world, using whatever skills and talents you have. Speak your truth to those who can take your truth forward beyond your time."

Since I turned eighty five years ago, my "truth" has been expressed in this line, which has become my mantra: "Meaningful work through the last breath."

What I know both from research and from personal experience is that all of us are healthier and feel better about ourselves when we are doing something that gives us purpose and is fulfilling.

- "Work" is much more than employment. It's productive effort that benefits you, your family, and/or your community. Throughout life, we are both learning and teaching productivity — as students, parents, homemakers, employees, volunteers, and citizens.

- "Meaningful work" is purposeful work that requires focused effort, produces results, matches up with your interests and skills, and stimulates learning.

Much of the value of meaningful work, however, depends on us recognizing its value and maximizing opportunities for a full range of productive effort. Our consumer society focuses on the value of paid work that generates monetary income. Too often, we as individuals and our institutions undervalue unpaid work such as parenting and grandparenting, volunteering, craftmaking, and family caregiving. That attitude creates a sharp divide at the time of "retirement." I once heard my late husband say, "Work is my life, and when I retire I will have no life." The U.S. Census Bureau goes further and identifies all retirees as "dependents." Residents in long-term care facilities are usually seen exclusively as recipients of services, who are discouraged if they offer services to fellow residents. When nursing home managers bring in plants and pets and daily responsibilities, everyone's morale goes up.

I earned my PhD at age sixty-nine with a survey report on "Productive Aging in Rural Communities," small towns with high proportions of older adults. It was a surprise to find that residents were still keeping their shops open and running for public office into their eighties. Echoing other research, "the older adults engaged in productive activities, whether paid or unpaid, were more satisfied with their lives."

Purposeful lives enhance the well-being of older adults and their communities. With 72 million baby boomers coming into retirement age this decade and next, communities need more volunteers for nonprofit and public agencies strapped for resources. They need more caregivers (30 percent of boomers don't have children to care for them). They need more advocates to ensure age-friendly communities, and more tutors and mentors for our underserved youth. Our cities and towns need more help from those of us who are still healthy and active into our eighties.

My talk about "meaningful work through the last breath" may sound ludicrous to you. My late husband showed me that the process of dying is both a learning and teaching experience. He learned from a near-death experience when he was resuscitated after a heart failure, then involuntarily intubated for several weeks, and then leashed to an oxygen machine for three years. At the end of that time, he gradually withdrew from his books and TV and food and ultimately told his doctor that he was ready for imminent death. My son and I took him home, where, six hours later, his breath faded away. His work was done and he had taught us how to die. So now I know that we are both teachers and learners from birth through to the end of life.

36

Ways to Earn a Little Extra Money and Avoid Boredom

By Art Koff

Art Koff graduated from Dartmouth College in 1957 and did his postgraduate work at the University of Chicago Executive Program. He started his career with the *Chicago Sun-Times*, after which he spent forty years in advertising. Art appears often on TV and has been quoted as an authority on the new developments and challenges that affect older Americans in such major newspapers and magazines as the *Wall Street Journal*, *Business Week*, *Money Magazine*, and *Fortune*, and on hundreds of Web sites. Art writes a monthly column for Dow Jones MarketWatch. He founded RetiredBrains.com in 2003 and the site has developed into a major destination for retirees, people planning retirement, and Americans with responsibilities for older family members.

I was in my late sixties when I founded RetiredBrains .com in 2003 after "retiring" from forty-plus years in advertising. I intended the site to provide content for older Americans in every area where this demographic had an interest. What I did not know at the time was where their interests lay.

Now, some thirteen years later, I am able to check the traffic to each area of the site and not only see how many people visited, but also how long they spent on each page. What I have found out is somewhat surprising. Many older Americans are interested in continuing to earn money — even those in their eighties and above. I suppose this should not be surprising as we are living longer — actually much longer. The Centers for Disease Control and Prevention (CDC) Reports show that in 2015, life expectancy for men was 78.8 years and for women 81.2; however, what is important for you readers to know is that a man who has already reached sixty-five can expect to live, on average, until age 84.3. A woman turning age sixty-five can expect to live, on average, until age 86.6. In couples where both reach sixty-five, one member is likely to live into his or her nineties.

So what, you might ask, are the kinds of things someone my age or older might do to earn money and to keep themselves challenged? The best way to answer this is to tell you which pages of my Web site are getting the most traffic. They are as follows:

1. **Work at home** (retiredbrains.com/work-at-home). This is unquestionably the most visited area as it is

Art Koff

easier for a senior and particularly for a senior in his or her eighties to stay in their home and work. Okay, you might ask, but what kinds of jobs? They are varied and the list that follows is in order of the most to the least visited. Writing or editing, tutoring, direct selling, selling online, becoming a virtual agent, freelancing, telemarketing, medical transcription. There are all kinds of opportunities in each of these areas and the site provides links to each.

2. **Start a small business** (retiredbrains.com/ employment-assistance/start-your-own-business). Most who visited this area were interested in starting a small business enterprise with a modest capital contribution, as people did not wish to dip into their retirement funds at this stage of their lives. While communicating with those who actually got their businesses off the ground I asked if I could list them on the Web site so that others might see if they could use one of these ideas to start a business of their own. I took all this input and compiled a list, which is available at the URL address at the top of this section.

3. **Take a part-time, temporary, project-based** or **seasonal job** (retiredbrains.com/job-seekers). There are some in their eighties who continue to work full

time like I do, but most who wish to continue working are not interested, and some are not able, to spend forty-plus hours a week doing so. There are many opportunities to work less than full time. Seasonal jobs are particularly attractive, whether it be working for a retailer during the holidays; for a tax preparer during tax season; on a golf course as a starter, ranger, or even driving the ball pick-up machine at the driving range. There are winter jobs at ski resorts, at lodges, and fall, spring, and summer jobs at ranches and resorts and on tour boats where you can work as a cook, in reception, as a guide, etc. There are opportunities in national parks working for the concessionaires who run the hotels, restaurants, gift shops, and marinas. In Alaska, there is need for seasonal help at resorts, and fishing and hunting lodges, as well as for transportation and tourism companies. CoolWorks.com has a list of these kinds of jobs specifically geared to what they refer to as the "Older and Bolder" seasonal job seeker (coolworks .com/older-bolder/). Here you can find out what it's like to work at some of these jobs, and also talk to older workers who are willing to share their experiences and what they learned with you.

4. Volunteer and, in lieu of getting paid, get free or discounted accommodations and travel. (retiredbrains .com/employment-assistance/volunteering). This section of my Web site has information on traveling and volunteering and lists many organizations looking for interested seniors. There are also volunteering jobs that allow you to work from home, particularly if you are computer literate. Jobs may include mentoring inner-city high school students, helping promote awareness of certain diseases, and doing fundraising. Some cruise lines look for "hosts" to be a fourth at the bridge table, dance with older single passengers, and fill in when there is an emergency if you are a physician or have medical skills.

If you are a healthy, alert octogenarian or even in your nineties, and you're looking for a new challenge, you may be able to find an encore career that will help you make a bit of extra money on the side!

37

My World at Eighty

By Robert Matulonis

Robert Matulonis is a retired international consultant. He held management positions in leading American firms. As VP of operations in Frankfurt, Germany, he was responsible for automating the Department of Defense military banking system. Subsequently, he became president of an artificial intelligence firm, Knowledge Management Group. He has lived in Amsterdam, Frankfurt, London, and Zurich for more than a decade. He now resides in Cumberland, Maine. He is a member of the World Affairs Council of Maine. He keeps busy as a writer and is working on his second novel in a series of thrillers involving world affairs and cybertechnology.

As a youth, I remember walking home after school through fields where a system of watering pipes crisscrossed the rows of a farm. Sometimes, I'd stop and place my knees over one of the pipes so that my head dangled below my knees. From this hanging position I'd look up at the infinite sky and watch the clouds drift by. It was a time for me to wonder what the world was really all about. My upside-down view never really provided me with much insight, but the Zen-like moment of harmony with the universe always left me with a feeling of euphoria.

Times changed dramatically, with the country involved in the Korean conflict and threatened by a Cold War with Russia. I was called into military service in my sophomore year at university. The transition from urban life to military discipline was an abrupt eye-opener for me.

I remember arriving by troop ship at Bremerhaven, less than six years after the end of World War II. I looked down at the scurrying German dock workers, who until now I had thought of as the enemy. Traveling by train, I arrived later that day in Augsburg, a large industrial city in Bavaria. My first assignment involved radio communications training. Life after training fell into an orderly routine. I took every opportunity to travel, to escape from the monotony of army life.

Two destinations stand out in my memory. One is the city of Zurich, the location in a film called *Rhapsody* that starred a young Elizabeth Taylor. While Liz looked great, it was really the charm of Zurich I fell for! So, at the first opportunity to leave the base,

I took the train to the city I had dreamed of visiting since my youth.

The next trip I took was to Dachau, a place often reported about in Movietone News clips. The memory of seeing the horror of war firsthand at the age of twenty-one still remains with me.

It was almost a year into my tour of duty when I met my wife. A whirlwind romance was followed by our marriage in a German civil ceremony. *The vows we took have seen us through sixty years of marriage.*

Returning to the United States, we moved to Michigan where I entered university. The school years rolled by quickly and upon graduation I accepted a position with a leading technology corporation. The job was filled with challenges. But, after a few years, I realized a sense of excitement was missing in my life. Fate stepped in at this pivotal moment and offered a choice: to complete my thesis for an MBA, or accept a management position in Europe. I chose the latter and the die was cast.

Married, and now blessed with a young daughter, we flew to Amsterdam and settled into life in Europe. I was on a learning curve doing business there, and

I needed to hold my capitalist instincts in check when working with managers in socialist countries. For almost a decade, we lived in and experienced the culture of several countries. But all good things necessarily come to an end. The oil crisis in the '70s hastened our return to the U.S.

I started an international consulting practice that kept me busy for the next twenty years, until my retirement. With time to pursue other interests, I joined the World Affairs Council of Maine to stay abreast of global events. I also realized I could share my experience, learned during several decades in the world of business. I joined SCORE, Service Corps of Retired Executives, and helped budding entrepreneurs to realize their business dreams.

My most rewarding activity was as a mentor at Freeport High School. I was assigned three teenagers who needed help in overcoming their limitations. It was refreshing to see the world through their eyes. For three years, I coached them along until they graduated. Natasha was offered several scholarships upon graduating. I nominated Crystal as a mentee who benefitted most from the program. Crystal, along with other nominated mentees in the state, was selected as one of the outstanding students in the program. I drove with Crystal to the state capitol building where she proudly stepped forward to accept her honorarium presented by Governor John Baldacci. The broad and happy smile on Crystal's face truly made my day!

Now, at the treasured age of eighty, only a few items remain on my *eighty things to do* list. Somehow, goals no longer seem pressing. Ever a lover of words, I now use my time writing novels, populated with compelling fictional characters. My first book, *The Seventh Floor,* is an international thriller that deals with advanced government technology. The next is a work in progress I call *The Damocles Solution,* and it covers Iran's nuclear ambitions. I've dedicated these books to my grandchildren, the next generation. May they follow their dreams in a complex and rapidly changing world.

38

Aging into Selfhood

By Richard Anderson Bamforth

Richard Anderson Bamforth, a retired priest of the Episcopal Church, grew up in coastal Massachusetts and graduated from Bowdoin College in 1951. After a year as a high school teacher, he enlisted in the army to avoid the draft. Three years of military service then drove him to seek holy orders and he earned a graduate degree from Berkeley Divinity School at Yale. Richard served churches in Missouri and Massachusetts and in his fifties he earned an additional graduate degree in education from Boston University. In retirement he has found endless opportunities for teaching, preaching, and writing. He was co-editor of *Iron Jaw: A Skipper Tells His Story* (2002) and wrote numerous articles and reviews for church periodicals. Currently he is working on a memoir of his life as a substitute teacher and pastor. Richard and his wife, Patricia, parents of two daughters and grandparents of three grandchildren, live in Maine and spend summers reading and writing at their secret lakeside hideaway called "Someplace Else."

W hen I retired in my sixties I tried to hide from my previous life as an Episcopal priest and pastor. I needed to be free from 24/7 responsibilities and availability. I had to do something different so I signed up as a substitute teacher in the local school system. I chose the high school level and, after a few disastrous forays into middle school, I stayed with the upper grades where I felt more at home. For the most part, when I pretended that adolescent teens were really adults, they responded accordingly.

I had a graying beard and they enjoyed calling me "Colonel Sanders" or "Abe Lincoln." Playing with my surname, some even had the nerve to address me as "Mister Bam Bam." I enjoyed their acceptance and we chuckled together. When they spied me entering the building they called out, asking, "Who are you in for?" or simply, "Who are you today?" That question became the prevailing mantra of my life. Who, indeed, was I presuming to be? What role was I playing? Who was I becoming?

My new job brought previously unused talents out of me, enlivened gifts I didn't know I had. I loved it when students asked me questions about my life and the world I grew up in. They had a hard time believing how one could grow up without television, copiers, computers, and cell phones. They couldn't comprehend a world in which hot dogs cost a dime and candy bars a nickel. As they tried to imagine life in my past, I relived my earlier days and grew into a new appreciation of my present being.

My subbing days were to last almost a decade but halfway through the first year I was asked to fill in for ministers at one church after another. Having found school substituting to be an energizing sport, I also came out of clergy hiding and rediscovered the joys of pastoral ministry. It became clear that there was nothing boring about retirement. On the contrary, I was being needed, sought out, and appreciated by both my local school and church. Some in the latter even called me "Father Bam Bam." To make things even better, all administrative details were being handled by others. I was aging into mature selfhood, entering into both the educational process of the young on weekdays and meeting the spiritual needs of myself and others on weekends.

Other opportunities multiplied. I was asked to serve on challenging committees, to mentor other adults, to lead prayers in secular settings like the state legislature and a college commencement. While my gray hair gradually turned pure white I became more of what I was made and gifted to be. I was beginning to answer the high schoolers' question, "Who are you today?" with the realization that I was becoming a richer, fuller self.

I collaborated with my brother and my wife in editing a book about the life of my sea captain father. I wrote numerous articles and reviews for church publications. I've been reading up a storm lately, catching up on books I missed while I was "working." I'm also spending more time now with my wife and children and grandchildren. I have left school and Sunday subbing to others. I'm getting a bit unsteady on my feet, and thinking about using a cane, but nevertheless I'm enjoying my ever-emerging self.

At eighty-six years old, I am still in process or, with apologies to Descartes, I am becoming, therefore I am.

6

KEEPING THE
CREATIVE JUICES
FLOWING

39

Looking Forward

By Caroll Spinney

A puppeteer since he was eight years old, Caroll Spinney has been the man inside Big Bird and Oscar the Grouch since *Sesame Street* began in 1969. Since achieving worldwide renown, he has had the opportunity to travel the globe with his characters and has been honored with six Emmy Awards (one being the Lifetime Achievement Award), two Grammy honors, two gold records, four honorary degrees, and a star on Hollywood Boulevard. He was also named a Living Legend by the Library of Congress! Caroll has written and illustrated his autobiography, *The Wisdom of Big Bird*, and most recently he had a full-length documentary made about his life story called *I Am Big Bird*, which was produced by Copper Pot Pictures and distributed by Tribeca Films. Caroll calls New England home and has been living there with his wife Debra for forty-three years.

Now that I am eighty-two years old, I realize how important one thing can be — and that is to make plans. Always have something to look forward to. It has gotten me through life and has given me so many wonderful memories to look back on.

For example, when I was a young boy of eight years old, I saw my first puppet show. Right then and there I decided I wanted to be a puppeteer and I set the plan in motion.

My mother made me a flannel snake and I bought a monkey puppet for five cents. I made some bench seats and put up signs: "Puppet show in Spinney's barn — 2 cents!" Sixteen people came to see my show and when it was all over, I counted my thirty-two cents and made plans to do another show!

All through my school years, I performed with my puppets, always adding a new puppet or storyline so I eventually had quite a repertoire. My plan was to be on television. Sure enough, I landed a job on *Bozo's Big Top* in Boston. For almost ten years, I played Bozo's sidekicks — Mr. Lion, Grandma Nellie, Kooky Kangaroo, Flip Flop, and many more. And of course, I put on puppet shows.

However, although it was a lot of fun, I was feeling like I wanted to do something more meaningful and important.

So, in 1969, I drove to Salt Lake City to attend the Puppeteers of America's annual convention. I had built an elaborate show using new puppets and animation that I had designed and filmed. I wanted to mix the two mediums. My plan was to wow everyone with this new way of putting on a show and I had hopes of it leading to something bigger and better.

At first, that didn't happen. Someone had turned on a huge spotlight that washed out my animation so I couldn't see the background that my puppets were meant to interact with. It seemed like a total disaster and I was so disappointed. Nothing had gone as planned.

But as I was packing everything up, I heard a gentle voice behind me say, "I liked what you were trying to do!" It was Jim Henson.

We talked awhile and something bigger and better *did* happen! He said he was scouting for a puppeteer to play two characters on a brand-new show called *Sesame Street* and would I like the job? I nearly fainted . . . but I said, "Yes!" Big Bird and Oscar the Grouch were born that day!

I had always dreamed of traveling the world and certainly *Sesame Street* helped with that. But it was always for work and always when and where they said it would be.

It wasn't until I met my wife, Debra, that I found my true traveling partner. We both have wanderlust in our veins. At any given point in the year, we are planning a journey for the future.

Naturally, when we were younger, it was easier to navigate the globe. Just pack things up, get on the plane, train, or automobile — and go!

The years have flown by and I still don't let Mother Nature get in my way. We are eagerly looking forward to going on a European river cruise this summer. The anticipation is so much a part of the trip. And since I fell and gave myself a nasty concussion that affects my balance, I am planning to bring along a cane and a folding wheelchair! We've made plans and we are going — by hook or by crook!

Looking forward to something, whether it be a trip somewhere or a visit to the people I care about, is what gets me excited about life. It's been a philosophy that I have always followed and will continue to do so. I wonder, where will we travel to next year?

40

Strike Up the Band

By Elaine M. Decker

Elaine M. Decker is a social satirist and recovering Type-A personality. After graduating from Brown University, Elaine, a New Jersey native, worked in New York City. Following an early career in computers, she climbed a Fortune 500 ladder into consumer marketing, then dabbled in communications. She relocated to Providence, Rhode Island in 1992. Continuing on her debatably logical career path, she migrated into nonprofit management. She finally retired to write, blog (retirementsparks.blogspot.com), and take saxophone lessons. She has a regular column in *Rhode Island Prime Time*, a magazine aimed at older adults. She is the author of three books, *Retirement Sparks*, *Retirement Sparks Again*, and *Retirement Sparks Redux*. She now lives and jams in Connecticut.

Many studies confirm the importance of socializing and keeping active for maintaining mental and physical health. As we get older and life takes its turns, it's hard to hang on to even our most dedicated friends. My husband and I recently downsized to a peaceful condo with lovely views, leaving most of our social circle behind.

Once the move and the unpacking were behind us, I did a lot of nothing for quite some time. If you think I'm exaggerating, check out the indentation in our couch. After a while, the peace and quiet wore thin, and I realized I needed a hobby, preferably one that would help me find new friends.

I decided to take up saxophone again after a hiatus of half a century. My friend, Lynn, inspired me. She began playing clarinet late in life, eventually adding sax. Lynn and her husband retired to bucolic Ladysmith, British Columbia, where she plays in community bands, as well as in Dixieland and swing groups. Music has become her late-life passion and that reminded me that music was a big part of my school years.

Playing in a band is a social experience. I remember this fondly from high school. My bandmates were among my best friends and I'm still in touch with several of them. The prospect of finding similar camaraderie late in life is a siren call for me. If you've never been part of a musical group, I hope you'll be inspired to find out what you're missing.

Taking saxophone lessons after such a long absence presented several challenges. I had to find an affordable and convenient place to rent a horn and schedule those lessons. The closest studio wanted my Social Security number before they'd rent an instrument to me. Despite (or perhaps because of) my fond recollections of the boys in the band, there was no way I was giving out my Social to a shop full of young musicians. I finally found a place that accepted my credit card.

If you embark on a similar journey, look for an instructor with whom you'll have good chemistry. In my case, that meant someone who remembers Ol' Blue Eyes and for whom the lure of marijuana has long since lost its luster. That done, I was ready to get reintroduced to the saxophone.

Surprisingly, my wind capacity isn't an issue, and no doubt there's a joke in that somewhere. But other things are more difficult at my age. On the sax the left thumb rests near the octave key. The left hand curves from the octave around side levers to reach the upper keys on the main body. I struggle to avoid those side ones when I use the octave. Apparently my height isn't the only thing shrinking with the years. My fingers seem to have become shorter as well.

Eventually, I bought a quality used alto from a friend

who had it stored in his basement. You'd be surprised how many folks have instruments stashed away, ones they might sell at a good price if you decide to join the musical parade. You might also be surprised at what's hidden in musicians' cases, but what happens in the band room stays in the band room.

I've found a community group that let me join their jam sessions. They range from young folks to my peers. The intergenerational mix adds to the appeal. They're welcoming and blessedly nonjudgmental. It could take a while until I'm a "ready for prime time" player, but I expect to keep at this for years.

Still not convinced that you have a future in music? Throughout my musical journey, I've discovered other seniors who are taking up instruments later in life or relearning ones from their youth. A college classmate in Vero Beach, Florida, plays banjo in a Dixieland band called The Elderly Brothers. At my music studio, I met a mature man who was starting vocal lessons so he could join a church choir. He said he's not much into the church part of it, but he wanted to sing with a group. The Lord works in mysterious ways.

One thing missing from my new foray is my childhood

Beagle howling along with me. As I prepared to practice recently, I noticed a neighbor walking his dog. I popped outside to warn him that the dog might bark once I got going. Turns out my neighbor played alto in school, too, and his horn is stored in his basement. I didn't ask what else might be in his case. I'm lobbying him to take up his instrument again, if only to socialize. Okay. I admit it. I'm really hoping to recruit a neighborhood jazz group.

If you think you're too old to begin a musical adventure, think again. No matter what your decade, it's never too late to strike up the band!

41

There Is Still Sex and Romance at Eighty!

By Desiree Holt

Known as the world's oldest author of erotic romance, Desiree Holt has produced more than two hundred titles in nearly every subgenre of romance fiction. She has won the EPIC Award for action/adventure, the Authors After Dark Award for Author of the Year, the Holt Medallion, and she has been featured on CBS *Sunday Morning* and in the (*London*) *Daily Mail*, The Daily Beast, the *Village Voice*, *U.S. News and World Report*, and The Huffington Post, to name a few. Her stories are enriched by her personal experiences, her characters by the people she meets.

A t a time in my life when I'm sure my family thought I'd be reading on the back patio and watching television with my cats, I managed to fool them all. Why? Because I gave in to my addiction to romance novels. Not just reading them but writing them.

Becoming an author was a longtime goal of mine but it didn't happen until I was closing in on seventy. I like to tell people it's because I had to spend all those years gathering information and preparing myself for stories that would melt people's hearts. Actually, it was the first time in my life that I could sit down and give my imagination free rein.

My first books were simply good romance tales, because I have always been about the "happy ever after." But after I began creating my stories and developing my characters, I realized there was a lot more to heat up than their hearts.

I didn't start out to write in the erotic romance genre. My original love was (and probably still is) romantic suspense. But a few years ago I was invited to submit to a publisher noted for the erotic romance genre. I discovered, after that first book, that I loved exploring all aspects of a couple's relationship. And it's fun, giving my characters the opportunity for sexual experimentation. Showing how it really enriches the relationship. After all, sex is at the very heart of any good relationship, so why avoid it?

I'm frequently asked why a woman who is eighty wants to write erotic romance. First of all, I ask them, who would have more experience to draw on than someone my age? Secondly, age is a positive rather than a negative here. Just because you move from one decade into the next doesn't mean that sexual desire disappears. I think that's the primary reason I moved into erotic romance — to let my contemporaries know that at any age and in any decade there is still sexual desire between two people.

As people age, their love ages with them, burnished by the passage of time and shared experiences. Erotic romance is my way of letting people know that age is no boundary to a satisfying relationship. Not to mention the fact that I enjoy it. I love creating the stories where the intimate scenes between the characters don't stop at the bedroom door.

Writing erotic romance has also been a way for me to increase my outreach and connect with a lot of readers. I am constantly amazed at the number of people past so-called retirement age who read my books and write to me about them. I smile when I read e-mails from people who say my books have shown them there is still spice in their lives despite their age. That my books have opened a whole new world to them. With every e-mail I am inspired to continue writing more books.

And it's fun. Yes, fun. Taking two people and exploring every aspect of their relationship, from the initial meeting to the steamy bedroom scenes, gives me a lot of pleasure. I enjoy showing readers that at any age a relationship can be enjoyed to its fullest. Each day as I sit at my computer I lose myself in the lives of my characters and in their feelings for each other.

Also, it keeps me young. It's impossible to feel old when you are writing erotic romances and heating up cyberspace with your stories.

I've had so many funny things happen when people meet me and realize I fit well into the Senior Citizen category. I guess they think if you're over forty-five you don't know what romance is. I tell them that is when it just begins. I'm even writing a series for couples fifty-five and over. It's never too late to write and it's never too late to love.

I expect to be doing this for a long time to come.

42

Anyone for Their Own Toy Theatre?

By Ann Stokes Neff

Ann Stokes Neff did her undergraduate work in kindergarten-primary education and received her master's degree in business. She has been employed as a teacher, computer programmer, telecommunications manager, and international consultant. As a writer, Ann has had articles on toy theatre published in the journals of the British Puppet and Model Theatre Guild and UNIMA-USA, an international organization of puppeteers. Currently, she manages operations at Dr. Neff's Incredible Puppet Co., Inc., and putters around rural South Jersey pursuing her varied interests.

I propose to you a pastime for the leisure of your eighties; one that has brought great pleasure to me. The pursuit of "toy theatre" could actually provide you with your very own personal theater! (Note: When writing about toy theatre, it's customary to use the British spelling for theater since that's where it all began, back in the early 1880s.) The benefits of this pastime are many — mental stimulation, creative endeavor, absorbing activity, new-found skills, friendships, a true sense of accomplishment, and probable applause!

And just what is toy theatre? As the folks at Great Small Works, an American toy theatre collective sing, "It's got an arch, it's miniature, it's made out of paper, the characters are flat, and you can do it yourself. This is what toy theatre is." It is a theater scaled down to dollhouse-size, with a proscenium arch, scenery, and a curtain. Traditional toy theatres are made out of paper and cardboard; a wooden frame for the stage, with mechanics, is often added.

What do you do with a toy theatre? You raise the curtain (always magical), slide the small cardboard characters around, read or say the lines of your play, change the scenes on your set, and tell a story! The whole production is often done by one person. The performances are intimate, the audiences small.

For my very first sleepover, my mom bought me a book to take as a gift to my hostess. The book opened up to become a theatre with cardboard characters to punch out and push around the stage, to tell a story about a frog. It was the first toy theatre I ever saw, and I found it was very difficult to leave it behind with my friend!

Although I have always been fascinated by the theater, I never quite considered myself "actress" material. But since I am creative and a storyteller, I can use puppets as surrogates to "put on my show." As it happens, I now have worked as a puppeteer professionally — at both the beginning and end of a long, successful career in the corporate world.

The latter work with puppets involved instructing elementary education undergraduates how to use puppetry in the classroom. I accumulated lots of puppet material, including books that changed into theaters with characters, which students could use to tell a story. I was teaching toy theatre!

At a puppetry festival one summer, I took a workshop on Toy Theatre and fell further in love with this two-dimensional form of puppetry. Sponsoring the workshop was a lively eighty-year-old woman, an avid fan and true devotee of toy theatre. Under Gigi's tutelage I began to discover the depth of this historic and worldwide pastime — known also by the names "model theatre" or "paper theatre."

I was then approached, via the Internet, to build a

wooden stage for a woman halfway across the country. During the process, my art professor husband, an older man who has pursued puppetry far longer than I have, ventured down to our studio workshop, and asked if he could help. Together we designed, built, documented, and shipped out our first wooden toy theatre. Before we were finished, my husband was already planning a theatre with all the features he wanted to build for us!

And so the partnership began. My husband and I have produced and performed toy theatre plays designed by others — simply cutting out the parts and characters and putting it all together. We have modified others' designs. From scratch, we built a toy theatre version of Washington Irving's *Rip Van Winkle* — with traveling theatre, script, characters, and soundtrack! We have taken our shows on the road and performed them in homes, churches, universities, and festivals. Toy theatre has given us great pleasure.

My husband, who is now in his mid-eighties, told me he enjoyed doing toy theatre because it involves many of the activities he likes — writing a script, developing characters, drawing, painting; bringing it all to life in a performance. To that I must add that a toy theatre is more easily managed than a full-scale puppet show, both in creation and in terms of lugging it around for performances.

Though not as experienced an artist or actor as my husband, I too can find satisfaction: conceiving a production, designing the theatre, and working out the mechanical challenges. In addition, I have discovered I have a talent for watercolor and have increased my skills with character "voices"!

But you do not have to be an artist, or a Method actor to be a producer of toy theatre! Your personal theatre can be made simply. The basic materials and equipment are easily obtained: a box, heavy cardboard and paper, scissors and glue, with a gooseneck lamp for lighting. Once you make your theatre box, you may cut out characters from magazines or photographs and use calendar art for backgrounds.

However, there are other methods of obtaining your personal toy theatre. On the Internet are ready-made model theatres with plays. There are books of instruction and kits for theatres to punch out and slot together. Some items can be downloaded free of charge. Older and sometimes valuable materials are for sale on used-book and auction-house sites. There are two stores in London, several web-merchants in Europe, and an emporium in Ohio that sell toy theatre sheets and equipment. We have amassed quite a collection of books, theatres, plays, and assorted paraphernalia during our pursuit of this pastime. We have also accrued wonderful friends, many well into their eighties! You may find this is a hobby you'd like to explore now that you are in your eighties. You may find you have hidden talents waiting to emerge!

Personally, there are many toy theatre projects on my to-do list. As I proceed into my eighties, my dream is a toy theatre set up in my home, into which I may invite a few friends to see my shows; make them wonder and laugh. In addition, I am curious if I just might be able to locate somewhere that ancient toy theatre book with the frog play!

43

The Cycle of Nature

By Barbara Boldt

Barbara Boldt was born in Germany in 1930 and came of age in wartime Europe. After World War II, she immigrated to Canada, married, and raised a family before learning to paint in her mid-forties. She embraced this late career as the work and passion of her life, and through her paintings she explores the world around her, the vanishing landscapes of British Columbia's Fraser Valley, and the intricate rock forms of the Gulf Islands. *Places of Her Heart: The Art and Life of Barbara Boldt* by K. Jane Watt in conversation with Barbara Boldt, was published by Fenton Street Press in 2012.

My eightieth birthday in July 2010 was celebrated by my extended family and close friends under the massive maple tree in my yard. I have lived in my modest, rented home in Glen Valley, British Columbia since I turned seventy. It is my studio, my gallery, my teaching location. My life has not changed in the last ten years! I am still painting, teaching, and inviting the public to view and —

hopefully — sometimes purchase a piece of my artwork. It is my livelihood!

A surprise came when I received a phone call during the 2010 Winter Olympics in Whistler, British Columbia. Longtime family friends from Germany were attending the events, and were staying at a hotel there. My friend Erivan called to tell me that they saw my ad in a magazine in their hotel room. "Isn't it about time," he asked, "that you write a book about your art and life?"

My response was, "I don't know how to write a book or publish it!"

Erivan said he would pay for everything. All I needed to do was to find a writer. Wow! That was quite something!

I searched for an author, and I remembered the historian K. Jane Watt. I looked her up in Fort Langley, we met, and she said she would be happy to work with me. For the next two years, we met once a week at my place and that's how *Places of Her Heart: The Art and Life of Barbara Boldt* was written.

My work was to dig back into all my journals and photographs, my writings and newspaper clippings. I also spent much time researching the writings and old photographs of my ancestors. When the book was launched in 2012, it attracted quite a few visitors to Fort Langley, close to where I live. Jane Watt and I celebrated my eighty-fifth birthday at a book fair there.

My life in my eighties has been as active as it was before. I am still painting and teaching, and doing commission work.

The act of painting and my love for the subjects I choose is not just a "job." It is a passion to honor the ancestral history of art. My great-great-grandmother and one of her sons were both artists. That knowledge has created a cycle for me, and it reflects what I feel about the cycle in Nature.

CYCLE OF LIFE

Never ending, ever creating
Cycle of life
Perpetuating existence on earth
By changing her face,
Yet never dying,
Knowingly vying
For higher planes
And brighter futures.
Awareness brings solace,

My *hungry heart.*
The circle closes
And I am *part!*

My poem above expresses the ongoing passion I feel for Nature's gifts to us, and my need to portray it in my works. Some of the landscapes around me that I have painted during my forty years of art have changed so dramatically that the fields and forests have turned into townhouses and commercial sites. The natural cycle, which we normally feel in our lives, has not continued in the same way.

I will hopefully continue to portray Nature as I always have. It lives in my memories of my eighty-plus years!

44

Writing for Your Family

By Willis "Wiz" Arndt

Willis "Wiz" Arndt has been in the business world at home and abroad for fifty years. He loves the world of ideas and enjoys writing and performing with friends in a series of events onstage (including reciting classic rhyming poetry, historical remembrances, and "Wit, Wisdom, Personal Insults and Put-Downs, All from the Past"), which have been greeted with loud and prolonged applause. He likes audiences and it seems that audiences like him. After being a successful CEO for a number of companies, Wiz retired in 2007 but he continues to write and his book "*Wizdom*" *Memos* is now published. He and his wife Esther ("Tweenie") live in Vero Beach, Florida, and Devon, Pennsylvania. He enjoys life and it seems life enjoys him.

What to do when you turn eighty? There's tennis, golf, heavy gardening, owning boats, skiing, and for all of these and more, I say: "been there, done that." I gave some of these up because of such things as rotary cuff problems, reduced stamina, or just lack of continuing interest.

For exercise, I walk with my wife, Tweenie, and our dog Maggie. We start in the early morning, seven days a week, and do a no-dawdling, solid forty-five minute walk and I'm always the one trying to catch up.

I am no exercise buff. I remember reading in the newspaper some time ago that coffee was bad for one's health. Then, more recently I read that the latest research says that coffee is good for one. With that in mind, every day I pick up the morning paper, hoping to read about the latest research saying exercise is bad for you. I am waiting but not counting on it.

The above not only describes how I feel but, in large measure, how my friends of the same age feel as well. Of course for all of us eighty and over, the question we must answer — to ourselves as well as to those who ask — is, "What do you do all day?"

Speaking for myself, there is one project in particular that I find has forced me to *become* busy because it is ongoing and always needing attention. This project is called "Wizdom Memos."

My nickname is "Wiz." It always has been. When I was a toddler, my parents gave that nickname to me. To explain "Wizdom Memos" and how they started, let me quote a paragraph from the Introduction to the book with that title, which will soon be published: "In December 2012, with family about for the Christmas holidays, I let go (as I am wont to do) with some observations, thoughts, remarks, even some advice about the here-and-there of daily life. One grandchild suggested I write down my thoughts and e-mail to all. Another grandchild, creative that she is, suggested I call them 'Wizdom Memos.' And so I started."

I e-mail two "Wizdoms" a month to an extended family of children, grandchildren, in-laws, stepchildren, step-etc., and some interested friends. Some "Wizdoms" are one-half page. Some are a full page. Others are much longer. Oh well, sometimes I just have a lot to say.

As for the contents of these "Wizdoms," a sampling of titles will give you an idea of the diverse range of topics: "How to Get an Informative Answer"; "Managing the Expert"; "Gossip vs News"; "Travel Directions, The Art of Giving and Receiving"; "You Are American, I Am Pakistani, Thank You for Thinking American"; "What Makes for a Very Successful Party"; "Big Words"; "Serendipity"; "The Emperor Has No Clothes"; "The Importance and Power of the Written Word"; "Business and Altruism"; "Atta-boy, Atta-girl"; "Immigration: One Coin, Two Sides."

As you can see, the subjects are all over the lot. A topic might just come to mind, but it's better than that. I continually am alert to a potential subject and, much to my wife's chagrin, once I'm inspired I immediately begin making notes no matter where I am. Remember at eighty, short-term memory is not my strong suit!

The definition of "serendipitous" is "an unexpected pleasant surprise," and the project of "Wizdom Memos" has been and *is* indeed just that, serendipitous! At times I get off schedule. How rewarding it is to receive an e-mail asking, "When is the next 'Wizdom'?"

For those who are reticent about writing or want to know how to start, I have an idea that, in addition to limbering you up, will be very well received by your children, grandchildren, and your whole family, all of whom are your audience. *Write a chronological timeline listing the events in your life for the past eighty years.* I would give my eyeteeth for my parents' and grandparents' timelines. Unfortunately they were never written.

By writing your timeline, all sorts of memories will come up, many of which you may wish to elaborate on. As you do, you may even want to record your "observations, thoughts, remarks, and even some advice." Why not?

I started this essay regarding my disappointment in not finding enjoyment in exercise. I end with an observation on exercise by Peter Stothard, editor of the *Times Literary Supplement*, where, in a recent article he referred to Cicero's essay on growing old, writing, ". . . yet fighting what we call aging (is) a necessity for survival, and . . . exercising the mind is a worthy substitute for the gym." I like that!

45

Looking at Life with a Comedian's Eyes

By Julie Kertesz, PhD

Julie Kertesz is an eighty-two-year-old grandmother of five, with a PhD in chemistry and a Distinguished Toastmaster award. She's a personal storyteller, writes two blogs, and has more than 11 million hits on her Flickr photo site so far. In addition, she's an award-winning 2012 stand-up comedian.

I've been in London for more than seven years now. Before that, I lived in and around Paris for forty-five years but my mother language is Hungarian.

When I first arrived in London, I felt very alone. Six months later I joined two Toastmasters clubs and made a lot of pals. I also got the courage to go outside the clubs and tell my personal stories to paid audiences.

I've told my stories for Spark London at the Canal Café Theatre and even in front of five-hundred people in Manchester. What I learned from playing to such a large crowd is that the more audience you have, the more energy they give back!

I discovered photography, joined Flickr, and began to share sets of my photos with an international audience. In addition, I started a blog called *Il y a de la vie après 70 ans* (*There Is Life After* 70) and proved to myself and others that there are so many different things to learn and to do after seventy. After eighty too. Now, I write regularly on my English blog *CompetentCommunicator* and I am very active on my Facebook page. In March 2016, I became a member of the newest Online Toastmasters group, Firebirds Collective.

Five years ago, while onstage performing one of my personal stories, "Mistaken Identity," the audience suddenly began to laugh. Why? I decided to learn how to make them laugh *when* I wanted rather than by chance, and I attended comedy workshops, one after the other.

At the age of seventy-seven, I discovered I had a funny bone.

I got the Silver Comedy Best Newcomer award for 2012, then went on to perform with success in at least seventy-seven different comedy clubs. They tell me, "Come back whenever you want to perform."

Of course, at eighty-two, I have no plans to stop now.

Last year, I was invited to Tallinn to give a Humorous Speech workshop for participants from eight countries. I love doing my stand-up comedy act (one of my highlights was making a group of young corporate women laugh when I performed in London!). I have offered a storytelling workshop online, and I was filmed in a one-hour performance, parts of which were featured in a television show in June 2016, demonstrating we are never too old to make others laugh.

After my first cataract operation, I remained home alone. I woke up with a huge headache and felt so lonely, like a lost child. I had to add drops in my eye but nothing came out of the eye-drops bottle. I was so sorry for myself. After my third try, I discovered: the cap was on.

Suddenly, I thought: *I can use this! I can tell this story in my act to make people laugh!* I realized I had developed "comedian's eyes."

Now, I look at my life through my comedian's eyes.

Whenever something bad happens to me I ask myself, *How can I can make something funny out of it*? Not only does this make things less heavy and easier to bear, but people around me laugh and see me — and old age — differently!

I learned a lot about what I can bring to make any speech entertaining and I've begun to understand audience reaction much better. Nowadays, I do not have to use (as I did at the beginning) four-letter words to make them laugh. I learned how to suggest and then make fun of it. For example, I say: "My favorite toy is always on the table near my bed. Because size matters. Well, not always, believe me. This is my favorite toy nowadays: my beloved Kindle. After my cataract operations, I needed big-size characters to be able to read!"

It works. I make people laugh when I talk about having to shave after fifty and then I show a selfie of me with shaving cream. I can even make an audience laugh when I describe losing my teeth (so cute . . . when you are eight. Alas, not at eighty!) or breaking my leg.

Recently, when I had to have surgery, I had my whole medical team laughing when I told them some of my funny stories. From then on, they looked at me with different eyes.

I have begun to teach people how to dig deep to tell their personal stories, to inspire an audience and make them laugh at the same time. I'm teaching them how to discover their funny bones and to develop their own comedian's eyes.

46

The Joys of Solitude

By Carol Hebald

Carol Hebald was an actress for twelve years on the New York stage before enrolling as an English major at the City College of CUNY, from which she graduated Phi Beta Kappa, magna cum laude in 1969. Subsequently awarded a Teaching and Writing Fellowship in fiction at the Iowa Writers' Workshop, she received her MFA in 1971. Having taught creative writing at the university level for the next thirteen years, she resigned a tenured associate professorship in English at University of Kansas in 1984 to write full time. She has since published the memoir, *The Heart Too Long Suppressed* (Northeastern University Press, 2001); a novella collection, *Three Blind Mice* (Unicorn Press, 1989); and four books of poetry: The long poem *Delusion of Grandeur* from Turning Point Press (2016), and *Colloquy* from Finishing Line Press (2015); and from March Street Press: *Spinster By the Sea* (2005) and *Little Monologs* (2004). Her novel *A Warsaw Chronicle* is forthcoming from Regal House Books in 2017. Visit her Web site: CarolHebald.com.

The death of my father when I was four left me an exceedingly lonely and unhappy child. My mother at work and my sister in school, I expressed need for attention to an overworked housekeeper who responded by locking me daily in a closet, where my fantasies had free reign. There, I dreamed my way out of the lingering pain of wanting by imagining my father still with me. Much later, I would learn to make constructive use of such fantasies. Mistaking them for reality in the meantime, however, allowed my mental illness to take root. Unable to listen in school or to read until I was nine, my teachers thought me slow, and my classmates called me stupid. As a result, I moved further and further into fantasy.

One day a kind teacher named Mrs. Kessler, who kept me in after school for misbehaving, took the trouble to get to know me.

"What does your father do?" she asked me.

"He died a long time ago," I told her.

"Do you remember him?" she asked me kindly.

I remembered only our last words:

"Daddy, what should I be when I grow up?" I asked him.

"Be somebody," he said.

Who? I didn't know. Mrs. Kessler asked me what I liked to do best. To pretend, I told her simply. What fun it was to discover — by a gesture of the wrist, a foreign accent, a limp — the different Carols I could be. No sooner had I confessed this, than my desire to act was born. After graduating from the Drama Department of the High School of Performing Arts, I landed my first professional job at nineteen.

I learned quickly that the first step in playing characters was to find them in myself. Experience was my hunting ground. I could use what I'd been through. As my teacher, the renowned actress Uta Hagen, constantly reminded me, "Use everything!" I had the gift, and enough success to see me through twelve years of playing on the New York stage before mental illness caught up with me again.

What went wrong? Jobs were difficult to find. I needed to be working all the time! I grew depressed. Instead of making rounds, I spent my days reading in the library. The theater had been my salvation. There weren't enough jobs in salvation.

By then, psychoanalysis had come into New York fashion. I saw my psychiatrist regularly.

"What about love relationships?" he asked me one day.

"They're not for me," I declared. "If only I could spend my life working, I'd die a happy old lady. Other people have each other; I have my work."

"You don't have anything now," he reminded me.

On the contrary, I had my relationship with him on whom I depended for care, and privately loved like a father. This had happened before with other doctors: I'd wanted my therapy to succeed. My stronger need to be nurtured overrode it. Every step forward brought me closer to losing him. The only answer was to lose them all! If I really wanted to get well, I'd have to do it alone.

"You can't do it alone," he told me. "No one can."

Although I never met a psychiatrist who disputed this, I am among the patients who have proved it largely, but not wholly true. A diagnosed schizophrenic for thirty years, I quit therapy and medication, and by so doing found my mind.

Eventually, I quit acting to go to college. Subsequently granted a Teaching and Writing Fellowship at the Iowa Writers' Workshop, I started publishing my first poems and stories.

A tendency to create in fantasy what I lacked in reality was the springboard for my written work. I composed fictional characters from different aspects of myself. If a character was distant from me emotionally, I searched her inside out like a robber to probe her intimate thoughts, persistent memories, and dreams. I asked, *What exalted, depressed, or bored her?* She told me where she wanted to go. My years onstage had taught me that only by a thorough investigation of my characters' inner and outer realities could I hope to bring them to life on the page.

What about my own life? There is no passion like the passion of thinking, as one grows older. And for me, to think has always been to remember. It occurred to me, if I could write a memoir that showed a direct relationship between the harm of early hurt and my subsequent errors in judgment, I would accomplish something of value, not only for myself but also for others. Having accomplished this in 2001, I turned into the happy old lady I promised myself to become.

Writing has become the central activity of my life. It has done more than help me to regain the equilibrium I had lost. In breaking free from the blows of the past, I had to teach myself again to feel: love, hate, shame —

even outrage from too much pain. Thanks to my acting training, I can tap these feelings at will, and with them truthfully endow complex fictional characters with the life forces that define them. By this I feel I am giving back something of what I have learned.

47

Retirement? Nuts!

By J. A. Pollard

J.A. (Jean Ann) Pollard is an artist/author who was born and currently lives in Winslow, Maine (after a few exciting misadventures in such places as Libya, Tunisia, Bermuda, the Bahamas, England, Russia, the Netherlands, and, oh yes, California). Illustrating many of her published books, short stories, and nonfiction works in pen and ink, she also creates large acrylic paintings in three series, including *Au Naturelle*, which consists of landscapes and close-ups of plants, animals, and insects; *The Reef Series*, which adds *bas relief* sculpture to the gleaming, magical world of coral reefs; and *The Gaia Series*, which presents our planet as seen from space surrounded by the sculpting of human inventions, activities, and dreams, and ranging from Darwinian evolution to Western and Eastern mythology to extinct and modern plants and animals. It's focused on Planet Earth and "talks" — in these days of climate change — about the need for awareness and planet-care.

Being an artist, it seems to me, is "talking" to people without words, without gestures, but with the excitement of placing colors and shapes and lines in a composition on paper, on walls, boards, bricks, whatever, all balanced with the same feeling as skiing down a mountain. Being precise. Focused.

As a child growing up in central Maine, running through fields and woods, I met no art. No paintings. No group of artists beyond a few involved in music. There was readin', 'ritin', and 'rithmetic, of course, plus a few history books hinting at something called the Sistine ceiling of Michelangelo, the *Mona Lisa* of Leonardo da Vinci, and European cathedrals soaring with stained-glass windows, but for a kid who loved to draw, the big world of fine art was a mystery . . .

. . . except for one important thing: lunching with my mother in a small Italian restaurant on Main Street, Waterville, in the 1940s, I was mesmerized by magical scenes of Venice on walls beside the booths. Scenes in paint! And while outwardly nibbling at a sandwich, I was actually tracing mental fingers over brush strokes, sinking into ultramarine and cobalt blues, and reflections that somehow caught on water. I was reaching . . . reaching for something I didn't know existed, but knew I needed to do!

I was lucky. The restaurant was called Diambri's, and

someone in the family knew how to capture visions with oil paint on canvas!

Like every youngster bent on self-discovery, one day I boarded a train heading south for Boston University where I joined a program that seemed removed from whatever it was I was seeking . . . but there were some courses in life drawing, gold leafing, the use of gesso, pen-and-ink illustrating, and, of course, introductions to the Isabella Stewart Gardner Museum and the Boston Museum of Fine Arts where I "met" John Singleton Copley, Gilbert Stuart, Charles Willson Peale, adventurous Thomas Moran (who gave Americans our first glimpse of Yellowstone), Thomas Eakins, Winslow Homer, and John Singer Sargent . . . so many American "greats" . . . none of whom were women (you understand?) but all of whom seemed to work with oil paints on canvas, like Turner in England, and Renoir, Monet, Klimt, and Picasso (of course) in Europe. Mary Cassatt, an American painter who settled in Paris, was one of the few (the very few) female Impressionists, but even she had a difficult time of it (naturally). What kind of artistic career would I have? I didn't even like oil paints.

I vividly remember a man demanding, "Why hasn't

there ever been a great female orchestra conductor or famous fine artist?"

To which I wondered, *Yes! Why not?* (But that was before my pregnancy, childbirth, and the twenty-year circus of child-raising. Also, before I discovered the kind of paint medium that spoke to me.)

By the late 1960s, frustrated with adventures in New York City and Washington, D.C., working at nearly anything to "support my art habit," including stints at biological and medical illustration, being a medical secretary, writing for newspapers and magazines, I met acrylic paints and (as such things happen) it was right back in Maine.

In fact, it happened on Main Street, Waterville, when landscape artist Tony Vajs inquired, "Haven't you tried acrylics?" at which I gaped, but immediately purchased three primaries plus white, and some jars of media and, as they say, "the rest is history." Acrylics allowed me to do what I wanted, from painting broad, flat areas of color to the finest details on gesso-covered sheets of sanded Masonite . . .

. . . to which I ultimately applied *bas relief* sculpting by mixing certain acrylic media with marble dust and other items.

Heaven!

At last!

Life, especially one that reaches eighty years, provides a fairly comprehensive view of what it means to be a human living on Planet Earth.

"But haven't you retired?" someone asked as I came crashing into my eighties.

From life? I wondered. *From work? From responsibilities that we've all created?*

For years I'd painted in three series, beginning with *Au Naturelle* (with landscapes and close-ups of plants, animals, and insects), then moving on to *The Reef Series* (after thrilling to snorkeling on coral reefs), and later, with climate change upon us, I created *The Gaia Series*, which combines acrylic paints and *bas relief* to "talk" about the magical, irreplaceable glory of our one-and-only home. I'm saying, "Be aware of climate change. Look at our planet, folks, it's wonderful! Precious! Take care of it!"

My paintings are now owned by people in Russia, England, and America, including NASA scientists. It's hardly the time for retirement!

48

Do Music!

By Karl Singer, MD

Karl Singer, MD, is a physician who is board-certified in Internal Medicine, Family Practice, and Geriatrics. Currently, his practice is focused on serving as an attending physician and medical director of a 220-bed nursing home. His major interest is in how we can slow the development of dementia and frailty, the two major issues of people in their eighties. He finds that one of the ways he approaches this issue for himself is to play in a chamber music group that chooses to work on a new piece of music every month.

I began to study the violin when I was about ten but I didn't develop a passion for playing until I joined the orchestra at the start of college. During my senior year, I decided I wanted to play chamber music. I taught myself viola because violists were hard to find. I have been playing chamber music ever since; and for the past forty-three years, I have been playing in the orchestra at Philips Exeter Academy, a private high school in Exeter, New Hampshire.

For the past fifteen years I have played chamber music with the same group, a violinist and a cellist. We invite other instrumentalists from time to time so that we can play a wide variety of pieces. We try to play lots of music that we have never played before and have worked on over one hundred pieces. Since we range in age from seventy to eighty-one, we call ourselves The Alzheimer's Prevention Trio. Because our strategy of challenging ourselves to learn new pieces utilizes so many different parts of our brain, we hope we are increasing our cognitive reserve.

Researchers have been able to verify that playing a musical instrument does, in fact, utilize many different parts of the brain. Using advanced-imaging techniques like functional MRI, it is possible to study how listening to and playing music involves the auditory system, the cortex, the visual system, and the parts of the brain involved in emotional processing. Music therapy can also be useful in treating many different neurological disorders including post-stroke weakness, Parkinson's disease, and Alzheimer's disease. While it can't cure these illnesses, it can mitigate some of their effects.

Music has such profound effects on the brain because it is a very complex activity. When you listen to or play music, you need to recognize different pitches and understand rhythm. Then there is the intellectual activity needed to understand the words of a song or patterns of notes, the emotional impact of the music, and the social aspects of listening or playing with others.

There are many different genres of music. While it is fun to enjoy old favorites, it is also good to expand your horizons and explore some of the many varieties available. Attending the Edinburgh Festival after graduating from college, I heard Ravi Shankar and fell in love with the complex rhythms and haunting melodies of Indian music. Recently, while taking a course on the history of the string quartet, I learned to appreciate the music of twentieth-century composers like Arnold Schoenberg and Alban Berg. I am looking forward to attending a performance of the new musical *Hamilton* and listening to the hip-hop music that it features.

In many cases, musical experience allows you to interact with people of varied ages. For example, all of the other members of the Philips Exeter Academy orchestra I play in are teenagers. I am also fortunate to be able to play music together with some of my children and grandchildren. I find interacting with young people to be both stimulating and fun.

Music is a wonderful way to become closer to other people and even to feel that you are part of something larger than yourself. For example, when my trio plays a beautiful piece of music and everything comes together, it feels like we are united with each other. The same kind of feeling can occur on a larger scale when you are part of an orchestra or choir.

As you try to learn new techniques or understand new music, you will hopefully be adding to your cognitive reserve and possibly be slowing down the loss of brain function. Almost all participation in music involves some physical activity, whether it is playing an instrument, moving your body with dance, or even just tapping your feet or swaying to the rhythm of music you are listening to. You may be improving your physical fitness.

So continue to play music if you have been enjoying it in the past or take up a new instrument, join a singing group, learn to dance, or just listen to some new or familiar music. Your world will be richer for the experience, your body stronger, and you might even help to prevent Alzheimer's disease.

49

Free to Have Fun

By Robert Urban

Robert Urban has worked in the advertising world and started a market-research business. For twenty years he helped national and international fresh-produce firms sell fruits and vegetables to American supermarkets. At the age of seventy-one, he sold his business and since that time he has been enjoying life with his wife, Judy, traveling, drawing and painting, and building objects out of wood and electronics.

W hen I turned seventy-one, I retired, sold my market-research firm, and turned my attention to the interesting projects that I'd toyed with for years but couldn't pursue seriously. When I was in college I'd studied art for a couple of years. Later I built a small desk with a few hand tools when we lived in a New York apartment. I owned a digital camera and a sound recorder and, between business trips, I used Adobe software to create fun stories for my grandchildren. So now I was free to play.

Maybe a better description would be free to work; free to devote serious effort to making things that interest me. I've built furniture, painted portraits, created animations, and assembled electronic toys.

Now that I'm eighty-eight, I make these little electronic sound generators, using analog synthesizers, which create odd digital sounds. They are assembled from small resistors, capacitors, and integrated circuits. It requires serious precision to design a structure that is small and that will accommodate many switches, wires, and circuitry as well as a speaker and a 9-volt battery. One circuit is connected to a colorful graphic sculpture that I've designed for the project. The sculpture may be a rocket ship, a family of pet dogs, or a fire engine. I use my imagination when creating these fun pieces. Each sculpture supports a variety of knobs and switches that control the sounds that come out of its speaker. Turn one knob and there's a whistle. Flip a switch and a whistle becomes a growl. It's great fun to experiment.

One hears about older people who have retired and feel lost, with nothing to occupy themselves. It must have been my childhood that spared me. My family situation was unusual. My father was extremely rich in my very early years and then began to drink heavily and died impoverished. My mother used our money to give me a spectrum of experience: life on a cattle ranch, travel by motorcar throughout the U.S., concerts, bookstores, an antique armor collection, and more. We lived in many places as the family fortune diminished and I attended many schools. I think that this experience taught me to look hard around myself and see novelty in my surroundings. So I have seldom in my life been truly bored. Instead, I like to create objects based on forms that have piqued my interest.

Last year, my ten-year-old grandson came to visit and I brought out an electronic fire engine that I had assembled from scratch. We turned on the power and I stepped away to let him fiddle with it. I was really pleased to see that he had a great time generating all manner of hisses, clicks, and siren music just by playing with the knobs and switches. That's one of the main reasons why, at eighty-eight, I enjoy building electronic sound generators!

50

A Second Life

By Roger Pepper, PhD

Dr. Roger Pepper withdrew from a successful career in science to follow his lifelong ambition of becoming a novelist. He now writes full time, lives in Maine, and is the author of two thrillers and a spiritual fantasy. Roger is active in the organization of writers meetings and workshops at the Maine Irish Heritage Center, the Scarborough Public Library, and the Falmouth Memorial Library. He is currently working on a novel based on the true story of his life in London, England, during WWII. With friends from the Appalachian Mountain Club, he hiked in the Austrian and Italian Alps, the Kangchenjunga and Annapurna Himalayan regions of Nepal, and traveled in France, Italy, Israel, Russia, and Central Asia.

My second life started early, at fifty-seven, and it's still going strong now that I've passed the big eighty.

I recall sitting in my office at an aerospace materials company years ago, wondering if I had followed the Peter Principle when I took the position of Director of Research, rising to my own level of incompetence.

Certainly, by not having time to work in laboratories, I no longer felt the excitement of creating something new. I no longer had an opportunity to work on materials like the carbon fiber reinforced aluminum I helped develop, which NASA used for the antenna of the Hubble telescope because it didn't distort when exposed to the thermal extremes of dark space and bright sun.

I was a successful scientist who had his fifteen minutes of fame, and was Director of Research. Great, you might say. Yet I grew tired of the lifestyle, traveling the country, estranged from home and family, living in hotel rooms and wining and dining people I had no desire to be around, all in the hope of landing another research contract. I was bored. I needed a fresh start, something that demanded imagination and creativity, a new beginning that could lead to a meaningful later life.

I had always dreamed of being a novelist, and I'll never regret starting to write fiction in my spare time. Spare time quickly became full time. I joined the ranks of artists, actors, writers, and others who pursued uncertain careers. Somehow, I plucked up a little of the nerve they had, courage I'd always admired.

When I took the plunge, I quickly discovered that to write good fiction, the author needs to be in the head of the principal character, be it a man, woman, or child, and have a clear picture of the story's place and time. But where would these ideas come from? And how to survive the later years with peace at home, as well as good health, when so many hours are spent at the keyboard, exercising only the fingers? I'm fortunate to be married to an avid hiker and skier. Together we have traveled to countries all over the world, France, Italy, Russia, Nepal, Central Asia, and I find this to be an excellent complement to writing. My most successful ideas have come in faraway places.

For example, on a flight from Moscow to Almaty in Kazakhstan, it struck me how beautiful the Tien Shan Mountains looked all covered in white, and how ugly they could become with global warming. But what about when the permafrost melts in Siberia, and prehistoric creatures, frozen in time, pop out of the tundra? Gradually, Corky Mason, the heroine of my published novel *The Brothers Cro-Magnon* materialized. Then she told me how Russia's secret police came within a swish of a mammoth's tail of proving their claim that she was the primitive sister of four murderous brothers.

While backpacking in the Dolomites, I tried to picture myself living high up in Italy's World War I trenches in the middle of winter, exposed to gunfire, starving, caught in a savage fight. The character of Carmela DeMitri emerged from a patch of mist, then stayed with me, sharing the story of her search for the love of her life on Mount Marmolada, and how he fought for the Alpini and survived a massive avalanche. I worked hard on this story for three years, and it became my novel *ICE*.

On the social side, I've never been one of those secretive people who keeps quiet about what they write. Rather, I enjoy being involved in writing groups, and my second life has become very active. Three good friends and I recently took over as the organizers of Portland Writers Group in Maine. We run the group through Facebook, providing meetings and workshops for over a hundred members at the Maine Irish Heritage Center in Portland, the Scarborough Public Library, and the Falmouth Library.

I am busier than I have ever been. My ongoing literary endeavor is a novel, entitled *Tommy's War*, based on my childhood in London, England in WWII. It's the story of a boy's tenuous relationship with an ambitious, class-conscious father. I've done the research, now it's time to write.

Creating characters and living closely with them and their full range of emotions and actions for months can be rewarding, especially when you have the writing skills to bring their story to a meaningful conclusion. I have worked hard over the years to acquire those skills, as have many authors, and even a modest level of success, such as mine, brings a strong sense of accomplishment. I wish you a worthwhile second life as well.

51

Pleasures

By Jennifer Birckmayer

Jennifer Birckmayer has been an early childhood educator, speaker, author, and trainer for forty years. She has retired from her position as Senior Extension Associate in the department of Human Development at Cornell University. Since retirement, she has been a consultant/trainer for Libraries for the Future, Family Place Libraries, the State University of New York Early Childhood Training Strategies Group, and several early care and education programs. With Anne Stonehouse and Anne Kennedy, she has published a book, *From Lullabies to Literature*. The crowning glory in her life are her four adult children, but she continues to miss her husband who died twelve years ago.

The first few months after my official retirement date were like an extended vacation. I slept late and rolled over in bed when it rained. I read novels in the morning, or sometimes late into the night. I went for walks whenever I felt like it and had coffee or lunch with friends. I'm embarrassed to admit that one of my simple pleasures was taking time to open a plastic bag in the produce department of the local supermarket. For years I had dashed in to grab a vegetable for supper, cursing my lack of small motor skills and often rushing to the cash register without bagging my purchase. It gave me enormous satisfaction to be able to take my time over opening the darn bag.

It was not until a dear friend from Australia came to visit that I realized a pleasure from my previous professional life was missing. Anne and I had worked together in the Department of Child Development at Cornell University and discovered a mutual delight and interest in children under the age of three. We didn't always agree but our discussions were stimulating, often filled with laughter and invariably provocative. During her visit we discovered a new mutual interest in the growing research on ways in which very young children learn language and become literate. I had been captivated by a statement from Kofi Annan, while he was United Nations Secretary-General. At an International Literacy Day (1997), he said: "Literacy is a bridge from misery to hope. It is a tool for daily life in modern society. It is a bulwark against poverty and a building block of development."

Anne and I believed that literacy skills begin in the

first three years of life and are based on a love of conversations, nursery rhymes, songs, stories, and books. We were anxious to share this belief with parents, teachers, and others who were interested in the development of very young children. So-o-o we decided to write a book!

At this point I was in my middle seventies and as unskilled in using a computer as I had been in opening plastic bags in the grocery store. Anne assured me that I could still learn and after she returned to Australia our adventure began. The rough plan was that, based on an outline we had developed together, I would write the first draft of a chapter and Anne would then add, subtract, and generally rework what I had written. Of course, it would all have to be done by e-mail. Anne bore with great patience e-mail messages from me like "The computer won't let me —" or "The computer has hidden half of this chapter —" or "How do you put something in italics?"

In spite of my technological ignorance we made good progress, until I was diagnosed with breast cancer and had to have a mastectomy. Undaunted, Anne persuaded a good friend of hers (also named Anne!) to join her, and, fortunately, this wonderful second Anne continued to work with us after I had recovered. She and I finally met when we presented the finished book (which was published by the National Association for the Education of Young Children in 2008) at a national professional conference.

We called our book *From Lullabies to Literature* and I began to use it in some of the consultant work I was doing with libraries, as they developed programs for families with infants and toddlers. In the process of this work I discovered that some librarians, skilled as they were at creating marvelous programs for children over the age of three, had less confidence and little training in their work with babies and toddlers — and these very young children were increasingly important visitors to libraries. It became clear to me and to the director of a national program called "Family Place" that we badly needed some visual aids so that we could show, instead of tell, librarians what an effective program for very young children looked like.

Almost miraculously (it seemed to me!) the dedicated Family Place director obtained grant monies, enabling me and a talented young videographer to create two videos, "Beginning with Babies" and "Terrific and Trusting Toddlers." Together we filmed young children and their families at home and in library settings. Together we edited raw footage. I then wrote the script and he directed me in the narration and managed all the production details.

It's been deeply satisfying to use the videos in training programs and to watch librarians "catch on" as they see the children, families, and libraries we filmed. Now in my eighty-fourth year I hope we can find funding to make a video about three year olds. Making and sharing videos is a lot more fun than opening plastic bags in the supermarket!

52

Writing Poetry in Our Eighties and Beyond

By Joan Peck Arnold

Joan Peck Arnold has lived for the last ten years in Maine. She has been published in several journals, including *Soundings Review* of the Northwest Institute of Literary Arts, *Slant: A Journal of Poetry*, and *Soundings East*, of Salem State University in Massachusetts. She also received an International Merit Award from the *Atlanta Review* and an Honorable Mention from *Writer's Digest* magazine. Also, as a result of a contest, and while she still lived in Gloucester, Massachusetts, she had the delight to be interviewed on a Boston Public Radio station, WBUR, where she read her poem, "Van Gogh's Universe" on their *Here and Now* program. It has been her privilege to occasionally study over the last twenty years with Charlotte Gordon, Marion Blue (online), Moira Linehan, and Valerie Nash. She is grateful for their poetic spirit in her life. Joan reads and writes poetry avidly in her search for truth and beauty in her life and the world.

"Poetry is my home," I often say. It is where I go to feel comfortable and where I do my self-exploration in writing. It is also where I go to be uncomfortable when my writing is changing or the subject matter is verging on the unfamiliar. I didn't consciously *choose* to write poetry. It just happened. One night I started writing because I badly needed to express myself and, much to my amazement, a poem emerged. Why a poem? I still can't answer that question.

Another question I can't answer is why after a short time of writing poetry, it just became something I *had* to do. Perhaps it has happened to you, too. You may be maneuvering through rush-hour traffic or some other unchosen time, when suddenly you find yourself thinking about yellow leaves falling on the lily pond, or the illness of your brother or husband, and before you know it a new poem begins to form. There is nothing to do but pull over at the next rest stop and start writing. Hopefully you carry a pen or pencil with you along with some paper. The back of the fuel bill will do. The love of words; rich, smooth, powerful ones begin to form when you write, and you are hooked.

Writing poetry can be invaluable in deepening your understanding of yourself and the world, especially if you are facing a gain or a difficult loss, as we all have done by the time we're eighty. So you write.

And you begin to find your way with using words either intuitively or purposely. You can even utilize the advice of others like I did when I brought to mind the mid-nineteenth-century poet Emily Dickinson's opening lines to a poem:

> *Tell all the truth but tell it slant —*
> *Success in Circuit lies . . .*

Although I had read Dickinson's poem long before I began to write, even studied it, I understood it only on a cognitive level. It was only after I had written poetry for a long time that I began to understand it experientially. I share the following story:

On February 19, 1995, I had my routine yearly mammogram. Afterwards, the oncologist came to the waiting room and tapped me on the shoulder, saying, "Can we talk in my office?" Immediately my knees started to shake, and my voice quivered and of course my intuition was correct. He showed me the results of my mammogram and there it was, the lesion in the milk duct in my left breast. What I had always dreaded. My mother had breast cancer before me so I had expected a similar diagnosis but had always prayed, *Please not this time.* But now was the time!

I slept little that night, and my mind had gone into its "awfulizing" mode. In the middle of the night, I got up, went downstairs, opened my journal, and started doodling. Doodles turned into words and words into a poem. My "awfulizing" scared the first-ever poem out of me — at sixty-three. I have revised it several times since, but this is all that I have left of the first version. As you can see, in the poem I focus on the décor of the waiting room to escape cancer's frightening reality for the moment. By doing so, I am also able to spare my readers the details of the cancer. "Telling it slant" has a real purpose here. It almost makes the poem more powerful. See what you think.

The Waiting Room

A *few women have companions.*
Silence and a discreet distance
separate those who don't.
The room is dressed
in safe colors; maroon
and gray with a dash of blue,
ashen blue.

A *watercolor hangs, just a touch*
crooked on the wall, picturing
paint tubes and flustered brushes

placed at odd angles as though an invisible
artist can neither clear the confusion
nor muster the courage
to continue her still-life

Sheer curtains by a cliff
of windows tremble and in the corner
a memorial black granite
sculpture kneels;
a naked woman still bears
her smooth polished breasts.
Her head is bowed, her eyes closed.

Now some twenty years after "The Waiting Room" was written, I can say what a multifaceted gift poetry has been to me and how satisfying and healing it has been to speak of life's gains and losses in this way. I intend to continue writing and I invite you to come along and write with me as we progress into our eighties. In other words, "Come home with me."

53

Last Acts

By Patrice Dotson

Patrice Dotson is an eighty-three-year-old great-grandmother from Eugene, Oregon, who has just finished writing two books. She has led a variegated life, having had many careers, from medical technologist to marketing director, with a bit of time thrown in as a massage therapist and outside sales. She has volunteered for many years in the Eugene area, working with the homeless and various other causes. When she was seventy-seven, she entered the world of stand-up comedy where she enjoyed appearing at the Actor's Cabaret and the Pacific NW Women's Comedy Event at the Wildish theater in Springfield, Oregon. She was the winner of the 15th Annual Laff-Off contest in Eugene in 2010. For several years she studied Chinese brush painting and her work appeared in several shows. Currently, she is marketing her books by combining her stand-up comedy routines with her book-signing events.

As I write this essay, I am eighty-three years old. When I was in my fifties I got the idea in my head that I was going to die at age sixty-two. Don't ask me why I chose that year. It just came to me to prepare. It seemed that I had done everything

I needed or wanted to do in life. There was nothing left worth living for. I retired from my job and filed for Social Security.

And I prepared. I got rid of a lot of "stuff," I bought and paid for my cremation, I wrote up a will and had it notarized, I moved to a small town on the Oregon Coast, and then I waited. And waited. Things were beginning to get boring.

Well, imagine my surprise when nothing even close to death happened. I didn't even have a cold that year, or the next. I felt very healthy and was walking three miles a day on the beaches.

While I was waiting for the inevitable I began to find things to do in the community. I took hospice volunteer training and had a few clients I helped to "pass on." Because I had no family nearby, I volunteered at the Mission on holidays. I took a writing class at the community college and I inherited a computer, my first, joined a computer group in the town, and learned to create cards, calendars, banners, and even a family recipe book.

At sixty-nine I moved to a larger town and I went back to work in a completely different field as a marketing director. I loved it, and worked in this position until I hurt my back at age seventy-two. That was when I was brought to the ground with a big dose of reality. Now I had to use a cane and sometimes a walker. Recovery was slow and showed me my limitations, no questions asked.

I took up Chinese brush painting, an art that required a peaceful mind and could not be hurried. I learned to sit quietly and patiently and create lovely brush strokes. I began to win ribbons for my art and I had some art exhibitions of my own and placed my work in local art shows and galleries. It was a lovely time — and then it was over. I had gone as far with it as I had wanted, and I was once more at a loss for something creative to do with my life.

I was seventy-eight when I took a class and began doing stand-up comedy, or rather sit-down comedy, with my walker. I was having the time of my life, appearing onstage, giving people a good time, and also doing a lot of volunteer work in the community. Who could have dreamed that I would be doing such a thing and having so much fun doing it?

Now I was eighty! Who could believe that I had come this far in years . . . and what was to be next?

Well, this is what came next. This past year I wrote and published two books! One is a novel I began eighteen years ago when I was sixty-five, but could not find a way to finish it. It took eighteen more years of living to teach me what I needed to know about life in order to complete the novel. *Well, You Just Never Know* is the title, and fast on its heels came my next tongue-in-cheek book titled *Dating Tips for the Septuagenarian*. I did all the illustrations for this book myself. It's loaded with tips for people who are alone, wishing they had a partner to share things with. It has time-tested advice and hopefully it will make readers laugh. Both books are self-published and available on Amazon.com.

I have been marketing the books myself, doing a stand-up comedy routine combined with a book-signing event in my city. I go to bookstores and retirement centers. Well, who would have dreamed all this could be happening at the age of eighty-three? I would have hated to miss all this.

I have to say, for those who are willing to hear it, that older is definitely better. In my sixties I still carried a lot of expectations about how life needed to be in order for me to be happy. People needed to change, circumstances needed to be different, so much was wrong with the world.

Today I know that nothing needs to change. I don't need to change, things are going to happen with or without my consent. But how I respond to what is going on makes all the difference in the world. I can choose to enter the arena and fight the battle or I can be an observer and watch it pass by. It is always my choice.

I'm so fortunate to have lived long enough to know that the best days of my life are the ones I am living right now, no matter what is going on around me. I wonder what ninety will bring . . .

STAYING ACTIVE

54

Axels at Eighty

By Richard ("Mr. Debonair") Dwyer

Though he's a beloved star in the glamorous ice-show business, figure skater Richard Dwyer prefers to think of himself as a sportsman. He is actually one of the great artists of theatrical skating. His legendary, crowd-pleasing routine as "Mr. Debonair," which has delighted his millions of fans as he's performed with "Ice Follies," "Ice Capades," and "Holiday on Ice," is still in demand. Backed, as always, by four lovely Dwyer Girls, "Mr. Debonair" was a highlight guest performer at the opening ceremonies of the 2016 U.S. National Figure Skating Championships. The audience and youthful contestants cheered eighty-year-old Richard, a sportsman after all.

I was so fortunate to celebrate my eightieth birthday at the Yerba Buena Ice Arena in San Francisco — yes, at an ice rink! What could be a more perfect place to see many of my friends from "The Ice Follies," "Ice Capades," and "Holiday on Ice"? What a great way to kick off this new decade!

My whole life has been connected with figure skating,

so it isn't going to stop now. I love the sport, and it keeps me going. Throughout my career I've been known as "Mr. Debonair" and skating has given me great joy. I started traveling with "The Ice Follies" at fourteen and a half in 1950, and performed with them for the next thirty years. I then joined "Ice Capades" in 1981, and worked with them through 1993, always on the road. I never got tired of traveling.

This year, my itinerary started with the United States figure skating championships in St. Paul, Minnesota. Next, I'll go to Knoxville, Tennessee. For the pro-skate auditions, I get to see all the up-and-coming talent. I find it so inspiring, plus it keeps me current on new skaters, all such great young people. I am invited to judge the Los Angeles Figure Skating Club showcase championships; this is a theatrical competition, with lots of "show biz." It's fun to see, but tough to judge. I take in as many local competitions as I can to support our skaters. It's so rewarding to see what they can do today. The sport is improving all the time.

In the summer, I travel to somewhere special to skate — Lake Tahoe, Sun Valley, and I always enjoy the experience of skating outdoors. In August, I go to the United States National Showcase Championships, another theatrical event. I sometimes present the trophy to the winner, and that's a real honor for me. In October, I always go to the Ice Theatre of New York fund-raising gala benefit, a special evening that honors a great contributor to our sport. I love New York City — talk about things to do! I go to shows, sports, galleries, museums, restaurants! It's a treat to just walk around, seeing all my favorite spots: St. Patrick's Cathedral, Central Park. I go skating at Chelsea Piers, Rockefeller Center, Wollman Rink, it never gets old. I love to visit and just take it all in.

I guess you might say I'm still on the road. I often drive to San Francisco. I spent thirty summers there, built a home in Marin, which I still have, so I have an excuse to keep tabs on it. Nowadays, I lease it out. And of course, when I'm in San Francisco, I get to see many of my ice show friends that live there. I always take my skates with me!

I love to visit Santa Rosa too, especially since I appeared in figure skating shows produced by *Peanuts* cartoonist Charles Schulz. He created the beautiful Redwood Empire Ice Arena in Santa Rosa. It is always great to connect with all the staff and skaters at the rink and to get on the ice with old friends.

I do have other interests besides ice-skating! I love cars. I have two old ones that need tender loving care. They run, but . . . !! I have always been interested in real estate, and I still have my fingers in it, too. It's a big job trying to keep the couple of houses I have looking good and up to date. I love to go to home shows, to keep up with new ideas for homes, and I enjoy visiting The Home Depot and Lowe's for new ideas and the improvement sections. I always make a point to visit the tool section as I still have the shop that my dad owned in Burbank. I bought the shop years ago — it's very small, but it is my spot to come to every day. That's where he made sets and designs for shows in Las Vegas, plus he did work for Barbra Streisand. He was a real artisan, and I keep it up to date. If you want to build props or sets out of metal, brass, copper, or stainless steel there, it's good to go! Going to my dad's shop keeps me busy. That's my answer to staying healthy. "What are we doing tomorrow?" my dad used to say. He had an unbelievable spirit. Like him, I am always looking forward to a new day and challenge.

I find that I can help other friends who do not drive anymore by getting them out once in a while. I love to read, and go to the movies. I am a real sports fan, so I love to attend a baseball, football, or hockey game.

I try to attend alumni functions and fund raisers at my alma mater, Loyola High School, and I do the same for the University of San Francisco. Because I was always living out of a suitcase, it took me twenty-two years to get my degree!!! I'm in their sports Hall of Fame, which is a great honor.

Life is exciting and I have been blessed with pretty good health, so I keep enjoying each day. I skate every Monday through Friday at the Pickwick Ice Arena in Burbank; having fun and trying axels. I guess you might say I have eighty things to do. I admire so many people and I think I am happiest seeing old friends, and making new young friends, who exude energy and spirit. I do know my limitations, but I try to challenge myself to stay at a happy level that I feel good about. Life is wonderful, and I am so fortunate to continue to be active!

55

Making the Most of Your Eighties: Be a Triathlete!

By Dr. Ruth Heidrich

Ruth Heidrich, PhD, although technically "retired," is an author, speaker, nutritionist, talk-show host, triathlete, and now "movie star" as she "starred" in the ground-breaking documentary, *Forks Over Knives*. Living in Honolulu, Hawaii, she trains in running, biking, and swimming all year round. Still competing at the age of eighty-one, she's won over nine hundred medals and was named one of the "Ten Fittest Women in North America" by *Living Fit* magazine. Her books include *A Race for Life*, which details her struggle to beat her fast-metastasizing cancer; *CHEF*, her cook/raw recipe e-book; *Senior Fitness*; and *Lifelong Running: How to Overcome the Eleven Myths of Running & Live a Healthier Life*. Her Web site is: ruthheidrich.com.

Turning eighty years of age is, first of all, something to be grateful for as you've just made it past the average life expectancy for people in this country. You've obviously had some healthy habits and luck to allow you to make it this far.

I thought when I started running daily at the age of thirty-three that this would assure me of living to one hundred — or something close to that. A diagnosis of stage IV breast cancer at the age of forty-seven immediately disabused me of that notion! I thought, *Wait just a darn minute!* I was the healthiest, fittest person I knew and was even running marathons by that time.

The luckiest I've ever been was when, right after that damning diagnosis, I came across a notice that a local doctor was starting a clinical research project to determine the role of diet in the treatment of breast cancer. He was looking for newly diagnosed breast cancer patients who had not yet started chemotherapy or radiation. His theory was that the Standard American Diet, known appropriately as "SAD," was causing our increasing incidence of breast cancer in this country and reasoned that if you got rid of the cause, the body could heal itself. He also knew from previous studies that chemotherapy and radiation really did not "cure" the cancer, that the incidence of relapse was high, and that these treatments caused permanent damage to the patient's immune system, just at the time when it was needed most.

Since I had just been diagnosed and was being transferred from Surgery to Oncology, I fit that category. Now, I had studied nutrition in college and thought I knew what a good or even the "best" diet was and had followed it ever since leaving college, which was about thirty years before. I thought here was a chance to "prove" that the SAD diet was not the cause, nor the possible "cure" of breast cancer.

Two days later, I presented myself to John McDougall, MD, armed with all my medical records, ready to take on this challenge. When he told me that his plan was to put newly diagnosed patients on a low-fat, vegan diet, I was pretty sure that this wouldn't work in my case; as I naïvely told him, I felt that my diet of skinned chicken, fish, and low-fat dairy was already good enough.

He turned around at his desk, pulled out a file drawer, saying, "Here's the research that backs up what I say." Here were animal studies showing that when tumors were implanted on rats with half of them fed a low-fat diet and the other half a high-fat diet, the tumors shriveled up and even fell off the rats fed a low-fat diet. With the rats on a high-fat diet, the cancer spread rapidly. The second batch of research consisted of epidemiological studies and population studies showing the same thing in many different countries. The countries consuming a high-fat diet had high rates of breast cancer, and the countries with a low-fat diet had low rates of breast cancer. This was enough to convince me to enter Dr. McDougall's research study that day!

From that moment on, no animal products or oils passed these lips! My bone pain subsided within days and my liver enzymes normalized by the next blood test three weeks later.

The second luckiest I've ever been was when I happened to see the Ironman Triathlon, which was taking place right here in Hawaii where I lived. I was transfixed by what I saw. First, they swam 2.4 miles right here off Waikiki Beach; then jumped on bicycles for a 112-mile race around the island, and *then* ran a marathon! I thought that since I could handle the marathon, I'd just add swimming and biking. Besides the disappearance of my cancer symptoms, I had noticed that my running got faster, and I had a lot more energy, which I was pretty sure was due to my new diet.

I did some checking and found that up to that point no woman as old as I was, forty-seven, had ever done the

Ironman and, of course, no cancer patient, either. So this became my quest: prove that this low-fat, vegan diet could not only reverse cancer but was powerful enough to help me complete what was then considered a "grueling" event that attracted "crazies" who were seeking a super-challenge. I was feeling so fit and healthy that just two years later, I crossed the finish line of the Ironman, impressing even Dr. McDougall!

Thirty-four years later, I'm still fit, healthy, with absolutely *no* sign of a breast cancer recurrence — and still doing my own mini-triathlons daily, never dreaming that I would be an eighty-one-year-old *triathlete*!

56

Stay in Shape: Eighty and Up

By Jameson Skillings

Jameson Skillings has been teaching, coaching, and personal training since 2003, working with a wide variety of clients who have their own unique needs and limitations. Jameson utilizes a full-body approach to personal training. By pinpointing muscular/structural imbalances in his clients, he helps them learn more about their bodies and how to improve themselves. A major theme in his work is meeting clients where they're at physically and mentally while focusing on the least invasive behavior change that creates the most positive results. Jameson has a BS in Kinesiology and is certified as a personal trainer, yoga instructor, spinning instructor, group fitness instructor, and a behavioral health professional. Please visit his Web site: jamesonskillings.com

As a certified personal trainer, one of my favorite things to do is to work with older clients. I have more than ten years of experience specializing in a high-risk population sixty-five years and over. I've helped clients lose over one hundred pounds slowly, safely, and maintain their practice to keep the weight off. I've seen them make incredible progress; getting so strong and improving their balance so much that they can stand up without needing to grab onto anything for the first time in years. Lower-limb amputees have relearned to walk again after training. Clients often rekindle excitement for exercise by getting back into activities they enjoy like yoga, strength training, golfing, or even tennis. Lots of personal trainers think working with professional athletes is the pinnacle of our profession, but they are wrong. It is within this highly nuanced and specialized population of older adults that the best work is being done in the field of exercise science.

For example, I often help my clients find the motivation they need to exercise, something that older adults in particular must do to stay healthy. I have an eighty-two-year-old married couple that has trained with me for three hours a week since 2014. They initially came to me, believing that exercise was not something you do for fun but only for the benefit. I told them that I would do the impossible and show them how to have fun when they exercise. We tried many different types of training programs before we discovered that nothing gets this married couple more excited to exercise than boxing.

It's not surprising to find that both their faces lit up with the prospect of punching their personal trainer! It was important for me to have them find something that they could look forward to doing. I know for a fact that if you aren't enjoying what you're doing, eventually you will stop doing it. Finding joy in an exercise program makes for healthier and happier people.

There are a multitude of benefits to increasing the amount of movement we do each day. Specifically, getting the right amount and type of exercise lowers the risks of several cancers, cardiovascular disease, some metabolic diseases, and premature death in older adults. People who exercise to build muscular strength; enhance range of motion; and improve agility, balance, and mobility can make strides no matter what their age.

During adulthood, people tend to gain body weight and fat while also losing muscle, height, and bone density. While this may be the norm, there is good news! An increase in body weight and body fat may largely be lifestyle-related instead of what was once thought to be part of the natural aging process. Getting out and moving more often is one of the best ways to get yourself feeling more energetic and lively.

The vast majority of older adults have a specific goal in mind: independence. For people in their eighties and older this is tantamount to success. Reclaiming or maintaining independence involves training for strength, mobility, flexibility, range of motion, endurance, and balance. Having an exercise routine that incorporates multiple aspects of fitness within a given training program is a surefire way to have success. Before jumping into a program, however, it is important to obtain medical clearance and assess your current ability levels.

Once medically cleared, meeting with a certified fitness professional is a great next step. Assessing your current fitness capabilities by way of a Senior Fitness Test is an excellent way to get started. With just seven test exercises, the Senior Fitness Test is completed in thirty minutes or less and gives the fitness professional multiple avenues in which he or she can help you improve physically and become more independent.

When following a recommended fitness program it is important to follow guidelines from a trusted and scientifically backed organization like the American College of Sports Medicine (ACSM). The principles regarding the frequency, intensity, time, and type (FITT) of exercise needed essentially applies to all adults across the board, not just those sixty-five and over. When older adults are unable to follow the recommended amounts of physical activity due to recurring issues, I show them how to modify their routines so they can still be as physically active as their abilities and conditions will allow.

In planning a fitness program, you'll want to get your heart rate up and move around five or more days a week at a level you would consider a five out of ten. It doesn't matter what you do for exercise as long as you avoid excessive stress/impact on your bones — keep the jumping on one foot with your eyes closed to a minimum! If you're the kind of person that does better with finite goals: aim for 150-300 minutes of exercise per week.

Building your strength up twice a week with a full-body, progressive-resistance training program that includes a total of eight to ten exercises, using ten to fifteen repetitions at a moderate to vigorous difficulty, will reap huge benefits for your bones, tendons, ligaments, balance, and muscular strength. Progressive-resistance means that over time you would increase the amount of resistance on your exercises as you continue to get stronger.

Be sure to incorporate at least two days a week of stretching each major muscle group. Hold each stretch for thirty to sixty seconds. Range of motion can sometimes be reclaimed if the lack of movement ability is from soft tissue. It is amazing what properly implemented static stretching and proprioceptive neuromuscular facilitation (PNF) stretching can do for immediate range of motion improvement. The majority of older adults often sit in a slouched position and have poor overhead range of motion, so focusing on stretching the hip flexors, quadriceps, chest, upper-body pulling muscles, and shoulders will prove to be the most efficient path to improved range of motion and independence. Do your best to maintain upright and neutral posture throughout the spine while holding all your stretches.

The most important takeaway is to get clearance from your doctor and to find a certified professional personal trainer to help guide you through the process. We're here to help!

57

Dance

By Naomi Goldberg Haas

Naomi Goldberg Haas is a dancer, master teacher, choreographer, and founding artistic director of the multigenerational company and educational organization Dances For A Variable Population (DVP), which promotes strong and creative movement among people of all ages and abilities, with a special focus on seniors. With DVP, Naomi has created site-related public performances at many of New York City's most iconic public spaces including The New York Botanical Garden, Times Square, Washington Square Park, and the Whitehall Ferry Terminal, and she choreographed the first commissioned dance on the High Line. She also leads DVP's education programs, including the organization's free community-based dance workshops that have served over four thousand seniors at thirty-five senior centers since 2009. Naomi has worked in concert dance, theater, opera, and film, and has collaborated with The Klezmatics, composer Michael Nyman, and Pulitzer Prize-winning playwright Tony Kushner. She holds an MFA from Tisch Dance at NYU, and began her career with the Pacific Northwest Ballet. In 2013, Naomi received the "Art + Action Award" from Gibney Dance. The Lower Manhattan Cultural Council awarded her the 2014 Presidents Award for the Performing Arts.

D ance. Dance every day. As fully and expressively as you can imagine. *Move*. *Move* and *move more!* In all ways you can imagine. When you are eighty celebrate the moving human that is you!

I am the director of Dances For A Variable Population, a multigenerational company and educational organization promoting strong and creative movement for adults of all ages and abilities, with a special focus on seniors. Our teaching artists and I meet and work with *many* vital and happy folks in their eighties. Our experience working with older adults has taught me that the older you are, the more deeply you understand yourself, who you are, and what makes you tick. You also gain a better sense of the ways you like to move. This understanding makes you unique in your movement, more defined in your body language, more alive in your presence in the world.

Your choices of how you move are tied to the essence of you. You have no concerns about what is cool or beautiful. What is beautiful is what is possible — from the practical ways you get up to the iconic way you gesture to the ways you bend to the ways you go from here to there. Your challenges, your limitations are a perfect place from which to start. They define you, and inside this sphere you are interesting, powerful, surprising, and beautiful. Exploring this essence is where we start investigating our personal movement vocabulary. What is possible is powerful. As one of the seniors who took our program said, "I always felt that I had a dancing heart, but I couldn't do anything about it before. Now it's my time and I will dance! I lose my inhibitions when I dance."

When you are eighty, what comes out is the beginning and the making of the dance that is uniquely and undeniably you. Martha Graham said, "There is a vitality, a life force, an energy, a quickening that is translated through you into action, and because there is only one of you in all time, this expression is unique. And if you block it, it will never exist through any other medium and will be lost."

As a choreographer making dances with older people, I am endlessly interested in the combinations of movements between people that they discover from their own personal vocabulary. Those are the most fascinating. My job often is to set up a safe environment and then to let folks loose! We discover treasures of movement with gorgeous strengths, which come from a place of knowing that is drawn from the older individual's years of doing movements that are comfortable, physical motion that is unique to each. Younger members of our company with far more movement variety work hard to be as interesting as the elder dancers in our company!

Having recently had an elbow replacement, my movement became limited; I am so grateful for all the possibility of this body of mine. As I strengthen and understand my new elbow, I recognize that it is now a defining part of me and I remember to honor all the layers of experience inside me. They have defined me and resonate with every movement choice I make, investigating and celebrating the essence of me.

58

Surprising Myself

By A. David Barnes, MD

Veteran A. David Barnes, MD, PhD, MPH, FACOG, is an obstetrician living in Salt Lake City, Utah, with his wife Mary and their seventeen-year-old daughter Brittany. His journey started in London, where he trained at the University of London, Kings College. He then attended the Royal College of Surgeons in Ireland, and Oxford, where he took a tropical medicine course. Dr. David then moved on to more training at the State University of New York. He graduated with a post-doctoral master's degree from the University of California, Berkeley, then rounded that off with a PhD, focusing on the discovery of the cause of cancer in the cervix. David is proud of the fact that he emerged from five universities debt free! His new book, *Insanity of Wars*, is an illustrated autobiography describing his work in sixteen different countries around the world. Visit his book's Web site: insanityofwars.com or e-mail him at: adbarnesmd@gmail.com.

Several of my medical school friends have died of cancer, car accidents, even HIV. A few have retreated to summer homes. Marty and Helene have bought a large boat and are texting pictures from their yacht in the Caribbean. But I love my work. What is better than delivering a healthy newborn for a young mother on December 25th and saying, "Happy Christmas"?

I surprised myself when I thought back over the years that I had never had a serious illness or needed an operation. I had enjoyed jogging, snow-skiing, cycling, and swimming. The idea of a rocking chair had not occurred to me. I decided I would cover other obstetricians who needed time for vacation, conferences, maternity leave, or sickness.

At seventy years old, I surprised myself again when I accepted a call to cover a physician in Sitka, Alaska, for Christmas. Upon arriving on a Wednesday I was asked, "Are you aware Saturday is Polar Dip Day?" An elderly doc whispered, "Don't do it! Heart attack waiting!" Three days later, I surprised myself by jumping into the freezing cold Alaskan icy ocean, then swimming for several minutes. My legs felt like lead pipes as the group exited the water. A lady doc shouted, "Let's do it again!" I had no choice. Our reward was a "Certificate of Insanity." However, after a hot bath, my whole body seemed rebooted and I felt twenty years younger.

Maybe that was why I surprised myself again by completing the Honolulu Marathon of 26.2 miles for my seventy-fifth birthday. The reward: finishing the race and stumbling into the waves at Waikiki Beach for the best massage.

Another telephone call: "Would I cover two OB/GYN practices in Pennsylvania for two weeks?" Three babies came between midnight and breakfast one morning. I thought I was in the movie *Groundhog Day*.

Weeks later I found myself the only OB/GYN for a one-hundred-mile radius in Montana. I was walking along the Lewis and Clark trail of 1805 when my good friend, Karl, a nurse who organized small emergency-plane evacuations, suggested we support and attend a group of Wounded Warriors for the day. Absolutely. They did not need much encouragement to practice sniper rifle fire on targets a mile away and enjoy the farm lunch. Horse-riding was available too.

I surprised myself this year by completing my first book, *Insanity of Wars* (insanityofwars.com), an illustrated autobiography. As a London Blitz survivor I grew up as a child hating Germans, despising Japanese, suspicious of Vietnamese, Koreans, and the dreaded communists in China. Now I count them among my sincere friends. Our new enemy is ISIS. *The insanity of war!*

I can't wait to be an octogenarian next year and complete my twentieth marathon in Honolulu, the paradise area, which allowed me to start my first 26.2 mile run at forty-one years old and my son's first at just ten years old. Lesson: you're never too young or too old to start jogging if that is what you identify as a key to longevity.

I have reasoned from my exploits above that while I keep fit, I remain capable of doing good work for others. I know the years will continue to bring surreal surprises, but I also realize it will be me who's primarily responsible (and grateful) for my own good health.

59

Wings, Not Weights

By Nancy King, PhD

Nancy King, PhD, author of novels, nonfiction, essays, and plays, leads workshops in storymaking, drama, and language acquisition in the U.S. and abroad. She also writes for the Web site: yourlifeisatrip.com. Type in "Nancy King" to read her articles. Nancy lives in Santa Fe, New Mexico, where she writes, weaves, plays guitar, and enjoys the proximity of culture and nature. You can read excerpts of her writing and learn about the work she does by visiting her Web site: nancykingstories.com.

When I was sixty-five, I traveled from Ardentown, Delaware, to visit Santa Fe, New Mexico, not looking to leave my job, my community, or move two thousand miles away. While there, I saw a triangular house with light pouring in from every window. A few hours later I bought it. Everyone I knew — from colleagues at the university where I taught for thirty-five years, to friends in the community where I lived for thirty-seven years, to family — all reacted the same way.

"You did what?"

"You don't know anyone."

"What will you do?"

"You're leaving your oncologist? What about treatment?"

Although my new house was only fifteen miles from a ski area, I thought I was too old to ski, especially since I hadn't skied in eighteen years. Then I met skiers in their eighties and nineties. SO much for that thought! Despite facing another round of treatment for a rare and anomalous form of leukemia that I've been dealing with since 1985, I bought new ski equipment. It was an act of faith. Afterwards, I discovered, much to my delight, that the new skis were easier and more enjoyable to use than my old equipment. I've been downhill and cross-country skiing ever since. When friends invited me to snowshoe I bought snowshoes and experienced the pleasures of whooshing down deep snow under a brilliant blue sky in sunny, snow-covered woods, although I admit, climbing uphill in snowshoes is hard work.

When I was seventy and recovering from yet another bout of chemotherapy, I joined the local branch of the

Sierra Club. After hiking for a while I signed up for an eight-mile hike, only to realize mid-way, and much to my dismay, that it was ten, not eight miles — and that it was a one-way hike. There was nothing to be done but to do it. As I put on my hiking boots after wading across a roiling, cold stream, I imagined pushing my doubts away, telling myself, I *can do this*, and I did, even scrambling over boulders at the end.

Recently, friends and I decided to hike up Santa Fe Baldy, a 12,622-foot mountain. The hike is fourteen miles in length, with an elevation gain of 3,600 feet. I put on my backpack, overwhelmed with worries. *It's been two years since the last time I did this hike. Can I still do it? There's a forty-plus mph wind approaching the summit and temperatures are colder than normal . . .* I could feel anxieties and fears settle in my body like weights, making each step burdensome. I didn't feel good — my stomach hurt. My head hurt. The lump in my throat would not go up or down. I thought about going only part way. I could sit and wait for my friends to return to where I was. Then I got mad at myself. I was in good shape. I'd climbed Wheeler Mountain, which is not as long but it's over thirteen thousand feet, in good time and shape. What was I afraid of?

I told myself to stay in the moment. I told myself I could do this hike. I envisioned the weights around my feet transforming into metaphorical wings. And then, much to my surprise, it wasn't an illusion. I outpaced my friends who are years younger. They said I was amazing, an energizer bunny, but I wasn't. What I was, was grateful.

I think there are three ages: *Chronological*, about which we can do nothing. We're born when we're born; *Physical*, which we can do a lot about if we face our fears and listen to our bodies; and *Psychological/Emotional*, which we can affect if we imagine ourselves vigorous and vital and don't listen to naysayers or pay attention to media images of people over eighty as white-haired, bent over, deaf, and half-blind.

There is another way we can stay vital, which I think has to do with the well-being of our spirit, and that is to find ways to challenge ourselves, to move out of our comfort zones. I face fears of performance anxiety by joining a guitar ensemble to make music in community. Even when I don't feel well or am dealing with the effects of chemotherapy, I push myself to walk in the mountains, knowing that being in nature raises my spirits and heals my body. Most recently I have chosen to deal with my emotional and psychological baggage by going on a vision quest — I will spend three days at the retreat center preparing for four days and four nights alone in the wilderness, then three days of processing back at the retreat center.

All my life I have walked on eggshells and lived on high alert. I want to be able to breathe easily, without fear, to walk on the earth and feel my feet on solid ground. I want an experience where I can look deeply into myself with no mediation or distraction as a way of marking my journey through life up to this point — finding who I am and who I want to be. I hope to jettison lifelong patterns and habits that no longer serve me. Thinking about doing the vision quest fills me with a multitude of feelings ranging from trepidation to exhilaration and everything in between. I have begun the complex preparation with once-a-month counseling with the vision quest leader that will continue until we meet at the retreat center.

I don't know what spending four solitary days and nights in the wilderness will require of me — that's part of the training. I do know that when I stay present, in the moment, I always have a choice. I choose wings, not weights.

8

TRAVEL: WHAT'S ON YOUR BUCKET LIST?

60

On Earthwatch Adventures

By Warren Stortroen

In 1996, two months after retiring from the Principal Financial Group of Des Moines, Iowa, Warren Stortroen was watching birds from a blind in Costa Rica's cloud forest. This was Warren's first Earthwatch expedition, and he was hooked. He has now participated in ninety-two of them, and at age eighty-four he's already signed up for seven more. Warren lives in St. Paul, and when he's home, he volunteers with the Minnesota Valley National Wildlife Refuge, Minnesota DNR Scientific & Natural Areas, and several related organizations.

I n February, 2013, I was on the Mississippi Delta as part of the Earthwatch expedition called "Loons and the Gulf of Mexico Oil Spill." We set out from the boat landing at dusk to capture loons for research. The first one was easy! Earthwatch volunteer Tracy found him with the spotlight and kept it on him until Hannah, the research scientist, brought him into the boat with one swipe of the large landing net. There, fellow volunteer Jill held him with his head under her arm while Hannah checked his health, took blood, feather, and fecal samples; measured and weighed him; and attached leg bands, while another volunteer, Barbara, recorded the data. It was perfect teamwork!

My teammate Ken and I just watched the first loon capture, but were rewarded by being involved with a second capture later that evening. After several loons evaded us by diving, I found one more with the spotlight. He dove twice just out of reach of the net, but on the third try Hannah brought him into the boat. He was quite vocal and when released gave a short yodel and rose up in the water flapping his wings in farewell. This project was a milestone for me since it was my eighty-first Earthwatch volunteer expedition, just before I turned eighty-one!

Then, in late June in the French Alps I was warmly dressed as clouds scudded overhead and a cold wind blew up the valley to the snow-covered peaks above. I was on a hillside of lush grass and brightly colored wildflowers, watching marmot burrows for the newborn pups to emerge. On the slope above me a herd of ibex, with their long, curved horns on display, crossed a receding glacier to feed in an alpine meadow. Suddenly, two fleet chamoix came racing along the base of the cliff in front of me and then bounded straight up the cliff face! They posed nicely for a picture before moving on. I didn't see any marmot pups, although several adults were browsing on the hillside and juveniles staged mock fights near the burrows, but I was very satisfied with my day in the field.

This was an Earthwatch expedition to assess the effects of climate change on marmots living at 9,000-feet elevation, in La Grande Sassière Nature Reserve near Bourg-Saint-Maurice. We stayed in comfortable chalet rooms in the ski resort of Tignes where the researchers, with some help from the volunteers, prepared great meals of rural French dishes, including tasty, local breads and cheeses.

In August, 2014, at Crow Canyon Archaeological Center near Cortez, Colorado, I was about to close out my excavation of a "discoloration," a dark area in the surrounding red soil, when I spotted a glint of blue at the bottom of the pit. I carefully scraped around it, removed the remaining dark soil and lifted out a beautiful piece of turquoise! It was about 2 x 2 inches and was nicely shaped and polished. After marking the location for measurement I brought it over to archaeologists Steve and Caitlin, who were delighted with the find. Only four pieces had been discovered in the area, and this was by far the largest and most nicely worked! Since turquoise was thought to be a link to sky and water, they speculated that it may have been placed at the bottom of the hole, under an upright rock, in a ritual ceremony.

The site where I found the turquoise dated from about 500 to 750 CE in what archaeologists term the Basketmaker III period. People of that period were in transition from a life as hunter-gatherers to a more sedentary agricultural lifestyle. They developed simple pottery and lived in a community, not of Pueblo structures, but of pit-houses — underground rooms with pole and adobe roofs — with a central plaza or great kiva for gatherings.

This was my second Earthwatch expedition in scenic southwestern Colorado, with the San Juan Mountains and Mesa Verde to the east and the imposing Ute Mountain to the south. On each expedition I've been lucky enough to make exciting finds of pottery, bone, stone tools, points, flakes (the stone cores left by flintknappers), and other artifacts such as the turquoise. On my third expedition I found a beautiful, small projectile point while excavating a circular kiva at a Pueblo II site dating from about 900 to 1150 CE. I've really enjoyed working on this project with the great Crow Canyon staff. They do a wonderful job of welcoming and working with the volunteers! And the accommodations at the Center are excellent.

These three stories are a small sampling of the many volunteer research expeditions that are offered by Earthwatch. To date, I have been on over ninety expeditions, all over the world — twenty-one of them since turning eighty — and I've thoroughly enjoyed them all! I highly recommend these rewarding projects for active retirees who are interested in traveling to exotic places and helping Earthwatch experts to sustain our planet. If you'd like to go on an upcoming expedition, information is available at earthwatch.org. I hope to see you at one of the Earthwatch sites!

61

Retire at Eighty? *Fuhgeddaboudit* — I'm Too Old to Retire

By Ed Perkins

Ed Perkins conducted and managed aviation, travel, and tourism research from 1952 through 1985, during which time he and his wife, Eleanore, traveled extensively. With their combined backgrounds in travel and writing, they founded a "don't give up your day job" travel newsletter, *Economy Traveler.* It was, as they say in show biz, a critical success but a box-office failure. However, in 1985, Consumers Union took it over and morphed it into *Consumer Reports Travel Letter* (CRTL), with Ed and Eleanore as coeditors. Under their leadership, it became one of the country's most respected and successful travel publications. Ed and Eleanore retired from CRTL in 1998 and moved to Ashland, Oregon, where Ed continues to write syndicated columns and contribute to smartertravel.com.

I spent the last twenty years of my preretirement life writing and editing, first a newsletter called *Economy Traveler,* and later *Consumer Reports Travel Letter* (CRTL). My wife Eleanore and I coedited *CRTL* until my official retirement, at age sixty-seven, when we moved to

Ashland, Oregon. Eleanore and I traveled a lot when we first retired, enjoying theater, opera, and great museums in the U.S., Europe, and Asia, along with driving through the countryside just about everywhere. But starting in the early 2000s, Eleanore's health deteriorated to the point we couldn't travel. Eleanore finally lost her medical battles in 2011, when I was eighty-one.

Thus, a year past the eighty-year mark, I faced solo life after forty-five years of a close-knit marriage. Fortunately, travel could remain a focus of that life. I currently write two weekly columns, syndicated by Tribune Content Agency, one dealing with general consumer matters, the other directed to senior travelers, and distributed to some two dozen newspapers and Web sites. I also contribute regularly to SmarterTravel .com, a leading online source of travel information. I especially enjoy keeping up with a bunch of bright young dot-commers even though I'm forty years older than my next oldest associate. And I support consumer initiatives — advocating travelers' rights and fighting deceptive advertising — in cooperation with Travelers United, the Business Travel Coalition, and others. Having what is, in effect, a regular job at age eighty-six is huge, keeping my mind active and engaged with issues of importance to travelers.

Neither frequent flyer miles nor eighty-year-old guys improve with age, so I started systematically working off the miles accumulated over many years. Since 2011, I have taken six extended international trips:

- In early 2012, I went around the world, visiting places I'd missed over the years (Seoul, Beijing, Dubai, Istanbul, and Kraków) and revisiting an old favorite, northern Italy's beautiful Valle d'Aosta.

- In early 2013, I traveled to London, then drove to French Switzerland, including Geneva to Lucerne with stops in-between, enjoying the unequaled Swiss scenery and filling up on Gruyère cheese right in Gruyères.

- In late 2013, I drove the Dolomites around Cortina d'Ampezzo, then up the spectacular Grossglockner highway to the lakes and hills of Austria's Salzkammergut.

- In late 2014, I made a driving trip around southern Italy, focusing on Bari, a low-key but historic part of Italy far too many American tourists ignore.

- In early 2015, I drove the Mosel Valley (one of Germany's thirteen wine regions), with its fantastic steep-hillside vineyards and great wines, while ODing on schnitzels at every stop.

- in late 2015, I drove all over New Zealand, visiting both the North Island's fascinating geothermal area as well as the South Island's spectacular Southern Alps, rugged coastline, and picture-perfect Queenstown. One big plus for New Zealand: there's no tipping in restaurants. But you don't go to New Zealand for the food.

I find that renting a car and staying in small hotels outside of big city centers is the most relaxing and easiest way to tour an area. Even driving on the "wrong" side of the road in New Zealand isn't stressful after the first fifteen minutes. If you have to go into a city center, park at a station and take a train. Of course, you don't drive when your stops are all big cities, as in the round-the-world trip. But fortunately every city I visited had an efficient public transit system, and — in the Seoul, Beijing, and Dubai metros — recorded announcements and signage in English along with the local language.

We chose Ashland for our retirement base because of its diversity of cultural resources (a wealth of enjoyable performances at the Oregon Shakespeare Festival, Southern Oregon University, and many smaller-scale venues) combined with village convenience. Shortly after we arrived here, Eleanore organized two "interest groups" with the local branch of the American Association of University Women: Musicals and Opera. Each group met monthly to view and hear a featured work. Because of our home's dedicated media room with its projection TV and good sound system, our place became the more or less permanent venue for these meetings. Since Eleanore's death, I have continued to host these gatherings. We even did Wagner's complete *Ring* cycle last year.

Like most eighty-six-year-olds, I have my share of physical challenges; tolerable, however, with the occasional work-around. The only real defect in what would otherwise be a contented post-eighty life is the loss of Eleanore, a huge void that I will never be able to fill. But when you get to your eighties, stuff happens, and better to stay active and engaged than sit around moping, "Oy, poor Ed." So far, that strategy is working.

62

How Was the Food?

By Carol Scott

Now in retirement, Carol Scott was a conservation commissioner in the town of Chatham, Massachusetts, for eleven years. She is also an ardent gardener, a dedicated birder, a golfer, a hostess, a house cleaner, a cook, a handywoman, a painter, a bridge player, a clam digger, and a compost-bin filler. Carol is not a Type A and actually has hermit tendencies. It may sound like she's busy, but she's just persistent when she takes on a project. In her 'before retirement life' she did a bunch of stuff: art teacher, worked for a book publisher, married, moved around the country a lot, had three kids, was a substitute teacher, did display advertising ads for a local newspaper, had a silk-screen business and made wallpaper, worked in admissions for a college, and then happily retired! Carol has a great husband and three wonderful kids who all tolerate her quirks and are the reasons for her to keep on trucking.

Birding travels began early in our marriage. My husband was the trip planner and I was the packer. My sister said we'd hit a wall in our eighties, but not so. We just kept on planning, and birding and traveling far and wide on the elusive hunt for a bird yet unseen. One of the wonderful advantages of birding is throwing oneself headlong into the culture of the countries we visit. We had just returned from a trip to Australia and Papua New Guinea and were catching up on our sleep when I got a phone call from a friend to welcome us home.

"How was the food?" she asked.

The food? The food? We had climbed high into the mountains of New Guinea and seen the most magnificent Birds of Paradise in the world. I swear, I never noticed what we ate. Wait a minute; we did have boiled potatoes in coconut milk with garlic once and I only know that because I asked. The Birds of Paradise? Never, ever to be forgotten.

My husband and I have been ardent birders ever since retirement. We've trekked the world, all seven continents, in search of birds we've never seen before. It is a fantastic and awe-inspiring passion of ours. I can picture every single magnificent bird we ever saw, and sometimes the exact location . . . but the food? Not so much; but that's the first question everyone asks when we get home.

In Venezuela we hiked miles up a mountain just to

look at a huge harpy eagle bouncing around in a nest as big as a kids' blow-up swimming pool. I know what harpies eat: monkeys. On the way up we encountered a snake called a fer-de-lance, one of the most poisonous in the world. How was the food? That morning we had a bowl of cold tuna with a tomato cut up in it, but I'll never forget that eagle or the snake encounter.

Sometimes I only remember what we drank instead of what we ate. We were first to spot an iceberg on our trip to Antarctica and won a bottle of champagne. But the whales, the penguins, and the albatross, I see them all as a video in my mind. Gaining altitude in the high Andes of Peru we would stop for a cup of cocoa tea sold by the natives. I remember that well. During that trip, I craved cocoa tea . . . mmmmm, it made me feel mellow.

Camping in Kenya and Tanzania was most exciting. We were there primarily to camp and see wildlife. We happened to have a guide who was a native Kenyan, had graduated from Stanford, and was an ornithologist! Our whole group of eight became birders by the end of the trip. Let's see; how was the food? Well, I do remember yummy braised cabbage. But I also remember chasing the lions out of camp that must have smelled it too. Or lying in our tiny tents and hearing something lapping water from our wash basins on the other side of the zippered canvas. Not to mention the loo outside the tent's back zipper. It was a hole in the ground with a pile of dirt and a trowel to cover most recent use. My husband dropped the trowel into the hole. I let him cope with that alone. I may forget the meals I had but the whydah bird doing his dance with his long, beautiful tail stays with me forever, along with the baby cheetahs.

A combined birding and antiquities trip thru Egypt continues to be mind-boggling. Egypt is the main flyway for migrating birds from Africa to Europe and Asia. To experience this from the Temple of Ramses, the Aswan Dam, along the Nile, the Pyramids, did we even eat? I don't recall. But never to leave us will be seeing the elusive pharaoh eagle-owl and her chick nestled in a crevice high up in the Step Pyramid (built 4,700 years ago).

Peru: ah, yes. What a beautiful country. Now here is where I can really tell you about the food. Do not, I repeat, do not bother to eat a guinea pig. It's not that it isn't quite delicious, but I have never seen as many small bones except in a fish. It takes forever to eat around each one.

I'm afraid my stomach doesn't recall a lot of food in our travels. We kept moving on to the next exciting discovery and what that might reveal. In my mind, however, I have devoured a feast of beautiful memories — colors, cultures, people, and rare birds — to keep me full, satisfied, and aware that I have been incredibly lucky for the rest of my life.

63

Cuba Is for the Birds

By Don Scott

Don Scott grew up in rural Western New York, and graduated from the University of Virginia and Cornell. He spent the bulk of his working career in general finance work in colleges and universities, retiring from Wheaton College in Massachusetts where he was VP of finance and administration. Don is married with three fantastic children and an even more fantastic wife. Now retired, he finds that travel to all parts of the world, birding, golf, and work around the house have kept him more than busy.

My wife Carol and I are among those lucky folks who were able to retire early — in our case, at the age of fifty-seven. In the twenty-three years prior to crossing the eighty barrier, birding became our avocation, leading us around the world and enabling us to set foot on all seven of the world's continents. There are some ten thousand different birds in the world of which we have seen about twenty-five hundred.

Could we identify all that we've seen? Not on your life, especially not the LBBs (little brown birds), of which there are many, with only slight variations that permit definite identification. But we'll never forget the thrill of the hunt and the final spotting of whatever birds we were looking for at the time. Birding is not easy. It entails lots of driving, walking, hiking, climbing, slogging, and waiting in place for what seems like endless hours. Accommodations are hardly of the five-star variety — not even one star in some cases. They often provide cold water only for daily showers, but always reward the intrepid traveler with good, locally based food, cold beer, and comfortable beds. What more could one ask for?

The older we became, the more we felt the strain of the requirements of birding. We were in Papua New Guinea, climbing a steep, muddy mountain in search of a rare Bird of Paradise, when we realized that our seventy-plus-year-old bodies just weren't what they used to be. After that trip, which also included Australia, we knew that such treks were no longer feasible for our aged bones to attempt. But the urge to continue to bird does not go away easily, and the ability to explore remote areas and observe different cultures never dies. So while perusing a catalog from a birding company located in South Africa, we spotted a trip to Cuba that seemed very attractive — it would be a small group, traveling relatively close to home, and it was not too expensive. Also, there wouldn't be any challenging mountains to climb. At the age of eighty-two, we both signed up and launched into what at that time was "the forbidden territory."

As one might expect, all of the birds of the world *do not* travel, like us, to the four corners of the globe. In fact, many species have extremely limited areas in which they live. Cuba, for example, is home to twenty-eight different species that are endemic only to that island, and are found nowhere else in the world, not even in a place as close as the U.S., only ninety miles away. This is especially notable when one realizes that many species annually migrate thousands of miles to reach a specific area where they breed, raise their young, and then, at summer's end, make the long trek back to what is home.

At the time of our trip, March of 2014, travel from the U.S. to Cuba was highly restricted. Basically the only legal way for an American citizen to reach Cuba was by taking a so-called "People to People" limited educational trip via a nonprofit group. One could also enter through another country (Mexico, Canada, Dominican Republic), taking the risk of having U.S. Customs confront you upon reentry and imposing a fine of $5,000! All seven in our group gambled on getting through without a fine — and won! But that is a story for another time!

We were met at the Havana airport by our leader, a native Brit, now a resident of South Africa, named Clayton Burne. Our group all hailed from the U.S., all women except for me. Compatibility was evident from the outset — a great step in the right direction. We then drove immediately to our hotel in Havana and, if we did not know better, we would have thought we were back home in the U.S. We ate, drank, and slept well and on the next morning headed into what was in many ways a visit to the U.S. of the late 1800s.

Cuba is basically an agriculturally based economy. As we drove past rolling fields and small villages, we were not prepared to see men in fields walking behind a horse or a team of oxen that were pulling a plow, like we might see in a museum. And the dearth of automobiles was replaced by men on horseback or people riding in horse-pulled buggies. We saw no poverty and no squalor, but we were stunned by the tiny houses, all government owned, that were rundown, and badly in need of paint and repairs. They illustrated what it was like to live in a totalitarian regime.

The people we met were friendly and we visited many interesting places as we birded our way across Cuba, including The Bay of Pigs, famous as the site of the U.S. government's failed invasion in the 1960s, and the burial site of Che Guevara, the famous leader of the Communist revolution. We were also entertained by the endless roadside billboards featuring Guevara and the Castro brothers that we passed between birding stops.

And did we see birds! Of the twenty-eight endemics, we saw twenty-six and heard one — the elusive Zapata wren. Stars among these were the large Cuban trogon and the tiny Cuban tody, both amazingly colorful and quite accommodating. And we saw what is believed to be the smallest bird in the world — the bee hummingbird (whose name fully describes this tiny gem) — and these beauties are found nowhere except on the small island nation called Cuba.

We ended the trip with a tour of Old Havana, basically charming but clearly showing evidence of a tired city that was once a major historic attraction. Whether Cuba ever returns to its former vibrancy in the modern era remains to be seen — but to us and our friends, it was a wonderful experience.

64

An Eightieth Birthday Gift I Gave Myself

By Judy Mage

Born in the Bronx in 1935, Judy Mage (née Hollander) moved eight times before she turned nine. These frequent moves, although always in the Bronx, possibly stimulated her zest for travel. After graduating from Antioch College, Judy embarked on long trips to Europe and North Africa, and she's been to many destinations around the world ever since. During her checkered career, she has been president of the New York City Social Service Employees Union, which she helped organize, vice-presidential candidate of the Peace and Freedom Party in 1968; epidemiologist for the Poughkeepsie Health Department; educator for Planned Parenthood; and a social worker for a special-education program. As a single mother, she has raised one son, and she became a first-time grandmother in March 2016.

I've enjoyed traveling for most of my life since college. Working for a year after graduation, my then husband and I had saved enough to spend fifteen months in Europe and North Africa. Ten years later, in between jobs, my friend and I explored Mexico, Central and South America, returning home via California and the national parks after nine months abroad. Over the years my wanderings have taken me to Slovakia, the Czech Republic, China, Poland, Croatia, and Turkey. Almost all of these trips were self-organized, and involved travel by public transportation, even at times hitchhiking. Accommodations included camping, youth hostels (long after I was no longer a youth), and cheap, sometimes grungy, budget hotels.

In addition to going to churches, ruins, chateaux, museums, and the usual tourist attractions, I always made sure to make time for such activities as hiking, biking, swimming, cross-country skiing, and canoeing.

The one place I had never been and had been yearning to visit was the Galapagos Islands, off the coast of Ecuador. I could not find any inexpensive way to travel there, and I was intimidated by the cost of trips as advertised by a variety of travel companies.

The Galapagos interested me above all because of their role in Charles Darwin's research. I knew that their unique flora and fauna had inspired Darwin and had been key to the development of his theories of evolution through natural selection.

Then in February 2014, when I had just turned seventy-nine, my eighty-nine-year-old friend Dorothy called and raved to me about the joys of her recent trip to the Galapagos Islands with Road Scholar, formerly known as Elderhostel. They are a not-for-profit company specializing in "experiential learning opportunities." I imagine they changed their name to appeal to younger people who might prefer not to think of themselves as "elders" in our youth-oriented culture.

Dorothy had had no real problem, she assured me, transferring from the boat deck to the raft that motored to the shores of the islands. She'd had no problems with the daily hikes, and she'd loved the swimming and snorkeling. The food had been fresh, nutritious, and very good. Admittedly, my friend is still agile and strong from a lifetime of hiking and canoeing, but so was I.

And, finally, I realized three things: 1. The cost of the trip, which had deterred me for years, was *not* going to go down. 2. My income was *not* going up. 3. I was *never* going to be stronger or healthier than I was at that moment. It was then that I hatched my plan: why not celebrate my eightieth birthday on shipboard in the Galapagos?

I talked this over with my son, and with my partner Tona. Both thought it would be an excellent and dramatic way to become an octogenarian. Tona decided to accompany me, and soon after I telephoned Road Scholar to book the tour.

The twelve-day trip, including eight days at sea, turned out to be wonderful. Of the sixteen passengers on our small ship, I was the second oldest, but not the slowest. Every day beautiful sunrises and sunsets blazed in the unobstructed sky. The rolling motion of our ship motoring between islands soothed me to sleep as we lay in our bunks at night. I could manage the stretch across from the deck to the eight-person rafts that carried us from boat to shore, with the assistance of the strong arms of the crew. I could manage the wet landings and the dry landings, as well as the hikes on uneven terrain. The only thing I could *not* manage was to stay awake after dinner during the "educational" portion of the day, a part of most Road Scholar trips. I was a far better roadie than scholar.

I returned home with hundreds of photographs of the fascinating creatures of the islands: blue-footed boobies displayed their bright blue feet; colonies of marine iguanas lay heaped in great piles, and some occasionally heaved themselves into action to slide into the ocean where they searched for food. These are the creatures Darwin called "hideous" but I found compelling in their very ugliness. Sea lions nursed their infants, unfazed by our presence just yards away. A giant tortoise lumbered across our trail. Once nearly extinct due to their capture by sailors hunting for fresh meat, the tortoises are being replenished by a breeding center, which we visited on one of the islands.

We hiked over black sculpted lava fields, and peered down into extinct volcanoes that had created the islands and in some cases were still doing so. Then we returned each day to our floating home, drawn often to the top deck to admire the magnificent frigatebirds soaring above our heads.

On our last night on the boat the cook baked a delicious cake and my shipboard companions sang a raucous "Happy Birthday" to me. I can't imagine a more auspicious entry into my eighty-first year.

NEW DIRECTIONS: PLANNING FOR NOW AND THE FUTURE

65

Making the Most of Technology in Your Later Years

By Sally Abrahms

Sally Abrahms writes on boomers and aging, specializing in fifty-plus housing, caregiving, retirement and aging-in-place technology. Her work has appeared in *Time*, *Newsweek*, the *New York Times*, the *Wall Street Journal*, *USA Today*, the *AARP Bulletin*, and the *Washington Post*, and on Forbes.com and The Huffington Post. She is the author of two books and contributed to *Not Your Mother's Retirement*. She also blogs for, and consults to, companies that focus on boomers and seniors. Check out her Web site at sallyabrahms.com.

When you haven't grown up with technology, it can seem daunting. But what if "aging-in-place technology" were easy to use, fun, and, most important, allowed you to live independently and be in control? What if it enriched your life, made you feel safe, and kept you healthy and socially connected?

What if you could watch your grandson's soccer game in real time on your home TV screen?

Today, MedicAlert-like devices with multiple functions can look like snazzy jewelry rather than large, unsightly necklaces and bracelets that screech, "I'm old and infirm!" Products have become smaller, smarter, and subtler. Now, all ages sport wearable gadgets (i.e., Fitbits and Apple watches), leading to "device cool" rather than "device stigma."

These technologies are not just for seniors who want to stay independent but for their adult children, too. Many live long distance and want to know that Mom and Dad are okay — and if something is wrong, have the comfort of knowing they will be notified.

Warding off Loneliness and Isolation

Feeling connected and valued by others is critical to well-being. With Viber and WhatsApp, you can talk free anywhere in the world using your smartphone, tablet, or computer. The Internet, Skype, Facebook, the iPhone's FaceTime, Google Hangouts, and Google Chat (Gchat) can help keep you in the loop with family and friends and engaged with the world.

Options for staying connected are limitless: catching

up via e-mail, video chatting, or texting with grandkids, playing games online, listening to opera, or taking free classes from home. There are AARP's e-learning courses; Coursera, a university and college consortium; and Open Education Database (OEDb).

Some gadgets are geared specifically to seniors. These include grandPad, a simple tablet with preloaded technology so you can make phone or video calls, use e-mail, and view photos, among other functions; AARP's RealPad tablet; GreatCall's big-button Jitterbug phone; Samsung Galaxy S5's Easy Mode; and Sprint's Active Senior ID pack comes with Easy Type and even Senior Match for those looking for love!

While not specifically made for seniors, Amazon's Echo voice-activation device responds to oral questions of all kinds (for instance, "What are the best grandparent/grandchild trips?"), à la iPhone's Siri, as well as connects to major audio-streaming services ("Please play Pavarotti").

Uncomfortable with technology? Ask your grandchild or a friend to explain things to you. Mac owners can take free lessons at an Apple Store. SeniorNet has age fifty-plus learning centers around the country; AARP TEK (Technology, Education, and Knowledge) offers workshops; and the Connections program teaches classes at urban libraries, senior centers, senior-housing developments, and public schools.

Prefer learning at home? YouTube has how-to videos, and Techboomers.com offers free lessons about sites and apps, including YouTube, Twitter, and Gmail.

Staying Organized

With sharing and storing Web sites, technology is a way to keep all your important papers in one place, or let others know where they are in case you get sick or worse.

You can upload the documents themselves, details about them, or where they can be found. Keeping accurate files on these storage Web sites is an easy way to track such important information as your:

- health-care directive
- power of attorney
- Social Security card
- birth certificate
- passwords
- telephone and account numbers
- insurance policies
- statements for stocks and bonds

- pension and retirement accounts
- will
- deed to your house

These Web sites should be encrypted for safety. Some allow full access to the site for those you designate; others let you limit sections to certain people, or access under certain conditions (after you die or are incapacitated). Some popular sites include Everplans, Estate Map, and The Torch.

If you or a family member gets sick, needs care, or has an emergency, Web sites like CareZone allow people you choose to have access to your health information (medications, appointments, updates from caregivers, test results). Family, friends, and neighbors can go to such Web sites as CaringBridge, Lotsa Helping Hands, and CareCentral to volunteer to help with errands, meals, or transportation, and you can post requests on these sites as well.

Feeling Safe and Secure

A "PERS," as in personal emergency response system, is similar to a MedicAlert. Some only work when you're home but increasingly, mobile PERS, meant for use when you're on the go, are gaining fans. Check out

Philips Lifeline's GoSafe mobile medical alert service, GreatCall Splash, Mobile Help, and Numera.

PERS capabilities vary: they might detect a fall and automatically summon help, schedule lights and lock doors, or double as a cell phone.

Sensors are gaining ground, too. Placed on a favorite chair you use daily, the refrigerator, bathroom, or front door, they are able to alert family members if something seems amiss. Products include Evermind, Alarm.com, Mother by sen.se, and OnKol.

Have mobility issues or just want to make life easier? "Smart homes" let you or a family member remotely control doors, heating, air conditioning, lights, TVs, appliances, and audio and video systems from another room, or another state, with a phone, tablet, or computer. Nest has "smart" products, from thermostats to cameras to smoke detectors. Comcast's Xfinity, Sprint, and Verizon have systems that can allow you, or your adult child, to see what's going on in your house, without even being there.

Keeping Healthy

Wearable fitness trackers like Jawbone and Fitbit,

and smartphone apps and pedometers, can keep you motivated. Part of staying healthy is taking your medication. Some gadgets and apps remind you to take your pills via text or e-mail messages, phone calls, or recorded voice prompts. Some let you dispense pills at specific times. MedMinder flashes when it's that time, while MEDBOX and OnTimeRx are downloadable apps. PillPack packages and delivers medication. WatchRx is a watch that signals when it's time for your medication. And Reminder Rosie lets a family member record a message such as "Grandpa, time to take one green pill and two purples."

Remote monitoring, or telehealth, is used to monitor a chronic condition or a transition from the hospital to home and can transmit your vitals to your health-care provider. Video chats with doctors and nurses reduce office visits, as do health check-ins via FaceTime, Skype, or an online medical portal.

Envisioning the Future

In the next few years, look for major strides in the field of aging. Among them will be:

- social robots to help with household chores and to converse with you;

- virtual reality that lets you "participate" in a trip abroad with the family via 3-D glasses;

- ingestible pills with an embedded chip that have the name of the medication and dosage. When you take the pill, the chip dissolves and sends a signal to an adult child or health-care provider's smartphone;

- driverless cars that can take you to the store, a movie, or a relative's home.

These and more exciting discoveries are ahead! But even the most beneficial devices will not be helpful if you are isolated and lonely in your high-tech home. Technology is a way to stay independent, but community is essential as well. Finding the right balance is the goal for each of us, no matter our age.

66

Planning to Be Eighty

By Andrew Carle

Andrew Carle is a thirty-year health-care and senior housing executive whose work has been featured in numerous media, including CBS News, CNN, *Time*, and NPR. In 2001 he founded the first academic program in the nation in senior housing administration and has been nationally recognized for his work in developing "university based retirement communities" as well as defining a new category of "Nana" technology. He currently serves as COO of Affinity Living Group, a national leader in senior housing and retirement communities, as well as an adjunct professor at George Mason University in Fairfax, Virginia.

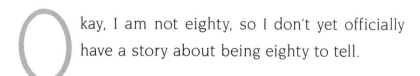kay, I am not eighty, so I don't yet officially have a story about being eighty to tell.

But I am someone whose profession over multiple decades has brought me face-to-face with thousands of individuals who are or were eighty and older. Whether as a health-care executive or director of the nation's only university program in senior housing, I have been able to share my days and collective efforts in the octogenarian world.

In terms of the topic of "aging," I've learned a lot. I've experienced life in an assisted-living community up close and firsthand. I've been able to research and in some cases even help develop new models of senior housing and technologies that can improve quality of life for older adults. I've come to understand both the clinical and emotional effects of Alzheimer's, and the toll it takes — not just on those afflicted but on everyone in their life. I am versed in "issues of aging"— from government policy, to Medicare, to AARP.

But what I've learned most hasn't come from a business plan, research study, or text, but from the octogenarians with whom I've been able to share time. It's come from sharing a joke, a round of golf, sitting together on a porch, and sometimes from just holding a hand to steady someone while they walked.

I learned from Joe, who skipped a scheduled showing of the movie *Pearl Harbor* in his retirement community. When I asked him why, he calmly explained because he was there and already knew what happened. What followed was a story of far more significance than any movie could portray.

I learned from Sarah, who at 108 (!) told me about her father, an architect who designed many of the buildings in Washington, D.C. As I was thinking of asking which ones, I realized some may have been built in the 1800s and were now registered as historical landmarks — I could look them up.

I learned from Marie, who agreed to try using the then newly released iPad as part of a review I was completing for Apple. Despite having never used a computer, she learned in minutes how to navigate the functions and access the Internet world. Since Marie was a frequent visitor to Atlantic City, she not only found my gambling app but happily lost "$3,000" on Roulette.

I learned from Rose, a concert pianist who was one of the first African Americans to play at Carnegie Hall. Despite advanced Alzheimer's, she could sit at the baby grand piano in the lobby of her assisted-living community (a piano she daily forgot existed) and perform from memory a piece so complex and beautiful it would make you believe in miracles.

And the lessons haven't just come from those I've encountered through my profession.

There was Gus, the father of a good friend, who for nearly thirty years treated my family like his own and never missed attending the Super Bowl party at our home.

There are my own in-laws, Dick and Beverly, who in their sixties purchased a fifty-five-year timeshare at Walt Disney World Resorts — sharing an optimism a nearly ninety-year-old Mickey would love.

Through my work and relationships I know aging eventually comes at a price. I've seen its effects on the body and the mind, and even to someone's dignity. But I've also seen how those who reach a certain age can both accept as well as simultaneously *refuse* to accept its consequences. How they can handle themselves with quiet — or even loud — pride. How they can exercise and socialize and seem far younger than their years. But how they also understand that you can come into the world hairless, toothless, and incontinent and — if you do everything right and catch a couple of breaks along the way — it may still require you to leave it in exactly the same way four or even five generations later. That to do so doesn't mean you've lost . . . it means you've *won* in the game of life.

So what I've learned has helped me not only plan to be eighty, but be excited about it. These are the lessons of Joe, Sarah, Marie, and Rose . . . and of Gus, Dick, and Bev:

I plan to share my history with others.

I plan to appreciate the gift of longevity.

I plan to try new things.

I plan to love and listen to music.

I plan to extend my love of family to others, even if I already have a family of my own.

I plan to stay young at heart.

I plan to *live*.

Harvesting Our Wisdom

By Joanne Turnbull, PhD, MSW

Joanne Turnbull received her MFA from the University of Southern Maine and MSW and PhD from the University of Michigan. She has worked as a family therapist, teacher, researcher, administrator, and is Executive Director Emerita of the National Patient Safety Foundation. She created *Your Write Mind* to help people find their creative voice and tell their stories. She is a certified Amherst Writers and Artists facilitator, Life Legacies Facilitator, a licensed clinical social worker, and is completing an internship to become a Certified Sage-ing® Leader. Joanne serves on the board of the Maine Hospice Council. She has numerous publications and has coauthored two books, *To Do No Harm* (with Julie Morath) and *The Grieving Heart* (upcoming with Claire Willis).

Most people hear the word *legacy* and think about preparing a legal will. There is, however, another aspect of legacy that is equally, if not more important: passing wisdom and blessings on to those who come after us, letting them know what matters to us and who we really are.

Traditional societies honor their elders as wisdom-keepers, entrusting them with the sacred task of linking past to present and future. These Spiritual Elders pass on ancestral stories and by telling their own stories, they transmit important values and lessons learned.

In western societies, the role of Spiritual Elder was lost during the Industrial Revolution. It remains undervalued in our culture's obsession with work and youth, but it's reemerging, thanks to the Conscious Aging movement.

Conscious Aging — also known as Sage-ing®, Positive Aging, Vital Aging, and Elder Spirituality — goes against the prevailing view of aging as a time of diminished capacity and isolation. Rather, Conscious Aging considers the last half of life to be a period of awakening and inner growth and a time to harvest wisdom.

Harvesting wisdom is rooted in the medieval Jewish tradition of the ethical will, a written document of instructions passed from father to son. Contemporary versions — usually referred to as the spiritual will or legacy letter — have the same intent as the ancient ethical will, passing wisdom to future generations.

However, they also express blessing and love to anyone who might benefit from such messages.

An intentional legacy includes these elements, but also conveys the essence of who we are and what matters to us. Intentional legacy is a conscious process that begins by connecting with the wisdom that each of us carries within. This inner, authentic self is awakened and strengthened by contemplative practices (meditation, recording dreams, and long walks) and creative activities (music, dance, and poetry). Intentional legacy also entails looking back to identify important people and events in our lives, and it is this process — integrating inner awareness with key events and people — that transforms experience into wisdom and helps us to discern the purpose and meaning of our lives. Through this process, as an appreciation develops of the ways that past, present, and future are connected, we are able to see how our identity has been shaped and strengthened over time. Questions, such as the following, can help to focus the memories and reflections that emerge from contemplation:

What events have been turning points in my life?

Who are the people who have shaped the person I am today?

What personal qualities and skills define me as the unique person that I have become?

What have been my biggest challenges? What lessons have I learned in trying to meet these challenges?

How have I dealt with my weaknesses?

What values are most important to me?

There are many ways to express intentional legacy. Some people capture their essence by creating pieces of art or music. Others record audio or video to convey ancestral stories, traditions, or pass along wisdom through lessons learned. We try to let those we love know about the things that provided us with a sense of fulfillment and meaning. Many, myself included, preserve these thoughts in letters of appreciation and legacy letters.

Letters of Appreciation. There are people, whose paths cross ours during our life journey, who provide vital support or guidance. These people bestow a horizontal legacy. If still living, we can express gratitude to them. If not, their stories can provide lessons for future generations. In tenth grade, I was identified as not working up to potential and assigned to an experimental class in which a young teacher nurtured my writing and encouraged me to apply for an award that changed my life. Four decades later, I wrote to her and explained what she had meant to me. She responded immediately, moved by my remembrance.

Legacy letters. Legacy letters, often written for special occasions, usually tell a personal story that transmits a lesson and ends with a blessing. My father died when I was seven months pregnant with my son. Andrew is the only child in the next generation who did not know his grandfather, and I wrote him a legacy letter in which I described a few of the many ways that his grandfather helped others. I also shared some questions I wished I'd asked my father when he was alive; questions that might have helped to shed light, albeit weak, on fragments of his life. I ended my letter by letting Andrew know that from my observation he seemed to have inherited his grandfather's intelligence and sensitivity. I told Andrew how much my father had looked forward to meeting his grandson and gave this blessing: *May our family stories provide you with lessons that help you choose a fulfilling path. May you always know how much I love you.*

We offer our loved ones a priceless gift when we harvest wisdom. By creating an intentional legacy, we are making a statement that our lives matter and that we matter; it is a gift we give ourselves. *May you honor your legacy by harvesting your wisdom and creating an intentional legacy for those you love.*

68

Look in the Mirror

By Timothy M. Vogel, Esq.

Timothy M. Vogel is the senior shareholder of the Portland, Maine law firm Vogel & Dubois, PA. He focuses on Elder Law, as well as Estate and Trust Planning and Administration. He is the Chair of the Education Committee of the Elder Law Section of the Maine State Bar Association. He writes an Elder Law column for the *Maine Lawyers Review*. He is a graduate of Brown University and Case Western Reserve University School of Law.

L ook in the mirror
Not at the familiar, but character over time.
Look deeper at your spirit
Search for the dear essence of loved ones.
How to care for body and spirit
Spouse, partner, family, and community.
Fit together self, interests, goals, love,
Abilities, responsibilities, resources.
Accepting help or becoming a burden
Being in control or getting in the way.

Commonsense planning bringing peace of mind
Discovering the legacy you will leave.

For over thirty years I have helped older persons and their families through my Elder Law practice. Many people have come into my office and asked what they need to do to plan responsibly for their future. I congratulate them for taking the first step to ask for guidance, instead of putting it off "for another day," or merely relying on "the word on the street."

Commonsense concepts are the foundation for successful legal planning. Make decisions for yourself, and document those decisions in understandable, legally enforceable documents. If you do not make decisions for yourself, persons who do not know you may make major decisions about your future. Do not expect your children to make up your mind for you. Entrust them to carry out your instructions.

Who will provide for your spouse and loved ones if you are no longer able to? Who do you trust to make decisions for you if an accident or illness disables you? How do legal documents (Last Will and Testament, Durable Financial Power of Attorney, Power of Attorney for Health Care, and a Trust) function to protect you and your loved ones?

Be comfortable with the life planning you and others are doing for your future. Some middle-aged children are in denial that anything could possibly happen to their parents or family elders. Others become "planners" who believe their parents' future should tidily fit into a three-ring binder.

Many clients ask me how to find, get, and pay for quality care that they, a spouse, or a loved one needs. In America the legal, health-care, and financial systems often do not make sense. There are elder-dedicated professionals who can help you understand the issues and options that impact you and your loved ones. Find a financial planner who understands your situation and goals. Talk with an Elder Law attorney about how to provide financial security for a spouse at home, even when the other spouse needs long-term care services.

Begin your search for elder-dedicated professionals by asking friends and acquaintances who has helped them with legal planning and documents or retirement planning? Who did they turn to when a wife or husband was diagnosed with Alzheimer's?

Which professionals in your area go beyond general information to focus on helping elders and their families? A true measure of a lawyer, financial planner, or real-estate agent is how comfortably you are able to talk with each one. Do they make sense when they answer your questions? Finally, professional organizations have Web site information and member directories, such as the National Academy of Elder Law attorneys at https://www.naela.org.

As you turn eighty, have fun. Enjoy meaningful activities with loved ones and friends. Take time to ponder your legacy to family and community. It is possible to plan for successful aging. Find that peace of mind for yourself and your loved ones.

69

Aging2.0 — New Technologies Are Changing Aging for the Better

By Stephen Johnston

Stephen Johnston, MBA, is co-founder of Aging2.0, a global innovation platform for aging and senior care, and of the Innovation Leaders Fund, a global equity fund focused on innovation. He is coauthor of *Growth Champions* (Wiley, 2012), a book about sustainable corporate growth. Stephen serves on the boards of Older Adults Technology Services (OATS) and Music and Memory, 501c3 nonprofits focused on improving the quality of life for older people. He has an MA in Economics from Cambridge University and an MBA from Harvard Business School where he was a Fulbright Scholar. He lives in San Francisco, California.

Startups — Meet Seniors

When you think of "tech startups" you may well think of millennials texting, chatting, swapping pictures, and oversharing things they may regret later.

While the "digital native" youth are clearly major consumers of technology, one of the more interesting recent developments is the growing number of technologies focused squarely on the needs of older people. This has been driven by the unprecedented aging of our society (the proportion of people over eighty globally will quadruple by 2050) along with plummeting costs and ubiquity of smartphones, sensors, and connected devices. While health and wellness are important topics, there are plenty more interesting things that older people want to focus on rather than just their health — their families, communities, and passions, for example. We've been tracking hundreds of startups over the past four years, and find they generally fit into the following four categories — mobility, independence, mind, and care, which we'll look at below.

Mobility

One of the most important issues we hear about for older people is mobility — getting around and staying active in the community. Two thirds of people over sixty-five in the U.S. don't have access to public transport. Mobile app-based car services Uber and Lyft have products, Pool and Line respectively, which allow people to share rides with others — lowering costs and providing an opportunity for social interaction. Personal mobility and exercise is also a strong area — Sword Health has a three-dimensional wearable device called a "tracker" to help digitize exercise and rehab and to ensure you're doing the right movements. Personal activity trackers such as FitBit, Misfit Shine, and CarePredict provide stylish wearable devices that track steps and sleep, even swimming strokes, with remarkable accuracy and require little to no maintenance or set up.

Independence

Over 90 percent of older Americans want to stay in their homes as they grow older — and new services are emerging to help make this easier — although as startups many of these are not yet available nationwide. Over 10 percent of room-sharing company Airbnb's hosts are over sixty years old, and startups Room2Care and Silvernest have created new senior living options that allow people to make use of the spare rooms in their house to earn extra income. This provides a new income stream for hosts and also provides crucial social engagement. On the financial side, True Link helps older people remain in control of their finances using a smart debit card that can inform the family of suspicious activity. On-demand shopping (Amazon Fresh, Google) and groceries (Instacart) deliver essentials to people's doors in hours.

Mind

There is overwhelming evidence that keeping people engaged with a rich social life goes a long way in keeping them happy and healthy — both the clinical benefits and the "business case" for laughter are very strong. Startups SingFit and Music & Memory (a non-profit operating in more than two thousand nursing homes nationwide) use music to stimulate and engage people, creating not only an enjoyable experience but also clinically validated improvement in happiness levels, often requiring lower usage of medications. New York City-based nonprofit Older Adults Technology Services (OATS) provides tech lessons to people over sixty — one of their recent graduates, a tech-newbie in her seventies, set up an Etsy online store to sell her own handcrafted gifts. Technology can also provide innovative ways to keep our aging population safe. When seventeen-year-old Kenneth Shinozuka noticed that his grandfather with Alzheimer's was frequently wandering and getting lost, he became concerned.

Shinozuka developed a wearable GPS device called SafeWander to track his grandfather's movements whenever he got out of bed. It's now a successful product on the market that is meeting a real need for thousands of people.

Care

Care is becoming everybody's business and Daughterhood and Daily Caring are two Web sites that are designed to make it easier for family members to be caregivers by providing online education and content as well as building local communities of support. Also, Roobrik is an interactive Web site that asks people a number of relevant questions and provides a personalized "decision support" for families. Reminder Rosie is a small alarm-clock-like device that sits in someone's home on which family members and caregivers can record reminders (locally or remotely) in their own voice to ensure their loved ones take medications or remember key appointments.

Coming Next — Robots, Drones, Wearables, and More

There are really interesting technologies in "adjacent" areas, often not focused on the needs of older people today, but they can give a glimpse of where things are going. Artificial intelligence, robots, and sensor technologies are converging to make the home a new, smart, connected hub that will give people easy access to all manner of services at the touch of a button, or not even that. For example, Amazon's new Alexa product takes voice commands and controls other things that are connected to the Internet, such as Spotify music services or smart lightbulbs ("Alexa — play some jazz music" or "Alexa — turn the lights down"). Robotics company Jibo provides a similar ability for people in their home to seamlessly interact with services, and Jibo also comes with a screen, a personality, and a sense of humor. Despite it being "just" a robot, early tests have shown that it increases older people's feelings of connection and a sense of well-being.

Get Involved!

One of the things that excites us is the potential to unleash the wisdom and experience of older people to act as creators and innovators themselves, not just consumers. Older adults can get engaged in a number of ways.

Advisor: Help startups improve their ideas. At Aging2.0, we created the role of "Chief Elder Executive" to give older adults mentorship roles with startups. Both sides benefit tremendously from the experiences.

Investor: Angel groups allow people to get together to focus on new investment opportunities — new groups for angels interested in this market are emerging.

Entrepreneur: Encore.org is building a platform to allow people to more easily change careers and retrain to a different career altogether, and it is working with corporates to make this a new benefit for their older workers. The Global Institute for Experienced Entrepreneurship (GIEE) provides skills (such as improv lessons), networking, and education to improve the entrepreneurial skills of older people.

We think that anyone, whether they're eight or eighty, can be an innovator. What's clear is that all sides benefit when younger and older people start having conversations about innovation. For more information, sign up to receive the Aging2.0 newsletter at aging2.com. So don't delay, dive in and get involved!

70

How to Age Like a New Yorker

By Audrey S. Weiner, DSW, MPH

Audrey S. Weiner, DSW, MPH, is President and CEO of The New Jewish Home in New York, a multisite geriatric care system serving over twelve thousand people each year through its post-acute rehabilitation, long-term skilled nursing, senior housing, certified home health agency, adult day health care, and care management services. She received her doctorate in Social Welfare Administration from the Graduate Center of the City University of New York and her master's in Public Health from Yale University. A leading figure in the movement to make person-directed care the preferred model of 21st-century nursing home care, Audrey has co-edited three books on the subject: *Culture Change in Elder Care* (2013), *Models and Pathways for Person-Centered Elder Care* (2013) and *Culture Change in Long-Term Care* (2003). She is co-chair of New York City's Age-Friendly NYC Commission, past chairperson of the national organization LeadingAge, and a member of the board of the Continuing Care Leadership Coalition of Greater New York.

A s a baby boomer, just a few years short of Medicare eligibility, I have often looked at the prospect of what it will be like to turn eighty as somewhat daunting. That may be a surprising admission from me since aging is my "business." At The New Jewish Home, where I am President and CEO, we learn every day from people in our care what it means to grow older, deal with health challenges, cope with unexpected frailty — *and* be active, engaged, and growing all the time. New York is one of the most demanding and diverse urban environments in the world, and we are determined to deliver the kind of health care and home care our communities deserve. That means turning the practice of eldercare upside down: celebrating older age, not fearing it. And yes, that has positive potential for me! At The New Jewish Home we are committed to transforming eldercare for New Yorkers so they can live meaningful lives in the place they call home.

To help call attention to both this attitude — and this transformation — we created an annual fundraising event called Eight over Eighty: Celebrating Eight Remarkable Lives. As I write this in 2016, we have had the privilege in three short years of honoring twenty-four inspiring people, eighty years of age or older, who are living lives of great significance and currency. They include philanthropists, artists, businesspeople, performers, teachers, writers, activists, volunteers — each a dynamic example of what we like to call "aging like a New Yorker." New York is a vibrant town and so are the amazing achievers in their eighties and nineties whom we have paid tribute to in our Eight over Eighty galas.

Little did I realize when we created this event that we'd learn so much, be inspired so deeply — and that I'd look forward to being eighty! Okay, maybe I should say, to be a little less anxious about it. Here are but a few of those twenty-four compelling stories.

One is the great jazz pianist Barbara Carroll. You may see this diminutive ninety-two-year-old treading carefully down a crowded or slippery-when-wet New York City sidewalk. But when she steps onstage (which she does most Saturdays at 6:00 p.m. at the legendary jazz club Birdland) she plays with such muscularity and joy that what you see and hear is the Barbara of the 1940s when she was one of the very few women in bebop jazz. Her talent transcends time, as exciting and inventive today as she has always been. As Barbara says, "Every time I sit down at the piano it's a new experience. The boundaries are endless. It's just the best fun in the whole world." *That's* aging like a New Yorker.

Chuck Diker is the managing partner of an investment firm that bears his name and the founder and chairman of a successful medical company. He goes in to the office every day (at eighty-three) — *and* exhibits and tends one of the greatest collections of Native American art in the world. When we first met, Chuck explained to me the kinship he feels with Native American people, a kinship both cultural and aesthetic. He approaches his own work with a boundless sense of creativity — and responds to the creative process in art, a synchronicity he relishes. "Being active at eighty-three? I enjoy it," Chuck says. "I think people in their eighties should work as hard as they did in their twenties, which is what I'm doing." *That's* aging like a New Yorker.

Jacques d'Amboise joined the New York City Ballet at the age of fifteen and by seventeen was a soloist beginning a three-decade career as a principal dancer. Forty years ago he founded the National Dance Institute and to this day (at eighty-one) he continues to teach some six thousand New York City schoolchildren each week. I was astonished by his dance performances onstage in the 1960s, and I continue to be moved beyond measure watching him teach in 2016. His talent and grace — and sheer force of will — are as strong as ever. Jacques's message to his devoted staff and me is this: "If you know something well, if you have a passion for something and you have skill in it and have done it, what are you going to do next? *You've got to pass it on.*" Now *that's* aging like a New Yorker.

And then there's Edie Windsor. Yes, the Windsor of the Supreme Court case *United States v Windsor.* Always an iconoclast, in 1956 Edie began what would become a two-decade career working with mainframe computers, much of it with IBM. The first IBM PC delivered in New York City was to Edie. For five decades — and counting — she has been an LGBT activist, organizer, and supporter. And in 2013, just days after her eighty-fourth birthday, the Supreme Court overturned the Defense of Marriage Act (which banned LGBT couples from hundreds of federal benefits), thereby granting same-sex couples all the rights and privileges of any other couple in the U.S. As Edie has said of the historic decision, "It's the beginning of the end of stigma, of lying about who we are. It's a different level of dignity than we've had." Edie Windsor is proof that trailblazing is ageless. *That's* aging like a New Yorker.

But remember — you don't have to be a New Yorker to age like one. These honorees are iconic in the creativity, passion, and determination they share. They inspire me . . . they inspire generations. If they represent what being over eighty is all about, count me in. They have taught me to look forward to the wonderful possibilities that can await us as we reach this milestone age. I aspire to be like them — now and when I am eighty. I want to age like a New Yorker.

71

Eighty! OMG!

By Rick Kimball

Richard S. (Rick) Kimball is a Maine-based freelance writer and photographer. He and his wife Tirrell own and operate Green Timber Publications, a small press producing curricula for use in Unitarian Universalist religious exploration programs. Rick began his writing and editing career as a reporter, columnist, and city editor at the Guy Gannett newspapers of Portland, Maine. He next became a full-time writer and editor for J. Weston Walch, Publisher, producing supplementary educational materials for secondary schools. He has created religious exploration programs for the national Unitarian Universalist Association, and written in the areas of creativity, local history, and human sexuality. He often speaks his own truths in Unitarian Universalist worship services, usually with a dash of humor thrown in. He holds a bachelor's degree from Harvard College, and a master's from Columbia University Graduate School of Journalism.

Here it comes — my eightieth birthday.

What do those words bring to mind? Let's try multiple choice:

A. Young Nell Fenwick tied by Snidely Whiplash to a railroad track and alarmed by a distant train whistle.

B. A sun-blinded outfielder waiting for a high fly ball to drop from the sky.

C. A tired old cat watching a bird and wishing for the energy to pounce.

D. An announcer counting down to the lottery selection of a single winner.

E. An announcer counting down to the lottery selection of thirty million losers.

F. Are you kidding? Who can remember five things at once?

None of the above? Then you're on your own, just like me.

Jay, a twenty-something friend, recently asked my age. "Seventy-six," I told him. "Oh my god," said Jay. "You're almost eighty!"

The woman who cuts my hair also asked my age not long ago. She looked stricken when I answered. "Oh my god," Beth said. "Here I've been flirting with you, and now I find out you're old!"

Something about aging brings out the OMGs. Here's another of mine: OMG. How did I get here? Just the other day I was twelve.

How can I cope with the OMGs? Partly through prompting from Dizzy, our fifteen-year-old cat. My wife and I came home one day to find him very sick, so we ignored his protests and hauled him off to the vet. Three hundred dollars' worth of tests showed that Dizzy is aging and slowing down. Three hundred bucks? OMG. We already knew he was old.

Later I Googled the human equivalent of a cat's fifteen years. Wikipedia's answer was quick and clear: seventy-six. OMG. There's a message.

While Dizzy was fighting off whatever it was that the tests didn't show, I spent some time kneeling next to him and offering comfort — mostly to me. Dizzy didn't seem to need it. He could barely walk. He threw up the little he managed to eat. He had no strength to climb the stairs and join us on our bed. He shunned water. He failed to fight back when the sister he had bullied for most of his life sensed his weakness and bullied him instead. And yet when I came downstairs at 2:00 a.m. to check on him he lifted his head and purred.

"Oh my god!" I said. "You're old and you're sick and you're purring! What's that about?" He gave me a look with sure meaning: "Let's both go back to sleep."

He did, but I did not. I lay in bed reflecting on the message of his purring in his illness, the message of acceptance. OMG! Dizzy had purred that "it is what it is," those words that drive me so nuts. "It is what it is." Okay. And it isn't what it isn't. And it wasn't what it wasn't because it was what it was. And it will be what it will be because it won't be what it won't be. I get it, OMG, I get it.

But I also fight it. My memory revises the past so it becomes what it wasn't. My mind contorts the present into a vision I can tolerate, a vision of what really isn't. My hope says that I and not some omnipotent "it" will shape my future and my eighties.

I'm on the far side of seventy now, and here comes my eightieth birthday chugging along like young Nell's train. OMG. I hope I'll be ready. I can be if I follow Dizzy's lead and accept my aches and pains. I can be if I divorce myself from the millions of people who fight change, who fight change with ballot and with bomb, with facelifts and with wrinkle creams, with hate and with horror directed at everything new and everybody different. I can be if I understand and prove that it won't be what it will be without at least some input and control from me.

Because OMG it's so simple. Aging is changing. If I stop fighting change, if I accept change, then I too can move on with a purr. I can do most of what I do now, with new freedom to be better, new freedom to be worse. Who cares? "After all, he's over eighty."

I can join the octogenarians who write and photograph, who laugh at aches and pains and increasing forgetfulness, who create, who accept with pleasure as much as life provides, who say "yes, it is what it is, but with just a little effort, maybe I can make it better." I can be among the changing who cause changes of their own.

Here it comes — my eightieth birthday. OMG I hope I reach it! Let me at it! Bring it on!

But not too fast.

72

A Fulfilling Life Is About Attitude, Not Age

By Bob Lowry

Bob Lowry retired in 2001 after a career as a researcher, and program and management consultant to hundreds of radio stations and major broadcasting companies. He has written two books on retirement and has been a guest contributor to several others as well as a frequent guest on podcasts. He writes the popular *Satisfying Journey* blog and lives with his wife in Chandler, Arizona.

I must admit, it is a little disconcerting to look so far into the future and speculate about my life. After fifteen years of retirement, most of the plans I made for this phase of my life have gone through major revisions. I discovered a powerful passion for prison ministry that was an important part of my life for several years. I fulfilled a dream to travel the country in an RV. I wrote two books and began a successful blog about retirement. Importantly, my life is so much more than I dreamed it would be: more creative, more spiritual, and filled with more relationships that bring meaning and happiness.

When my eighties arrive I imagine I will be quite thankful that I am alive to experience my ninth decade. Life has been every bit as joyful, demanding, uplifting, disappointing, satisfying, and mundane as one might expect. It is logical to assume that by then I will have experienced some health or mental challenges that place certain limits on me. I trust that my faith will sustain me through whatever happens. I will adapt and find the path forward.

I have every hope my marriage will be as solid and full of love as it is today. By the time I turn eighty we will be a month away from celebrating fifty-three years together. I imagine we will spend that special day like we spend every anniversary: thinking about our life together and enjoying a dinner at a favorite restaurant.

Even though I still love the music of my youth (think the Beatles and British Invasion artists), I hope that I will continue to embrace the changes that are inevitable, in music, technology, healthy living, relationships, and how America fits into the world of the 2030s.

One of the joys in my life now is the ability to keep my mind active. Reading anything and everything, taking online courses in subjects that stretch my comprehension, and finding local lectures and discussion groups are vital steps in fending off a loss of mental acuity.

Thus far I have been striving to not allow my chronological age to define my "attitude" age. I believe it's important to make such an approach part of who I will be in my eighties. There are few things sadder than encountering someone who remains convinced that everything good happened in the past and thus, refuses to learn and change.

Whatever legacy I hope to leave will pretty much be what it will be by the time I reach my eighties. My fondest wish is that my children and grandchildren will think of me as a man who loves them deeply, provided for them to the best of my abilities, and continues to cherish our time together. By then my kids will be in their fifties and my grandkids will be out of college. Hopefully they will be building a life that is meaningful and satisfying and maybe, like me, they'll be starting to think about the mark they hope to leave on the world.

I would love to live long enough to see some of the hurt and distrust that makes up too much of our daily discourse be replaced with an acceptance of differences as something to encourage, not fear. The advances in human development and quality-of-life improvements have come from those who refuse to accept what is. Those who question what a limit is today are the ones who help us all find new parameters for tomorrow.

Ultimately, my eighties will be spent, in part, looking forward to my nineties. Coming from a line of folks who made it that far, there is no reason why I shouldn't be one of them. My faith assures me of a future that has no end. I look forward to that eventuality, but am in no rush to get there. Too many opportunities and experiences await me here.

So when I think of my eighties, I say bring it on!

10

SPIRITUAL LESSONS

73

My Turning Eighty "Day Walk in Nature"

By Rev. Patricia Hoertdoerfer

Rev. Patricia Hoertdoerfer is a professional educator and a retired Unitarian Universalist minister who practiced her leadership in academic institutions, congregations, community organizations, UU camps and conference centers, and interfaith communities over the past forty years. As a certified Sage-ing® Leader she is currently sharing her ministry with elders while engaging in service to future generations. Partner to Manfred for fifty-plus years, mother to four adult children, and Oma to seven grandchildren, Pat enjoys retirement living in the Lakes Region of New Hampshire. Through her many decades she has lived her passions of sharing stories around a campfire, engaging multigenerational spiritual growth, and participating in cross-cultural adventures.

Turning eighty is definitely a significant milestone on our life journey. Milestones along my life journey have been as frequent as my annual birthday or as rare as my ordination into Unitarian

Universalist ministry. Milestones can be personal, familial, or communal. They include public celebrations of our heritage and culture and private ceremonies defining intrinsic values and our spiritual commitments.

I will mark my Turning Eighty milestone with a "Day Walk in Nature." When crossing other thresholds in my elder life, from becoming a grandmother to entering retirement (again), I spend a day of reflection in nature. It's a personal tradition with me. Turning Eighty is the time to mark this milestone toward becoming my true self. By sharing my Turning Eighty "Day Walk in Nature," I invite you to design your own unique milestone activity.

Crossing the Threshold to "Day Walk in Nature"

I begin by symbolically crossing the line from my home base to open space, leaving normal life and entering sacred space and sacred time.

Letting Go

I walk meditatively up the dirt road to a small mountaintop in my neighborhood. I reflect on the gifts and challenges of the previous decades of my life. With gratitude I walk in love for my spouse of fifty-plus years, my four beautiful and skilled adult children, and my seven curious and creative grandchildren. I pause to wipe away tears of joy. With measured steps I recall my many years of professional accomplishments, some missed opportunities for service, and a few unresolved problematic relationships. My forgiveness work with others and myself continues every day. Honestly, I am ready to let go of unhealthy relationships and unfinished business to make room for a new way of being at eighty.

Letting Be

When I reach a clearing on the mountaintop I lay my backpack down and unroll my small blanket. I pause to enjoy this view and new perspective as I drink deeply the water from my canteen and eat hungrily my mixture of fruits and nuts. With a sigh I take out my journal and begin to write what I am ready to let go of. My list includes opportunities for personal recognition, positions of public status, names of those with whom I've had unhealthy relationships. Soon I stop and tear out these pages, rip them into little pieces, and stuff them into my pockets.

Then becoming very quiet, I lay back and gaze at clouds in the sky, trees on the horizon, colorful plants blossoming, insects buzzing, and birds darting to and fro. I offer a prayer of gratitude for the beauty and power of this day and my life in this amazing interdependent web of life.

Slowly I rise and begin to walk around, gathering stones to make my meditation circle. I greet the four directions, pray silently, chant softly, and sing songs of justice and peace. Hours pass and I feel refreshed in body, mind, heart, and soul.

Letting Come

Gathering up my belongings, I bid farewell to the living things on this mountaintop and head down the road to the river less than an hour away. While walking I focus my attention on the new decade beckoning to me when I turn eighty. I wonder what will come, whether by intention or by surprise. As I slow my pace, I become acutely aware of the variety of sounds, sights, and smells around me and the diversity of feelings inside me. There are fears about physical diminishments and social isolation. And there are anticipated excitements of adventures to foreign lands and wild places, of my seven grandchildren maturing into their unique selves, and of active hope that I will be of service to future generations.

I sit down at the water's edge and watch the river flowing by, different every hour and every minute. All my senses have opened to the gifts of nature that surround me every day — the fertile earth blossoming with new life, the wind carrying messages of wonder, the sun brightening our days and stars brightening our nights, and this clear fresh water enabling a great diversity of life. What a blessing! A new river every day, every day a new river of life!

Give-Away Homecoming

Standing on the shore with my toes in the water, I give away the pieces of paper from my pockets to the river and let go of an old way of being. With a prayer of gratitude and humility, I bow to the Great Spirit, the Great Mystery. With arms wide open I stand on one foot and invite the coming years to bless me, my kin, and my life. I ponder: how will I keep my balance, physically, mentally, emotionally, socially, spiritually? Surely I'll keep my commitments to family, community, and Mother Earth. Yet how will I meet the surprises? How will I find peace?

With the gifts of life from nature, from loved ones and from meaningful work, I will turn eighty and come home to myself.

Letting Go, Letting Be, Letting Come,
Turning Eighty, Living an Eighty Miracle, Becoming a Sage.

74

Find Your "One Thing"

By LaTron S. Brown

LaTron S. Brown graduated from Virginia Tech with a BS in Psychology and Biological Sciences. He also holds an MBA from Averett University. He is a member of the Alpha Phi Omega service fraternity. LaTron continues to dedicate his life to giving back and empowering others. He is passionate about senior living and health care. Currently, he is the owner of Senior Lifestyle Concierge, a geriatric care management service, providing the highest level of personal attention and guidance to ensure that seniors' needs are truly met. He was the cofounder of the Cultural Arts for Excellence 5k, which raises funds for the afterschool program and promotes health awareness. LaTron serves as a board member with the Roanoke Chapter of the Virginia Tech Alumni Association.

The celebration of eighty years is an expression of the gratitude for all the emotional rollercoasters of life — the highs and the lows, the excitements and the disappointments, the loves and the heartaches. These dichotomies are the very things that have shaped who you are. But remember, as you turn eighty, you still have work to do — to discover your "One Thing" — the something special that is your unique gift.

The world has changed drastically over the years. Some of the changes have made you gasp. Other changes, you have wholeheartedly embraced. With our borderline narcissistic, fame-driven, technology-obsessed world, my generation — the Millennials — has disconnected psychologically, spiritually, and completely rejected many of the core virtues of life: delayed gratification, long-term marriages, and career longevity. We jump from one idea to another with the mentality that if anything is too hard it is "not meant to be." If it is not "making us happy" at all times, then we need to switch careers, marriages, and lifestyles. The belief in instant gratification is leaving many of us sad, desperate, and alone.

We are seeking guidance. While information may be readily and literally at our fingertips, I have learned that there is no better resource than someone who has endured a lifetime of lessons. Fortunately, there are many of us who still honor the teachings of our elders. We are eager to learn and ready to engage.

During my life, many of the greatest lessons have

come from older individuals. Some eighty-year-olds have more life than some thirty-year-olds! You are a treasure trove of knowledge. You have been tested and tried over time. While one person does not have all of the answers, each person has that "One Thing" that has transformed him or her. When shared, it can proliferate into a timeless message for generations to come. Your wisdom, based on a life of experience and intuition, continues to get you through difficulties. Imparting that wisdom, your own "One Thing" is the gift you can give to others.

I have been the recipient of such gifts from my elders many times. One of the most profound moments I recall occurred when I was a junior in high school. After church, a woman who knew my grandmother slowly came walking up to me with her hand motioning me to meet her halfway. She gave me one of the biggest hugs with her tiny frame. Then, she took both of my hands in hers and she looked me squarely in the eye, saying, "I know you are a quiet young man, but I just want you to know that you are destined for greatness."

She began to tell me some of the things that she went through in her life, from having children when she was not ready, enduring abuse, escaping through divorce, and suffering homelessness, to obtaining her education, starting a career, and eventually ascending the ladder in her successful career before retiring. It was as if everything she had learned through her years of struggle and achievement, the knowledge that was her special "One Thing," she was passing along to me. At that time, I was B student, just going through the motions, but after hearing her stories, it lit a flame in me that continues to burn today. She told me, "Whenever I see potential, I do not want it to be wasted." She reminded me every time we saw each other that she expected me to live up to my potential. From that first meeting on, I became more serious about life and started to get extremely involved in school. I joined the Spanish club, two pre-college prep clubs, and began volunteering. I graduated as an Honor graduate and Graduate of Merit. Even in college and to the present, I continue to be involved holding leadership roles and volunteering! Little did this wonderful woman know how our little talk sowed seeds of excellence within my own spirit. For that, I am forever grateful. We all like moments where people tell us how proud of us they are, but this one was special because almost fifteen years later, I am still trying to make her proud!

Wisdom is not complex and never boisterous. It is so simple that is leaves us speechless. It unlocks a hidden truth that can have an impact on us for years to come! I urge you to think about the "One Thing" that is your gift and impart your life lessons to someone of a younger generation. Your wisdom has the power to shape lives, as the words of my grandmother's friend shaped my life. Remember, I honor you, respect you, and love you, and I hope you use your "One Thing" to ignite a flame in others.

75

Successful Aging Needs Spiritual Meaning

By Gilbert Leclerc, PhD

With PhDs in theology and education, Gilbert Leclerc is a retired professor of the Department of Psychology and the Research Centre on Aging of the University of Sherbrooke (Quebec, Canada). He is still an active professor at the Doctoral Degree in Gerontology and the Third Age University where he gives three different courses on Spirituality and Aging. His main research interests and publication areas are: successful aging, self-actualization and aging, spiritual development in aging, life meaning and adaptation to retirement, widowhood, and disabilities.

Success and aging: two terms apparently contradictory. One involves ideas of happy outcome, gain, accomplishment; the other suggests images of decline, loss, deterioration. How can we be successful in aging when we know aging is not a winning game? It ends with death, sometimes preceded by disease and disabilities. How is it still possible to talk of success?

That's where life meaning comes in. Everyone agrees that life without meaning is not worth living and leads to unhappiness, sadness, and despair, while life with meaning brings vitality, creativity, and joy. When meaning is missing, even health and wealth can be unbearable; when meaning is present, even the worst hardship can be overcome. My question is: how can we find meaning in life not only when we're healthy and active but when we lose our vitality and experience disabilities? Is there a deep meaning that can resist the vicissitudes of the aging process?

To answer these vital questions, I have learned to distinguish two levels of meaning: *personal* and *spiritual*. *Personal meaning* is what gives fulfillment to my life as an individual. For example: loving relationships, warm friendship, personal development, professional accomplishments, or a satisfying social life. *Spiritual meaning* is what gives purpose to life in general, not just to my own, but to the life of all beings. It implies a commitment to values broader and more universal than my own personal concerns, transcending myself. These values make us open to our inner spiritual being and, through it, to communion with all beings.

Advanced aging gradually weakens our main sources

of personal meaning. Work, family, friends, personal development, and social life tend to fade away or disappear. So, the question of both personal and spiritual meaning arises with more acuity than ever. What can still give meaning to my life?

This process of decline and loss forces us to look for meaning elsewhere than in appearance, possessions, achievements, knowledge, social influence, or personal prestige. In a word, it leads us to rise above our ego and find meaning in something deeper: an openness to our inner being or deeper self, a dimension filled with peace, awareness, joy, and gratitude that is intimately connected to all other beings by love, kindness, solidarity, and compassion. While life meaning related to the ego is concerned about the future or the past, centered upon accomplishments, often intertwined with doubts, instability, dispersion, and disenchantment, life meaning flowing from the inner self focuses on the present moment, accepts reality as it is, and brings stability and deep joy.

The good news is that this spiritual meaning can resist the vicissitudes of advanced aging. In fact, we need only to get in touch with our deeper self, or give full attention to the present moment to experience peace, stillness, and a sense of being alive. Just by being where we are, and doing what we have to do right now in the present moment, we can experience the blissful feeling of having reached the real purpose of our life.

The following example will help clarify what I mean. Suppose you're lying calmly in bed at the end of the day, having almost fallen asleep, when the thought of your precarious financial situation comes back to your mind. Rapidly, you find yourself striving to solve your problems; at the same time you begin to completely lose your sense of quiet contentment. Your worries will overtake you unless you're able to bring back your attention to the present and say: "In this very moment, I have no problem. I'm resting quietly in a warm and comfortable bed. Nothing really threatens me." If you switch back to the here and now, and get in touch with your deeper self, you'll discover a space of clarity, joy, and serenity that has always been there. But if you miss this moment because you're caught up in the past or the future, you'll become alienated from your true self and miss the profound meaning of your life because you're not where you should be: living in the present.

In addition, we don't need to be a member of a religious group or even to believe in God to get in touch with our spiritual being. Religion can help some of us to get there, but it can also be an obstacle for many others because it traps us into a series of beliefs and practices that can become serious barriers between us and our deeper self. Spiritual life often needs freedom and complete openness to blossom.

Why do I believe such a dimension really exists? For me the answer is because I get in touch with it in daily life. In fact, it is not a question of beliefs but experience. We can have direct access to the present moment or our inner being in any life situation as long as our mind or our ego doesn't interfere. And all of us probably had that experience many times in our life; for example, when we contemplate a sunset, a flower, or listen to the song of a bird that lingered and kept us in awe for a few moments without thoughts or words. Unfortunately, for most of us, this kind of experience does not happen very often or last very long. Usually we live a hyperactive life where moments of calm and stillness are rare. That's why we need some specific exercises to become conscious of our spiritual dimension on a more regular basis.

For me, the two most helpful ways to reach spiritual awareness are conscious breathing and meditation. I practice both every day. Being conscious of my breathing brings me back to the present moment and helps me have direct contact with my inner being. Breathing slowly, deeply, and being fully attentive to the air coming in and going out of my body yields an immediate stillness and calm. It's the sign that I am in contact with my inner spiritual being. Every morning I devote twenty minutes to meditation, which I find is the royal avenue to develop spiritual consciousness.

As we grow older, aging invites us to find a deeper source of meaning when personal sources tend to weaken. It seems evident that in its last phase, our life needs to be open to its spiritual dimension more than ever to remain successful.

Some useful books and CDs:

Adyashanti. *True Meditation* (book with CD included). Sounds True, 2006.

Almaas, A.H. *The Diamond Approach* (six CDs). Sounds True, 2009.

Blackstone, Judith. *The Realization Process. A step-by-step guide to embodied spiritual awakening* (six CDs). Sounds True, 2011.

Rinpoché, Sogyal. *Meditation: A little book of wisdom*. Harper San Francisco, 1992.

Tolle, Eckhart. *Stillness Speaks*. New World Library, 2003.

Tolle, Eckhart. *A New Earth*. Penguin Group, 2005.

76

Life in the Eighties: Mourn or Celebrate

By Lanette H. Thurman, PhD

Lanette H. Thurman, PhD, has taught in two colleges and served as administrator in two universities, including interim Vice President for Development and University Relations for Savannah State University. She was founding Executive Director of Murray State University's Personal Enrichment Center, Center for Leadership Studies, Leadership Murray (community leadership program), and Kentucky Governor's Office of Cultural Affairs. In addition, she served as Commissioner of Kentucky Department of the Arts, and has continued coaching, consulting, and promoting development of future leaders. After retirement, she was featured in an interview chapter, "Life Development: Personal and Business Success" for the book, *Leadership: Helping Others to Succeed*. Since her eightieth birthday, she has continued to take workshops and learn, as well as volunteer to coach nonprofit organizational leaders. She is currently passionate about Creative Aging, and advocating for women who, as elders, are often isolated. Lanette holds BS, MA, and SCT degrees from Murray State University, and a PhD from Vanderbilt University.

As my eightieth birthday approached, I began to realize that I had a choice: *mourn* or *celebrate*! I had heard stories of gloom and doom, and aches and pains. So I could choose to mourn growing older, or be proactive and celebrate the wisdom, experience, and security that aging can bring. Since I don't suffer gracefully, I chose to celebrate! I decided to throw myself a party. Hearing that, a former student secretly planned a surprise dinner party, inviting close friends and specifying "no gifts, just cards, notes, or letters." My book club held a party, naming me "Queen for a Night," complete with a crown and robes. I didn't have to throw myself a party, and I ended up celebrating for weeks!

My two priorities for my eightieth year were *health* and *spirituality*, and I was surprised at the wonderful opportunities that resulted from setting these as intentions. For my focus on spirituality, one of the things I chose was to attend a retreat on forgiveness led by a Buddhist and a rabbi. Forgiveness was huge in my healing process. Joining a book group, Head and Heart, led to meeting new people and broadening my understanding of my own spirituality.

Healthwise, I chose to engage in twelve weeks of physical therapy, with mild stretching, gently increasing movement, plus walking. I have continued the exercises and am taking longer walks. Allergy and food-sensitivity tests led me to eliminate most of the "bad" foods I was eating, such as dairy, wheat, corn, peanuts, and tomatoes. With continued natural food supplements, I had more energy. I was physically on a roll, yet I had not really dealt with the prospect of growing old.

Keeping my mind active is very important to me. While I declined offers to be an officer in a number of organizations, I did want to contribute in some way, so I volunteered to help a local retired teachers' group identify ways to involve members in planning programs and activities that would be of personal interest to them. Responses have been rewarding and members have become more involved.

By about age seventy-five, I had finally admitted that it was time to acknowledge the inevitability of aging. I am a seeker and want to learn more and more, so I enrolled in and completed educational programs in a variety of locations. That is when I became uncomfortable with this new stage of aging. You see, I no longer could "be" a job title — professor, administrator, etc. I was trying desperately to use what I had done to make myself important in conversations with new friends.

A very dear friend gently asked me why I felt the need to do that. Reflecting on her question, I realized I was not living in the "here and now," thus separating myself from important connections. This enlightenment motivated me to make personal changes in my approach to having conversations with others in a new environment. I began to focus on "them" instead of "me," to ask questions about their lives, and to avoid simply giving them information about my personal or professional achievements. I found this to be extremely helpful, as often people would reciprocate and ask me to tell them more about myself.

Eventually, however, I still feared being alone. Would I end up being a geriatric patient who would feel diminished, as I faced a future of one painful physical condition or another . . . transitioning from a nursing home to a dark and solitary end of life? That seemed like a grim scenario, but where were the role models for living in joy, rather than despair?

Medical science had extended my life; how could I be more joyous in those years? In my teens and twenties, I had role models, mentors, and encouragers. Now what? Who did I have to look up to? I had no manual to guide me in finding the best ways to enjoy these later years.

There seemed to be no set rules to follow, and no advice on growing old gracefully. I realized that I had to release a phase of my life that I had outgrown. From this realization, I consciously read more books, and went to informative meetings focused on aging and creativity. I participated in a *Fierce with Age* retreat led by Carol Orsborn, PhD, author of a book by that title. Carol has helped many, including me, to increase confidence and optimism while facing the challenges of growing older. She shares a frank and realistic assessment of her own aging process, and celebrates how far she has come. She has inspired me to let things go, accept, and even embrace, aging while experiencing it as a spiritual path.

These newly discovered tools assisted me in my quest to celebrate my life, to strengthen my health, to search more diligently the depths of my spirituality, to improve my mind, and to acknowledge that my values have not changed, just my perspective. This is my new life: a celebratory life in my eighties to share with my family and new friends, both young and older.

"This Is Now"

By Lois C. Ernst, MSW

The eclectic career of Lois C. Ernst encompassed raising a family, owning a residential real estate business in Lexington, Massachusetts, in the '70s (when women didn't), and at age fifty graduating from the Bryn Mawr School of Social Welfare with an MSW. Subsequently, she did home visiting for the Natick VNA and the Hospice of Cambridge, specializing in the problems of adult children and their aging parents. In addition, she offered business counseling to inner-city minority businesses. At age seventy, Lois left Boston and moved to the Berkshires for seven years. There, in Tanglewood country, she opened and ran a charming bed and breakfast until she moved to Florida, where she now lives happily in semi-retirement. Her computer and Facebook enable ongoing connections with friends and family as well as new learning opportunities. In addition, there is also time for reflection, memoir writing, and the completion of projects. At eighty-eight, with the blessings of good health, her world continues to expand.

At age eighty-eight I am often asked the question: To what do you attribute your youthfulness? My stock answer was generated some years ago when a young doctor leaned forward in his seat and confronted me with this question. My flip response was, "Should I make it up or should I tell you the truth?"

Then I said, "It comes from 'giving too much,' always from a place of love, and never living in regret."

This has been my formula for having a satisfying life no matter what my age. As a corollary, I must note the concept that, to paraphrase a friend, although a person chooses to light the candle of another with his own light, he ne'er loses any of his own for having shared this gift.

Turning eighty has always had a certain sense of unreality for me. I knew but I didn't want to know. In the eight years that have followed, a look in the mirror at my youthful face and countenance has enabled me to live in a state of denial and obliviousness. That denial notwithstanding, I am clear about what I still want to achieve as I move on in life. I believe in the importance of being able to "let go of one's shit." I no longer allow my past to rule my present. Awareness, Acceptance, and Appreciation have helped me in this task.

My mantra is: "That was then, this is now." I have found inner peace through being totally present (a

Zen thought to be sure), coming to accept things as they are, and giving up unfulfilled wishes or fantasies of changing myself further. In addition, it has meant giving up the wish for things to be different and moving into a deeper appreciation of myself and the life I have been fortunate enough to have lived.

These days I am still an active, social, energetic person who continues to drive up and down the East Coast. I love the Internet and all the opportunities it offers to expand my world and also to connect with people from my past. I am blessed with good genes, good health, good eyesight, and still a good mind. I find there is always more to do in one day than can reasonably be done.

Most people would consider it a great gift to be eighty-eight and to look seventy, and indeed in most ways it is. But no one ever considers the other side of the coin: that my appearance and manner of being also present a conflict for my inner self in trying to figure out just exactly what my truth is.

For instance, when I meet someone new I often become an instant role model for them. When the "well-kept secret" of my age is revealed, I am met with "Oh, no, I don't believe you. Eighty-eight? Wow!" (This is when I pull out my driver's license.) Or someone says, "I want to be just like you when I get to be your age!" and so forth.

These reactions augment my state of emotional conflict. Shouldn't I be thinking about the fact that actuarially and actually I am now in my final years and need to plan for a declining future? Or should I just go on enjoying each day as if I had forever to live? This is a real dilemma created by the disparity between my visible self and the actual facts of my chronological age. I am sure these are questions that come up for many others as well.

My way is to straddle these issues. While going on with my busy life I am also planning for solutions should I become less mobile and incapacitated. However, I still harbor a sense of "unreality" about being eighty-eight and just trust that my end will somehow take care of itself. My mother always said there was a Guardian Angel on my shoulder and therefore I continue to trust that it will remain there and take care of me until my death.

78

Accept and Let Go

By Vimla Kaul

Vimla Kaul was born in Shimla and grew up in Delhi. She worked as a secretary for the All India Women's Conference (where she continues to serve as a life member) and the Delhi Social Welfare Board. Vimla has a total of eighteen years' experience as a teacher in convents. Her last post was with the Carmel School in Dhanbad. After retiring in 1993, she settled in Delhi. Then, in 1995 she opened a small informal school for slum children, in the village of Madanpur Khadar, near Sarita Vihar. This school, known as Guldasta, has been in existence for twenty years and has educated four hundred to five hundred children and received a number of accolades. Besides engaging in such social enterprises, Vimla has written three well-received books in English for students in grades eight to twelve.

To usher in this chapter of my life as an octogenarian, I recollect the adage, "Old is gold," and how the lucre of this will keep us shining and attractive. As we think about what to do when we turn eighty, the focal point we have to keep in mind is that we have lived our lives as well as we could and now it's time to give way and let go. If we do this, all else will fall into place.

It is understandable that we are possessed with our own individual way of looking at the world. So, adjustment seems an absurdity. However, all my agemates must remember that change is the essence of life. If we do not change with the times we are sure to lose out on this new phase of life with which we are gifted. Look down memory lane and ask yourself, wasn't I different from my elders too? So why should I resent it if a new generation is different from me? Learning to absorb change will benefit both me and them. Accepting change will always be the pivot of our happiness and will help us to age with dignity and grace.

At this age we are prone to believe that with our years we have a sea of experience. That may be true but we forget that our experience is of bygone days, most of which is now probably irrelevant. Moreover, friends, I daresay wisdom does not always come with experience. At times we don't always grow as we age. But we must remember that it is not about how many years of life we have had that is important but how much life we have put into our years.

A generation gap has to exist and it is not necessary that elders are always right. It is pertinent to note that we lived according to our social norms just as the generation of today lives by theirs. By remembering this we will be able to avoid unnecessary clashes of identity or ideologies, at home and out in society. This, to me, is one of the most damaging causes of strife that leads to divisions in many families.

When we were the working generation, the world was different. Some in our age group cannot understand the travails the young encounter. But we must learn to keep certain negative thoughts to ourselves and only offer advice if it is asked for. To put it another way, "Let there be space in our togetherness."

Our relations with young people may sometimes seem like walking on a razor's edge. There has to be a balance between taking an interest and becoming intrusive. You want to support, not interfere.

The nest for our young that we nurtured for so many years has disintegrated and the birds have flown away, some to raise families of their own. This leads us to suffer feelings of depression and loneliness. Most of us have not fashioned a place for ourselves beyond the nest. So, when the nest crashes down, we feel there is nowhere for us to go. If we had created an alternative outlet for our time, energy, and talents, we would not have time for feeling neglected or sidelined. When we experience the empty nest, we begin to tinker with the lives of others since we have nothing else to do. This, of course, is likely to lead to clashes. If, throughout the years, we had taken an interest in life outside the family, we would be able to make a smoother transition when the family is no longer the center of our attention.

It has to be remembered that with every passing day we will become more infirm, and thus, a support system outside our immediate family has to be developed. In order to do this, we need the young. We must embrace them with the warmth of love. This is not to suggest a selfish, self-serving act but to realistically acknowledge what will help us to steer through the next phase of our lives. If God is with us and our good sense prevails, life at eighty and beyond can be pleasurable and filled with honor.

So, let's be fair to our young. Let us take time to enjoy life while they work at building their lives.

79

Life Is a Gift — Live It Fully

By Rev. Margaret L. Clark

After her three children were all in school and she had painted the inside of her house several times, Margaret L. Clark decided it was time to find meaningful work outside the home. Her interests were mainly children and books. She felt she needed to be close to home so she applied for a job in the school district as a librarian. In this position, she would be close to home, have similar hours as her children, and have summers off. This wonderful job served her for twenty-seven years. As retirement approached, she was ready for something new. Philosophy was now her main interest so she began the long journey of studying for the ministry. After graduation, she became the minister at the Church of Religious Science in Seal Beach, California, until she retired from there at the age of seventy-five.

What does it mean to become eighty years old? In the process of living this long, we have made many choices and determined many likes and dislikes. There are so many joys in becoming this age, and there are disadvantages too. Most of the disadvantages are physical and the advantages are the freedoms we have to choose how we will spend our time. Once we are free from the responsibilities of work and raising a family, we are able to explore new ideas and take an interest in all the people we encounter in our daily lives.

We really do have wonderful opportunities to choose from and the time to indulge in them as much as we like. Now that I am in my eighties, I find it is a special time in my life and I intend to live it well. I'd like to share some of the activities that give me great pleasure in the three main areas of my life: body, mind, and spirit.

Body

The body needs feeding and exercise. Local hospitals have a variety of programs that teach about nutrition. My favorite one gave lectures on what foods to eat, and demonstrated how to prepare them. Then, they served the meal for us to enjoy.

Research tells us that getting exercise is one of the most important things we can do for our body — and our brain. I go to Weight Watchers once a week and Curves every morning at 6:30 a.m. Then I walk one mile around the park. I also keep physically active by traveling. Small ships that go on rivers work best for me. This year, I will visit France and the Italian Riviera. There is much to see without leaving the ship and short trips ashore that are optional. The number of passengers on these cruises is usually small and I find I meet many interesting people. There are also trips available for people that need physical assistance.

Mind

How do we keep our minds active? Again, we have many choices. One of the activities I enjoy most is going to Toastmasters International, one of the few organizations I know of where everyone participates in the meeting. This is very different from going to a lecture and just sitting in the audience.

In every Toastmasters meeting, the people in attendance get a speaking part in some capacity. You may be asked to present a prepared speech or deliver an extemporaneous talk on a subject that is given to you as part of the meeting's "Table Topics." The supportive atmosphere really helps members lose most of their fear of public speaking. And as a bonus, we get to know one another through so much interaction.

Other activities that are important to me are my book club and the discussion groups we have in my church community. Also, there are thirty-minute videos that we can view together, which feature a leading psychologist or theologian. Exchanging ideas is always an intellectual exercise that stimulates the brain.

The Senior University at Cal State Long Beach has given me the opportunity to take classes in a number of fascinating subjects that I had never explored before. I've learned to appreciate Shakespeare's plays, and study their meaning and beautiful language. There are also classes about other authors, bridge, current events, and a wealth of other subjects.

Spirit

For me, spirit is the emotional part of life. I find there is always something to appreciate. How I feel about my situation is entirely up to me. After centering my focus on the good things in life, I am able to turn my attention to others.

I really enjoy people. Visiting others every week who live in retirement complexes is part of my weekly routine. These well-planned environments are a gift to those who don't drive and are no longer able to shop or cook for themselves. The greatest gift of these places is that they offer community to so many who would otherwise live in isolation.

Life in our eighties has so much to offer. I'm able to spend time in ways that I choose. My life is enriched daily by the sharing of others, hearing about their experiences, interests, and ideas. This is a time that each of us can explore new meaning in what life is all about and pursue the rich opportunities it offers. Life is good and I choose to live it fully each and every day.

80

On Joining the Over-Eighty Club

By Donald F. Murray, MDiv, MTh

Donald F. Murray, MDiv, MTh, is a United Church of Canada minister, educator, workshop facilitator, and author, living with his partner Emily Kierstead, by Shortt's Lake, near Truro, Nova Scotia. He is now retired, having served pastorates in the Maritimes for thirty-two years and as program director and then executive director of Tatamagouche Education and Spirituality Centre for eight years. Don, having awakened to "the-death-of-God" theology in the early 1960s, has been an avid searcher. Following his theological education in the quiet 1950s he became a human relations trainer (with NTI) in 1971; a member of The International Transactional Analysis Association in 1972; National Training Institute Council of Fellows in 1989; attended Jean Houston's School of Sacred Psychology (better known as Mystery School), and in 1990 he discovered Carl Jung, "the psychiatrist of Christianity." He has authored three books: *For Unbelieving Christians* (1987), *Celebrating Eve* (2001), and *The Death and Resurrection of God: From Christianity to the New Story* (2014). Since 2001 he writes a religion column for the *Truro Daily News*.

The family were gathered, all thirty-one of them; from Winnipeg to Vienna. The sumptuous meal had been served. Many of the speeches were made. Then came the gala parade of the birthday cake, with the merry tune of "Happy Birthday" being sung lustily by all. In the center of that cake, surrounded by numerous candles, was a giant "80." "Happy 80th Birthday," actually.

It was, however, the "80" that seemed to be a pulsing light penetrating my consciousness. I have been on this planet for eighty years. I've seen it coming. I know it. It strikes me that the years have passed and I have indeed joined the over-eighty club. This whole ritual party, and the big "80," helps it sink into me a little more deeply. What *now*? is the big question.

The plethora of possibilities floods my mind. I quickly decide that this is not the time for grand new ventures. Life is always a crap-shoot but when you get to this stage it becomes more so. This could be the wrap-up decade. And that is fine. To have lived for eighty years and be in reasonably good health is a great privilege, but who knows what measure of time is left to me. I had better finish up projects, spend as much time as possible with family and friends, and enjoy being home with the companionship of my beloved partner Emily. She, too, although a bit younger, is on this journey of aging.

The usual advice at this stage of life is that one should be thinking about and preparing for heaven or eternity. I must confess that such thoughts do not weigh heavily upon my mind. I am more concerned with doing my best with life here. I hope that I have grown through the course of the years and that my life offers something of value to the world and to the yearning consciousness of the Universe.

I believe the goal of our existence is to become as whole and mature as we can be. Life may be full of mistakes, failures, roads not taken, a squandering of time and energy, and all sorts of things that make the journey incomplete. Our years will also have their blessings, accomplishments, joys, etc. It is important to find the threads that weave it all together and make it into a whole piece of cloth, whatever its blemishes and shortcomings may have been. Our task is to become the person we were born to be and to share who we are and what is ours to do in the world.

Only a few have a grand vision of what their life is about. Most of us muddle along doing our job and dealing with the everydayness of life. And that is actually the way we become the person that is in us to be. For the most part we don't grow by trying. Becoming more whole, mature, conscious, and all the things that make for a quality person is a side-effect of dealing with the responsibilities and challenges that life brings to us or we choose to take on. It is very important to accept and celebrate one's life as whole and complete, in spite of all the misadventures along the way.

To do so is especially challenging for those whose lives are cut short through disease or tragedy. We think of the multitudes who, through war, oppression, poverty, and social circumstances, have had little chance at life. However, for those of us who have had the opportunity to be present to the ages and stages of life there is a feeling of contentment, fulfillment, and completion that leaves us with no concern for the future. As I enter this roundup time of life I am profoundly thankful for the blessings the passing years have brought me. As I write this, Emily is composing a song, "Come home to yourself, love." And that is what life is about. In coming home to ourselves we come home to all that is, including the spiritual reality — God, if that image speaks to you.

I am in no hurry. I still have things to do. I enjoy the richness of my life; my partner Emily, our families, playing the fiddle, singing in Emily's choir, writing. However, whatever lies ahead, I have known the glory. I have made great strides in coming home to myself. What more could one ask?

ABOUT THE EDITORS

MARK EVAN CHIMSKY is the head of Mark Chimsky Editorial Services Unlimited, an editorial consulting business based in Portland, Maine (markchimskyeditorial.com). For nearly six years, he was the editor in chief of the book division of Sellers Publishing, an independent publishing company based in South Portland, Maine. Previously he was executive editor and editorial director of Harper San Francisco and headed the paperback divisions at Little, Brown and Macmillan. In addition, he was on the faculty of New York University's Center for Publishing, and for three years he served as the director of the book section of NYU's Summer Publishing Institute. He has edited a number of best-selling books, including Johnny Cash's memoir, *Cash*, and he has worked with such notable authors as Melody Beattie, Arthur Hertzberg, Beryl Bender Birch, and Robert Coles. His editorial achievements have been noted in *Vanity Fair*, the *Nation*, and *Publishers Weekly*. For Sellers Publishing, he developed and compiled a number of acclaimed books, including *Creating a Life You'll Love*, which won the silver in *ForeWord's* 2009 Book of the Year Awards (self-help category), and 65 *Things to Do When You Retire*, which the *Wall Street Journal* called "[one of] the year's best guides to later life." Mark also teaches in the Writing, Literature, and Publishing Department at Emerson College in Boston. In addition, he is writing the book and lyrics to several new musicals.

LAURIE MOORE SKILLINGS, associate project editor, is a creative consultant to Mark Evan Chimsky on many of his projects, including doing extensive research for his musicals in development. She has also created Web sites for numerous clients. She is a Senior Certified ADHD coach, parent and student advocate, and contributor to four popular books on ADHD. Visit Laurie's Web site at focuswithease.com.

ACKNOWLEDGMENTS

Anthologies are always collaborative efforts. This was certainly the case with 80 *Things to Do When You Turn 80*, and so I want to express my deep gratitude to all the contributors to this book, who generously provided their essays free of charge so that all royalties could be donated to benefit cancer research and prevention.

I would also like to thank associate project editor Laurie Moore Skillings who worked with me on researching and reaching out to potential contributors for this book. I couldn't have done such a wide-ranging project without her patience, good humor, and meticulous attention to detail.

Also, I appreciate all those who provided invaluable assistance to this project, including Karrie Allen, Roy Blakey, Chris Cappy, Sam Dalton, Judy Diamond, Kendall Dudley, Allan Glaser, Elaine M. Decker, Maryjane Fahey, Paola Gianturco, Jane Giddan, Kimberly Gladman, Heather Grabin, Cindy Hounsell, Deanna S. Hoss, Robbie Kaye, Savannah Lake, Lynne Martin, Mae Mendelson, Dorian Mintzer, Richard M. Morse, Greg Mort, Debbie Munn, Sharon O'Neill, Dr. Carol Orsborn, Bill Roiter, Debra Spinney, Kim Stegmeir, Richard Teller, and Robin Whitmore.

I am grateful to Ronnie Sellers, Mary Baldwin, Charlotte Cromwell, Megan Hiller, and the whole Sellers team for their amazing work. I also owe a huge debt of gratitude to Robin Haywood for her support.

Finally, I want to thank my parents Matt and Jean, for teaching me that time never dims the heart's love of literature.

CREDITS

"Turning Eighty" © 2016 Pat Boone; "It's All About Our Journey" © 2016 Tab Hunter; "Pay It Forward" © 2016 Sally A. Breen; "My Life Continues to Be an Adventure" © 2016 The Amazing Kreskin; "Keep On Keepin' On" © 2016 Elaine L. Newman as told to Kathy Stokes; "Cultivating a Happy Life" © 2016 Gordon J. Bailey, Jr.; "My Life: An Audacious Adventure" © 2016 Fred Weinberg; "On Turning Eighty" © 2016 Elisabeth Grace; "The Joy of Old Age. (No Kidding.)" by Oliver Sacks, originally published in *The New York Times*. Copyright © 2013 by Oliver Sacks, used by permission of The Wylie Agency LLC; "Eighty" © 2016 Robert Ellis Smith; "Changing Your Dreams: Talking About Life and Death" © 2016 Dorian Mintzer, MSW, PhD, BCC; "Recovering from Injury and Illness: It's Up to Me, It's Up to You" © 2016 Morton H. Shaevitz, PhD, ABPP; "How It Feels to Be Eighty" © 2016 Katherine Griesz; "The Stingray" © 2016 David Black; "Revisit the Dream, and Begin Again" © 2016 PJ Cowan; "Life Is an Adventure" © 2016 Jerry Witkovsky, MSW; "Be All You Can Be" © 2016 Roger Landry, MD, MPH; "The Gift of Wisdom" © 2016 George Wolf; "Eighty Is Old" © 2016 Walter M. Bortz II, MD; "Losing My Teeth" © 2016 Donald Hall; "How Your Work — and You — Can Live Forever" © 2016 George Lois; "Ruta's Rules" © 2016 Ruta Lee; "Retuning Your Life Portfolio" © 2016 William A. Sadler, PhD; "A Learning Life" © 2016 John O'Neil; "Life Lessons for Your Eighties and Beyond" © 2016 Betty R. Zimmer; "Rules for Old People" © 2016 Thomas Y. Canby; "A Letter to My Younger Self " © 2016 Florence Ladd; "Growing Young: The Formula" © 2016 Elizabeth (Betty) Finney; "The Heat Is Off" © 2016 Ginnie Siena Bivona; "A Work in Progress" © 2016 Rev. Margaret Stortz; "Seeking Wisdom" © 2016 Fran Morris; "All My Monsters Are Dead" © 2016 Betty MacDonald; "It